ORGANIZATIONS AND GROWTH IN RURAL CHINA

ORGANIZATIONS AND GROWTH IN RURAL CHINA

Marsh Marshall

MACMILLAN

First published 1985

Published by
THE MACMILLAN PRESS LTD
Houndmills, Basingstoke, Hampshire RG21 2XS
and London
Companies and representatives
throughout the world

Printed in Hong Kong

British Library Cataloguing in Publication Data
Marshall, Marsh
Organizations and growth in rural China.
1. China—Economic conditions—1949–
2. China—Rural conditions
I. Title
330.951'05 HC427.9
ISBN 0–333–38792–9

For my parents

Contents

Preface

An important part of the data used in this book was collected in China and a series of interviews there also provided vital information. The most helpful of these were with the following government officials: Deng Xiaoping (Vice-Premier); Zheng Zhong (Vice-Minister of Agriculture); Zhang Wu (Director of the Institute of Agricultural Economics of the Chinese Academy of Social Science); Wang Gengjin (Vice-Director of the Institute of Agricultural Economics of the Chinese Academy of Social Science); Wu Cheng (Deputy Head of the People's Commune Section, Office of Agriculture, Hebei Provincial Government); Lu Jinxin (Vice-Chairman of Jia Ding County Government, Shanghai Municipality); Li Shaoliang (Vice-Chairman of Fo Gang County Government, Guangdong Province); and Zhang Hua (Vice-Director of the Agricultural Commission of Guangdong Province). I wish to thank all of these officials and their staffs for their time and their help. They bear no responsibility for the views expressed in this book.

My interests in economics and in China were originally brought together at Stanford University. For encouragement to do this I should like to thank Victor Li, John Wilson Lewis, Walter Falcon, Bruce Johnston and Dennis Chinn.

I am most grateful to the University of Oxford for providing me with the motivation and the unrivalled atmosphere to think through the issues in this book. In particular, I owe an enormous intellectual debt to Amartya Sen and to Włodzimierz Brus. They have demonstrated that economics should be dealt with on a wider canvas. Their work shows that economists can draw important insights especially from history and philosophy.

I have spent many hours discussing the issues and details of this book with Keith Griffin and Cyril Lin. Their criticisms and suggestions have been of vital benefit and I cannot begin to thank them.

Valuable criticism was also provided by Jim Boyce, John Enos, Judith Heyer, Alec Nove and Maurice Scott. I have very much appreciated their encouragement.

Finally, there are many friends who have helped me in more practical ways to finish this book. They know who they are and I am grateful to all of them – especially to Alexa Wilson, Julia Lane and Michael Sissons.

London M. M.

Weights, Measures and Currency

1 jin	= 0.5 kilogram	= 1.1023 pounds
1 mou	= 0.0667 hectare	= 0.1647 acre
1 yuan	= 0.50 US dollar (1984)	

List of Tables and Figures

TABLES

FIGURES

Introduction

Most economies are composed of three structural elements: government, production organizations and households. Economists have long analysed the relationships between these three elements and have displayed considerable methodological elegance in the process. But in some quarters there is real doubt whether the conclusions of orthodox economics have usefully illuminated the most pressing economic problems. I am among those critics who believe that modern economists have failed adequately to explain the causes of and the solutions to unemployment and to inflation. They have failed, consequently, to prescribe a blueprint for sustained economic growth.

Nowhere is this intellectual failure more disturbing than in the developing countries: despite the rapid growth in many of these countries the horrors of poverty and malnutrition continue to rage. In recent years these conditions may even have worsened in the face of mounting foreign debts. Ten years ago Gerald Meier described the situation in words which are even more telling today:

> The World Bank now emphasises that the failure to achieve a minimum level of income above the 'poverty line' has kept some 40 per cent of the peoples in the less developed countries in the condition of life so degraded by disease, illiteracy, malnutrition, and squalor as to deny its victims basic human necessities. . . . The persistence of absolute poverty, despite respectable achievements in the rates of growth in GNP, is now of more concern than that of relative poverty, or of a 'widening gap' between the rich and poor countries.[1]

There are perhaps many reasons why economists have so far failed to deliver effective answers to the problems of unemployment and inflation in the industrialized countries and of poverty in the developing countries. In this book it will be argued that one important reason has been the lack of a proper framework for analysing the organization. Economists have traditionally dealt with the organization from a rigid methodological perspective. According to orthodox theory the organization is always assumed to be efficient in its decisions and actions. Perhaps surprisingly, most economists have displayed an interest only in the external affairs of the organization. After all, why analyse the *internal* decision-making processes in the organization if it is believed that every organization is efficient?

Yet an organization is an association of individuals, each of whom makes decisions which affect the collective performance. These decisions can vary over a wide range: from 'should I work hard today or should I take it easy?' to 'how much of the organisation's surplus should be consumed and how much should be invested?'. The point of departure in this book is that such questions can have profound implications for growth in an economy. I shall try to illuminate these implications by analysing the relationship between the structure of production organizations and economic growth and development. It will be argued that a crucial problem in growth is concerned with the organization's collective choices between investment and consumption. I shall suggest that an organizational structure which includes a wide degree of participation by its members in planning and decision-making can, under certain conditions, lead to an increase in the quantity and intensity of the input of labour, to a high ratio of accumulation to consumption and to the promotion of an equitable pattern of economic growth.

To lend descriptive and empirical concreteness to the arguments I will refer to the organizational arrangements in rural China. I do so for two principal reasons. First, with a population of approximately one billion people the Chinese compose nearly 40 per cent of the population of the entire developing world (and a quarter of the whole world). Moreover, about four-fifths of China's population live in the countryside. An analysis of China's rural organizations would thus seem to be useful for those readers interested in the relationship between organizations and growth.

Second, a study of China's experience gives one an opportunity to examine closely the sequential aspect of institutional change. For land reform in a developing country may not be enough. Perhaps equally important is the need to create an efficient organization of production. In China a substantial redistribution of land was undertaken from 1949 to 1953. While some important obstacles to growth were removed by the land reforms, other serious problems remained. This was recognized by the government and it moved quickly, from 1954 to 1957, to encourage the establishment of co-operative production organizations in the countryside.

It is these organizations which will provide an empirical basis for testing the propositions developed in this book. Chapter 1 will set out the main proposition involving the relationship between organizations and growth. This chapter will provide the theoretical framework for the rest of the book. Chapter 2 will discuss briefly the land redistribution in China and it will identify the most important problems that were left unresolved. This chapter will also describe the formation of co-operatives in 1954–7 and of the commune organization in 1958.

The structure and function of the rural organizations will be analysed in Chapter 3. This analysis will draw from the theoretical discussion in the first chapter. Particular attention will be paid to the problem of imperfect information and to the costs associated with screening and monitoring agricultural labour. Some insights from the literature on team production will be used in order to develop criteria for analysing the organization.

Chapters 4 and 5 test the empirical validity of the previous arguments by drawing on original material collected during a trip to China. Chapter 4 investigates the process of agricultural growth. Chapter 5 is concerned with rural industrial growth.

But many agricultural and sideline activities in China's rural production organizations take place not in the collective sector, but rather in the private sector. Chapter 6 therefore looks closely at this sector and provides empirical material to measure its importance. It is argued that the recent success of the private sector demonstrates the flexibility of the organizational structure and its ability to facilitate a rapid rate of growth in the rural economy.

Yet economists ought to be just as concerned with the pattern of growth as with the rate of growth. What effect has the structure of the rural organizations had on the distribution of income in rural China? Chapter 7 provides empirical information on the distribution of income in rural China and suggests an important connection between the structure of the rural organizations and a narrowing over time in the distribution of income. The effects of private economic activity and of the recent policy reforms on the distribution of rural income will also be analysed in Chapter 7.

Has the establishment of co-operative production organizations been sufficient to guarantee sustained economic growth in rural China? This question shall be tackled in the final two chapters. Chapter 8 reviews briefly the macroeconomic performance of the rural economy from 1949 to 1984. A critique of the 'ultra-left' periods in China (1957–61 and 1964–77) is also given in the context of the organizational approach of the book. The impact of the recent policy and organizational reforms on macroeconomic performance is also provided in Chapter 8. Chapter 9 will summarize the most important findings in the book and will offer some comparisons of China's rural performance with other developing countries.

Many developing countries have had revolutions of one kind or another – which have often created as many problems as they have solved. I have long been struck by how little economics has to offer on the subject of revolution and in particular on the problems which remain after the fighting ends. If this book can in some way help those who seek sincerely to tackle these problems, then it will have been worth every minute of writing it.

1 An Organizational Approach to Growth

1. INTRODUCTION

In this chapter an approach to the growth problem will be developed which emphasizes the importance of the organization. I will draw from three distinct areas of the economics literature. Each of these areas has addressed, from differing perspectives, the problem of growth and development. The first is the literature on growth theory and growth accounting. Recent criticisms by Maurice Scott and Richard Nelson are particularly important and these will be discussed in some detail.

Second, recent work in the economics of information will be reviewed, in order to develop insights into problems of team production. Joseph Stiglitz, James Mirrlees, Armen Alchian and Harold Demsetz, and Oliver Williamson, *inter alia*, have argued, for example, that the asymmetries of information associated with incomplete employment contracts in team production suggest that organizational structure and associated incentive systems are an important determinant of work effort by individuals, and, consequently, of labour productivity.

A third trend in the recent economics literature has featured a behavioural approach toward the relationship between the organization and labour productivity. The work of Herbert Simon and others from the Carnegie School of Industrial Relations, the 'micro-micro' approach of Harvey Leibenstein, and the diverse group of writers on participation theory and self-management (e.g. John Stuart Mill, Karl Marx, Carol Pateman, Włodzimierz Brus) will be discussed.

The aim of this chapter is to suggest an explicit relationship between organizational structure and economic growth. I will argue that a crucial problem in growth is concerned with the choice between investment and consumption; and that some organizational structures, on *a priori* reasoning, should lead to higher investment–consumption ratios, and thus, to better prospects for growth and development. It will be suggested that, in particular, a decentralized, collective organization can achieve a high rate of investment. In such organizations it is essential that investment–consumption decisions must be seen to be just and democratic where the benefits and costs are clear to everyone and, moreover, are internalized within the organization.

2. GROWTH AND INVESTMENT

In this section the underlying process of economic growth will be discussed. I shall focus on the importance of investment. First, however, certain aspects of the past treatment of growth theory and growth accounting will be criticized in order to identify important problems in that treatment for the development of my argument. Having isolated several crucial points from these discussions, a connection between growth and organization will then be indicated by emphasizing investment as an important determinant of growth.

The growth theory and growth accounting literature has been concerned, to a large extent, with the theoretical formulation and empirical testing of what Nicholas Kaldor has called the 'stylised facts of growth'. These are:

(i) output grows at a constant and proportionate rate;
(ii) the ratio of investment to output is constant over time;
(iii) the share of profits and wages are also constant over time;
(iv) a constant rate of growth of the labour force and of labour productivity; and
(v) a constant rate of return on investment.

The theoretical models which have tried to explain these 'stylised facts' have been derived from the theory of production and of the firm in perfectly competitive conditions. Firms face a set of alternatives with respect to the inputs they can procure and the outputs they can produce. These firms then make appropriate profit-maximizing (or present value-maximizing) choices. These choices reveal a time path of inputs, outputs and prices. These firms are then seen to be in a moving equilibrium, with their specific choices influenced by changes in product demand, factor supply and technological conditions.

This theory has generated a broad class of models, which have been divided by critics and writers of survey articles into two categories, depending upon whether technical progress is treated exogenously or endogenously.[1] These models have been concerned to stipulate the conditions for equilibrium growth by making appropriate assumptions from the theory of the firm and from production theory.[2] A critique of the structure of these models will not be presented here, as several such criticisms are available.[3] One should merely ask if the results obtained from the empirical testing of these theories explain in a meaningful way the underlying process of economic growth?

An important theoretical conclusion of the equilibrium growth models which treat technical progress exogenously is that most of the rate of growth of labour productivity is due to technical progress. This conclusion has been supported by a multitude of empirical studies which suggest that technical progress is indeed a very important factor in explaining productivity growth. Robert Solow's pioneering study in 1957 set a pattern for subsequent analysis. He assumed constant returns to scale, Hicks-neutral technical progress, the existence of a macro-economic production function and the validity of the theory of marginal productivity in analysing empirically the sources of industrial growth in the U.S. economy for the period 1909–49. He found that nearly 90 per cent of the doubling of outputs for this period could be attributed to technical progress.[4] Similar results were obtained by B. Massel, M. Abramowitz, S. Fabricant, among others.[5]

The size of this 'residual' (sometimes called 'coefficient of our ignorance'), and the fact that what seemed to be the most important source of productivity growth had been treated exogenously in most models, stimulated some economists to refine growth theory so that technical progress could be treated endogenously. It was thus thought that technical progress was not 'manna from heaven', but rather something embodied in capital inputs and labour inputs. This presented applied economists with a challenge: if these inputs could be specified in index form and measured more accurately then the residual should be reduced in empirical tests. As Dale Jorgenson and Zvi Griliches explained in an important paper in 1967:

> if quantities of outputs and inputs are measured accurately, growth in total output is largely explained by growth in total input . . .[6]

> our results suggest that the residual change in total factor productivity, which Denison attributes to advance in knowledge, is small.[7]

They argued that the great body of past research on total factor productivity 'is characterised by very substantial errors of measurement, equal in magnitude to the alleged increase in productivity'.[8]

Since the publication of Jorgenson's and Griliches's paper, efforts have been made by applied economists to reduce the 'residual' through more careful measurements and specifications. These efforts have involved the construction of indices by which to measure accurately capital and labour inputs. Labour inputs, for example, are seen to be a product of the total hours worked and the average labour quality per hour. Thus labour quality, expressed through an index, is meant to account for the level of skill provided per hour worked. Furthermore, skill is assumed to be determined mainly by education attainment and by demographic factors. Recent studies by W. Waldorf and P. Chinloy have suggested that more careful indexing can result in substantial reductions in the residual, and thus in a more accurate accounting of growth.[9] S. Star has argued further that 'the large, unexplained residual is caused by using aggregated rather than disaggregated data, and by incorrectly using value-added relationships rather than relationships implied by production theory'.[10] He corrects these biases and reduces the residual growth over the period 1950–60 in U.S. manufacturing industry from 47 per cent to 13 per cent of the annual growth of output. Star argues that any remaining difference between growth in measured outputs and growth in measured inputs is due to an inability to measure some of the variables correctly and to the difficulty in quantifying some of the variables. Star concludes his article with the following statement, which suggests a very important and unresolved problem in growth economics:

> The residual is a measure of our ignorance about only one aspect of growth. Growth accounting measures *what* changes have taken place, the most interesting question – *why* the changes occurred – still remains to be answered.[11]

If one could assume that all measurement problems, index construction problems, and production function specification problems were solved, what can growth accounting tell us about the underlying process of dynamic growth? It will be argued here, following Maurice Scott and Richard Nelson,[12] that this literature has not been able to answer this question, perhaps because it has never tried to answer it. Yet these studies often imply that growth accounts can *explain* growth.

There are several related reasons why this literature has not yet contributed to a better understanding of the process of economic growth. First, growth, by definition, implies dynamic movement. That is, growth like learning, is a process of experience. Therefore decisions and actions taken in the past should surely substantially affect results in the present. Yet this obvious feature of growth is often ignored in the growth accounting literature. This literature often poses the question in terms of the average contribution of capital, of labour or of technical progress to average yearly growth of output. Suppose one is interested in determining the contribution of capital (e.g. chemical fertilizer) to the growth of output (e.g. grain) during a year toward the end of an accounting period. It may well be that the contribution of this capital input to output is as large as it is because of labour mobilization, organizational change and certain investments (e.g. the construction of an irrigation network) during a *prior* period. Then, the 'average period' approach may be quite misleading. If one understands the process of economic growth to be to a great extent the result of past actions and decisions then growth is unlikely to be explained by the simple sum of the contributions of separate factors. As Nelson has argued, 'the contribution of technical change to growth, or the expansion of any particular factor, during any year is not independent of what happened to the other factors *prior to that year*'.[13]

The above qualification is strengthened by considering a second shortcoming in the literature. The process of growth is often an interactive one, involving important complementarities between inputs. This interactive and complementary nature of growth is particularly important in agriculture. Without substantial water control, for example, the 'green revolution', high-yielding varieties would not contribute, as they should in Asian agriculture, to the growth in grain yields. Indeed, effective water control is in Asian agriculture often a precondition for deriving the appropriate benefits from new varieties and from the introduction of chemical fertilizer. This sequential-interactive approach to growth is often lost in conventional growth accounting. It is perhaps more accurate to 'explain' the growth rate of output over time as the result of related and interdependent changes in the rate of growth of the capital stock, of the quality and quantity of labour and of organizational efficiency. Assigning a quantitative attribution to a particular factor is difficult because it is implied that growth still would have occurred substantially if the factor alone had changed. Because of the interactive and experienced nature of growth this may not be true: a product cannot be converted to a sum.

A third shortcoming in the growth literature concerns the use of an aggregate production function and the macroeconomic nature of most models. Limitations in the use of a constrained Cobb–Douglas function are well known: neutral technical progress, unitary elasticity of substitution and constant returns to scale are assumed. Indeed some critics allege that the phrase 'technical progress' is itself misleading when used in an aggregated way, for it may mask such phenomena as (i) substitution of capital for labour; (ii) economies of scale; (iii) learning by experience; (iv) increased education; (v) resource shifts; (vi) organizational improvements.[14] These are phenomena which have received little empirical attention at the microeconomic level. Indeed, Nelson argues that there is a sharp inconsistency between the macroeconomic growth literature and the microeconomic research on technical progress.[15] He argues that this inconsistency 'calls into question the basic tenets of neoclassical theory'.[16] Nordhaus and Tobin echo these sentiments: 'the [neoclassical] theory conceals, either in aggregation or in the abstract generality of multi-sector models, all the drama of the events – the rise and fall of products, technologies and industries . . .'.[17] In the theory of the firm it is assumed that the production set is defined by a set of known techniques which summarize the state of technological knowledge. Yet a considerable body of microeconomic evidence suggests that there are considerable differences among firms within an industry (and even within firms) concerning the technology used, productivity and profitability. In Nelson's words:

> In analysis of productivity growth considerable revealed conviction resides in the presumption that the production set is sharply defined and not bound by *experience*. Basic orthodox theory is mute regarding why the production set is what it is at any time; the set is a primitive concept.[18]

It would seem, therefore, that a better microeconomic understanding of growth and technical progress should illuminate the underlying process involved and thereby contribute to more robust and realistic macroeconomic studies in the future. A similar view is expressed by A. Heertje in a recent book, *Economics and Technical Change*:

> A macroeconomic analysis of technical change and scale effects must be mainly theoretical but it becomes considerably more meaningful at a microeconomic level. The discussion of the labour market in a macroeconomic context lacks substance, whereas a complementry microeconomic analysis can illuminate the effects of a technical change on the employee, the firm, and the entire industry. In short, while a macroeconomic analysis is useful for a preliminary sketch of the effects of technical change, a more profound under-

standing of technical development must ultimately be connected with human activities centred in the production process.[19]

Nelson concurs as follows:

> The diversity and change that are suppressed by aggregation, maximization, and equilibrium are not the epiphenomena of technical advance. They are the central phenomena. Thus before macro theorizing on growth can continue realistically and analytically, more must be known of the micro process of growth at the intrafirm level. In this way, choice of assumptions can be informed by what is known of actual firm behaviour, the micro processes of technical change, and the characteristics of selection environments.[20]

Such a microeconomic intra-organizational approach shall be pursued in the empirical studies in subsequent chapters.

So far it has been argued that the economics literature regards growth as resulting from larger stocks of labour, land or capital; technical progress is seen as a factor augmenting the quality of these stocks. Growth accounting considers how these stocks have changed over time and analyses the effects on output, on employment and on prices. In most of this literature investment is not given an important role in explanations of the process of growth. This neglect is a fourth serious shortcoming in this literature.

In recent work Maurice Scott has forcefully criticized such neglect. He extends the theory of J. Schumpeter in order to argue that investment plays a key role in the growth process. Schumpeter argued that development implies economic change, determined endogenously by the decisions of producers.[21] He argued that development is mainly concerned with 'the carrying out of the new combinations', meaning the 'different employment of existing supplies of productive means'.[22] Moreover, Schumpeter was very much concerned with the enterprise, as the appropriate unit in the economy to implement economic change and a rearrangement of existing resources.

Scott extends Schumpeter's ideas by arguing that investment should be defined as the '*cost* of change'; it therefore covers 'all expenditures which would not be made in a stationary state'.[23] He thus sees investment as an agent of change:

> It is the cost, in terms of consumption foregone, of propelling the economy forward instead of leaving it in a stationary state. Capital in

this sense is an *input*, an essentially backward-looking concept which we distinguish from its output. For the latter, we have the forward-looking concept of wealth, the present value of future consumption. Society therefore sacrifices present consumption in order to improve its prospect for future consumption. If we make the analogy with a person climbing up stairs, the effort he expends in climbing is his investment. . . .[24]

One can combine Schumpeter's ideas and Scott's notion of investment as the cost of change in the following way. Producers co-operate in order to 'carry out new combinations'. They create an organization which involves a different employment of the economy's existing supplies of means of production. Each organization is now confronted by new investment opportunities; moreover, investment itself creates further opportunities for future investment. The construction of an irrigation network, for example, can enable an organization to carry out, at a future date, new investment, e.g. purchases of chemical fertilizers and high-yielding seeds. The organization chooses between competing investment opportunities so as to maximize wealth. In this manner investment today contributes to growth tomorrow. Since technical progress is included within this concept of investment, outputs at any point can be accounted for accurately by measuring the inputs employed. Yet hidden in this accounting is the concept of investment, the agent and cost of change and the sacrifice of present for future consumption. This idea is represented in diagrammatic form in Figure 1.1. Assume that point *A* represents the position of one micro-

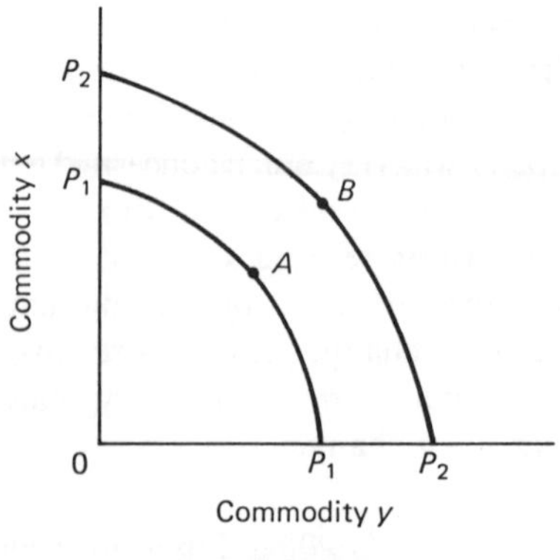

FIGURE 1.1

arrangement of existing resources in the economy. This organization is on the boundary of its production set. A different group of producers undertake a rearrangement of these resources: in Schumpeter's words; 'a different employment of the economy's existing supplies of productive means'. However, such an organizational rearrangement does not admit a 'free ride' from A on P_1P_1 to B on P_2P_2. But the organizational rearrangement allows the possibility of movement over time from point A to point B. A cost has to be incurred for this economic change. This cost is investment. Thus the organizational rearrangement may create investment opportunities (e.g. the mobilization of off-season labour in the rural sector) which can induce movement from A to B. A growth accounting at point B merely tells us what inputs were used at that time to produce the outputs obtained. Yet, underlying that particular accounting was first the important organizational rearrangement and second the investment undertaken to reach point B.

Since decisions to sacrifice present consumption are, by definition, implied in investment, the *process* by which these decisions are reached by the new organizational arrangement would seem to be very important in understanding economic growth.

3. ORGANISATIONAL STRUCTURE AND PRODUCTIVITY

Individuals form organizations, as Kenneth Arrow has recently written, 'because collective action can extend the domain of individual action'.[25] Indeed, as J. R. Commons argued, collective action 'means liberation and expansion of individual action'.[26] Within the organization each production plan can be viewed as a set of decision problems for each member; the sum of the individual choices then yields a pattern of collective action. Yet individual members of an organization may differ with respect to their valuation of a specific production plan, to the information they have and to their preferences. The organizational problem, therefore, is to determine a structure and a system of incentives which enable the sum of individual actions to yield organizationally optimal outcomes. This depends, as James Mirrlees has suggested, on 'personal relationships between members of the group'.[27] The organizational problem can thus be seen as a problem concerned with determining appropriate work relations of production.

In this section this problem will be discussed by drawing insights from three sources in the literature: (i) the economics of imperfect information; (ii) 'Micro-micro' theory and the organizational behaviour approach; and (iii) the literature on self-management and participation. I seek explicitly to describe a relationship between organizational structure and productivity. It will be argued that the extent to which the sum of individual decisions yields socially optimal group outcomes depends in an important way upon the structure of organizations in the economy.

Team Production and Incomplete Information

Each member of an organization has an important discretionary variable: his output of effort. Yet employment contracts are incomplete in the sense that the level of individual effort expended cannot be stipulated explicitly in the contract. That is, labour contracts usually allow a certain amount of discretion with respect to the *intensity* of work. They do not specify what each party will do in each state of nature. Hence an asymmetry of information exists: individuals know what level of effort they are providing, while employers do not have complete information about this discretionary variable. This dilemma, analytically similar to the problem of moral hazard and adverse selection in the economics of information, is particularly evident in team production.[28] In team production it is difficult and therefore costly to define or determine each individuals's contribution to team output. The output yielded by a team is not the sum of separable outputs of each of its members. Yet, for an organization, team production is efficient if the output of the team is larger than the sum of separate production by each individual. The employer thus faces a screening problem: estimating marginal productivity and making payments accordingly is costly. Moreover, such estimates are subject to considerable uncertainty.

How can employers minimize the costs of estimating the expenditure of individual effort and an individual's contribution to production? Spence has suggested a system of keeping performance records and re-evaluating *a priori* probabilities of each individual's expected contribution.[29] Terms of contract can then be revised *ex post* in order to include the additional information obtained from experience and from the performance audit. However, in the case of team production the costs of closely monitoring individual performance may outweigh the benefits of accurate factor payments. Indeed, Stiglitz associates such high costs with certain characteristics of information. The value of a given amount of information, for example, increases with the frequency of its use. He also argues that 'it can be shown that, in general, it does not pay to acquire just a little bit of information: a little information has negative net value, i.e. the costs always exceed the benefits. Thus it does not pay to monitor just a little; it either pays not to monitor at all, or to monitor at a finite level.'[30]

An important problem in the design of organisational structure is the prevention of 'free-rider' abuse by individuals (also known as 'effort-shirking'). Such problems arise because of potential conflicts of interest within the organization. To illustrate this, consider an organization with two groups of workers. Assume that each group's effort-output can be described by the characteristics θ_1 and θ_2, and $\theta_1 > \theta_2$, which are proportional to each group's marginal product. Assume, further, that the firm intends to pay each group of workers a wage equivalent to each group's marginal product, θ_1 and θ_2. To do so the employer implements a screening device to determine which workers belong to which group. The θ_2 workers, say, are unhappy with the prospect of identification and the consequent payment of the lower wage, θ_2. Assume that they are successful in forming a union and in convincing the firm to pay all workers the mean marginal product $\overline{\theta}$. The firm will continue to screen as long as the costs of screening, C, are such that $C < \theta_1 - \overline{\theta} < \overline{\theta} - \theta_2$. Moreover, if the firm could keep the screening information private, then it can earn, as a return to obtaining that information, the difference between the marginal productivity of θ_1 workers and $\overline{\theta}$. If this information remains private, however, θ_1 workers then lose incentive to expend a level of effort equivalent to θ_1. Their productivity regresses toward $\overline{\theta}$, thereby forcing $\overline{\theta}$ to regress toward θ_2. Moreover, as $\overline{\theta}$ regresses, θ_2 workers are again unhappy since they lose their 'free-ride' equivalent to $\overline{\theta}$–θ_2. Given such information asymmetries, and the costs associated with them, it is not surprising that unions act to guarantee that $\overline{\theta}$ in period 1 is at least equivalent in real terms to $\overline{\theta}$ in period 2, . . . , *n*.

Another important implication for organizational structure derived from the asymmetries associated with information concerns the importance of specialization within the firm. The larger the set of labour inputs about which performance information is collected within the organization, the greater the costs of collecting information. Thus, the larger the organization the more difficult and costly are efforts to monitor performance. To counter this problem Radner, Stiglitz, Alchian and Demsetz, Williamson and others have suggested that a large organization should be decentralized and specialized in order to reduce these costs.[31] Recent empirical research in industrial economics (e.g. Steer and Cable, Armour and Teece)[32] suggests that organizations which are structured in a decentralized way achieve better performance. Mancur Olson has argued, from a different perspective, that collective action is most efficient and productive when 'small groups' are involved.[33] In subsequent chapters these arguments shall be pursued and it will be suggested that 'small groups' production and specialization within a large organization is particularly important in agricultural production.

While economic theorists have pointed out the importance of organizational structure and related incentive systems in the promotion of technical efficiency and higher productivity, orthodox economics, unhappily, has had little explicitly to say about the relations between individuals *within* an organization. However, the suggestion that individuals within an organization have effort as an important argument in their utility functions, is in this respect an important step forward.

The Behavioural Approach to Productivity

A recent article in *The Times* described a situation which illuminated the central concerns of the 'micro-micro' and behavioural approach to productivity.[34] Ford Escorts were produced at two plants, one in Halewood in Britain and the other in Saarlouis in Germany.[35] According to the journalist (who visited both plants) the machinery in each plant was identical. The British plant, with 10 040 workers, produced 800 Escorts per day, while the German plant, with 7762 workers, produced 1200 Escorts per day. The writer attributed these differences in productivity to differences in 'mental attitude' between the two groups of workers, suggesting that the work relations of production in the German plant were more conducive to higher levels of productivity.

Advocates of the 'behavioural' approach such as Harvey Leibenstein often cite such casual empirical observations to support their claims that the orthodox assumption of technical efficiency in the theory of the firm is invalid. It is argued that the actual output of a firm is unlikely to be equal to the maximum output for given inputs. H. Arnold, M. Evans and R. House, members of the Carnegie School of Industrial Relations, wrote in a recent survey article that:

> Organisational behavior focuses upon the transformation process within firms, how these processes are carried out, how they are organised and how differences in intra-firm organization are related to inter-firm differences in effectiveness and productivity (given

identical inputs to the various firms) . . . what H. Leibenstein refers to as 'X-inefficiency' is, in fact, an article of faith or belief for organizational-industrial psychologists . . . if 'X-inefficiency' did not exist . . . there would not be need for . . . the discipline of organizational behavior.[36]

An outline of the behavioural model can be seen in Figure 1.2.[37] Fig. 1.2 shows the downward flow of influence in an organization from the external evironment to the decision-making process, to management practices and finally to individual responses. But the figure also shows that this influence can run in the opposite direction. Thus individual members of the organization evaluate the plans and practices of management and respond according to their personal reactions and judgements. Their responses, in turn, exert influence on management and may induce a change in the practices of management.

It is not hard to see why organizations such as Harvard Business School and the Carnegie School of Industrial Relations favour a behavioural approach to productivity. At Carnegie, writers such as

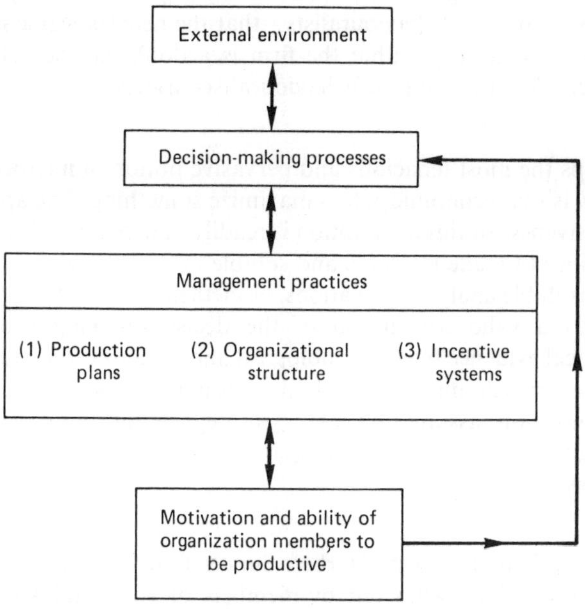

FIGURE 1.2

H. Simon, R. Cyert, J. March, among others, have introduced insights from psychology and personality theory into their behavioural theories of the firm. At Harvard Business School these theories are used to train young managers in flexible and innovative approaches to management. They are encouraged to establish a set of management practices which promotes better motivation in the members of the organization and consequently greater effort and higher productivity. It is thought that the more flexible and creative are management practices, the more responsive and productive will be the workforce.

Recent research in this field has centred on the problem of worker motivation. As Arnold, Evans and House argue: 'An important component of understanding work motivation lies in understanding how individuals make personal work-related decisions such as: should I really work hard today or should I take it easy?'[38] It is evident from Figure 1.2 that an important link exists between the motivation of the individual members of the organization and the decision-making processes within the organization. This raises the question of worker participation in the decision-making processes which determine production plans, organizational structure and appropriate incentive systems.

Before discussing participation the charge levelled by Harvey Leibenstein and the behaviouralists – that the neoclassical assumption of technical efficiency within the firm is a doubtful one – should be addressed. As one group of behaviouralists argues:

> perhaps the most tenacious and pervasive notion in microeconomic theory is that economic actors maximize something. The appeal and pervasiveness of this assumption is readily understandable in light of its ability to make tractable and soluble many otherwise intractable and insoluble analytic derivations. Nonetheless, it must be concluded that as a valid description of the decision-making process the empirical evidence from psychological and organizational research is now overwhelming that such an assumption is untenable. The maximization assumption assumed degrees of omniscience and computational sophistication that human beings simply do not possess.[39]

It is argued here, following Herbert Simon, that 'bounded rationality' implies 'satisficing' behaviour by members of an organization rather than maximizing behaviour.[40] However, it could be argued that members of an organization do maximize something, i.e. their utility.

This assertion necessarily implies a wider conception of utility (see, for example, A. Sen[41]) and a broader notion of technology.

In Section 2 it was argued that an important discretionary variable for each organization member is effort-output, of which complete information concerning this variable is known only to the individual. Thus one can conceive of a utility function with effort as an important argument. Individuals make decisions in response to their perceptions of the production plans, the organizational structure and the incentive systems which confront them. It could be argued that these are maximizing decisions, if, and only if, each individual acts to reach a utility equilibrium given the environment and constraints which he faces. Under these conditions the firm could be said to be technically efficient. Yet the behaviouralists claim that if a change in management practices yields a greater output for the same inputs, technical efficiency is an invalid assumption. But one could argue that a change in production plans, in organizational structure and in incentives systems can broadly be interpreted as a change in technology. In response to these changed conditions indviduals make choices with respect to, say, effort-discretion, such that their utilities are again maximized. If more effort is expended, productivity is increased, greater investment occurs (i.e. investment is the *cost* of change) and consequently the organization's production set is extended. It should be possible, therefore, to explain to an important extent, inter-firm variations in productivity within an industry (e.g. the two Ford Escort plants) by analysing intra-firm work relations. Moreover, this should be possible without having to abandon the assumption of technical efficiency and without having to create, in the manner of Leibenstein and the behaviouralists, an entirely new vocabulary.

The Participation Approach to Productivity

In the discussion of the behavioural approach to productivity it was suggested that an important relationship within an organization concerns that processes of decision-making, and workers' reactions to those decisions. It was suggested, further, that through more participation in the organization's decision-making by workers, these reactions may lead to an increase in the level of effort and consequently to improved productivity. The problem of participation will be examined more closely by drawing from three aspects of the literature on the subject: (i) the classical writers, (ii) the modern Western writers and (iii) the modern socialist writers.

An important concern of the participation theorists is the relationship between institutions and democracy. It is often argued that the existence of representative institutions at the national level is not sufficient for democracy. In order to proceed to a true democratic society democracy must be extended to decentralized levels, particularly to the work organization. Since most individuals spend a great deal of their time working within an organization, the exercise of democracy within the workplace can educate the majority of the population in the management of and concern for collective affairs and social welfare. In this way, it is argued, a person can gain experience in democratic procedures, which can only strengthen democracy at national levels. Therefore, as Carol Pateman states, 'if individuals are to exercise the maximum amount of control over their own lives and environment then authority structures in these areas must be so organised that they can participate in decision-making.'[42]

The Classical Writers

The foundation upon which modern participation theory rests is the writings of J.-J. Rousseau, J. S. Mill and Karl Marx. J.-J. Rousseau argued that through participation in decision-making individuals learn to be public as well as private citizens.[43] Through such participation Rousseau believed that an individual's freedom is extended since the individual is better able to control and determine actions which affect him by 'being one's own master'.[44] In Pateman's words:

> Rousseau thinks that individuals will conscientiously accept a law arrived at through a participatory decision-making process. More generally, it is now possible to see that a second function of participation in Rousseau's theory is that it enables collective decisions to be more easily accepted by the individual.[45]

And in Rousseau's words: 'so long as a number of men assembled together regard themselves as forming a single body, they have but one will, which is concerned with their common preservation and with the well-being of all'.[46] Rousseau's theory, therefore, suggests an interrelationship between the structure of authority within an organization and the attitudes of individuals toward work and society.

J. S. Mill extended Rousseau's theory into the context a modern social system. Mill argued that for individuals to engage effectively in national government, the qualities necessary for effective democracy must be fostered through local participation: 'we do not learn to read or write, to ride or swim, by merely being told how to do it, but by doing it. So it is only by practising popular government on a limited scale, that the people will every learn how to exercise it on a larger.'[47] In his later writings Mill included the workplace in his conception of 'a limited scale'. He thus saw the work organization as a political as well as an economic institution where individuals could gain experience in the management of collective affairs. Mill further argued that such organizations would inevitably become competing collectives, which framework would be well suited to the fostering of democratic participation and increased productivity. In his words workers will not

> be permanently contented with the condition of labouring for wages as their ultimate state. To work at the bidding and for the profit of another, without any interest in the work – the price of their labour being adjusted by hostile competition, one side demanding as much and the other paying as little as possible – is not, even when wages are high, a satisfactory state for human beings of educated intelligence who have ceased to think themselves naturally inferior to those whom they serve.[48]

Mill then argues in favour of an economy organized into production collectives:

> The form of association, however, which if mankind continues to improve must be expected in the end to predominate, is not that which can exist between a capitalist as chief, and workpeople without a voice in management, but the association of the labourers themselves on terms of equality, collectively owning the capital with which they carry on operations, and working under managers elected and removable by themselves.[49]

Under the traditional (and antagonistic) organization of production, Mill thought that workers' 'sole endeavour is to receive as much, and return as little in the shape of service, as possible'.[50] But in collective production work rules of production 'being rules self-imposed, for the manifest good of the community, and not for the convenience of an employer regarded as having an opposite interest, they are far more scrupulously obeyed, and the voluntary obedience carries with it a sense of personal worth and dignity'.[51] Mill further argued that collective production would foster work relations which would:

> increase the productiveness of labour, consist[ing] in the vast stimulus given to productive energies, by placing the labourers, as a mass, in a relation to their work which would make it their principle and their interest – at present it is neither – to do the utmost, instead of the least possible, in exchange for their remuneration. It is scarcely possible to note too highly this material benefit, which yet is as nothing compared with the moral revolution in society that would accompany it: the healing of the standing feud between capital and labour; the transformation of human life, from a conflict of classes struggling for opposite interests, to a friendly rivalry in the pursuit of a common good to all; the elevation of the dignity of labour; a new sense of security and independence in the labouring class; and the conversion of each human being's daily occupation into a school of the social sympathies and the practical intelligence.[52]

It is important to point out that by Mill's notion of 'friendly rivalry in pursuit of the common good' he means that collective organizations should compete against each other, with an efficient price system in operation to provide accurate signals and information. He argued that 'wherever competition is not, monopoly is; and that monopoly in all its forms, is the taxation of the industrious for the support of indolence'.[53] By promoting economy-wide efficiency, and, therefore, lower prices for consumer goods, Mill argued that competition 'between collective association and association would be for the benefit of consumers, that is, of the associations; of the industrious classes generally'.[54]

Karl Marx analysed the problem of growth and participation in a more abstract way than Mill; his discussions were independent of any specific social system. In the development model of Marx two categories are defined: production forces and production relations. The pace and pattern of economic growth depend on the relationship between these two categories.

Production forces are simply whatever is used in the production process, i.e. factors of production. The two major elements are means of production and labour power. Each is further subdivided. Means of production chiefly include instruments of production and raw materials. For Marx labour power was distinct from labour: labour power has the ability to develop, to acquire skills, to innovate, to gain education, experience, etc. Such knowledge and skills (especially science) are transmitted over time through labour power.

Yet for Marx man is more than labour power – he also stands in *relation* to other men and to other forces of production. He stated that

'In order to produce, [men] enter into definite connections and relations with one another and only within these social connections and relations does their action on nature, does production, take place.'[55] Relations of production, then, link forces of production with human agents. In his theory Marx divided production relations into two subcategories.[56] The first concerns ownership: such relations govern the control of and access of man to the forces of production and to output. *Ownership relations*, therefore, have a specific social and institutional form. The other subcategory, *work relations*, is concerned with the technical and social relations between men at the workplace, i.e. the organization of the production process.

Work relations are the relations which link labour power to other forces of production so that production can take place. The existence of work relations are independent of patterns of ownership and of historical considerations. They are technical in the sense that they are abstracted from specific social forms. The nature of these work relations can promote production or they can impede production. These considerations are a matter largely of the structure of the organization. As the production forces grow alterations in work relations within organizations are often necessary if new production possibilities are to be captured efficiently.

A very important element of Marx's model is the view that equilibrium growth can be disturbed when further development of the production forces is 'fettered' by inappropriate relations of production.[57] That is, ownership and work relations may no longer adjust smoothly to the development needs of the forces of production. Indeed, they can become obstacles. The possibility that bad relations of production can block further development of the productive forces does not refute the view that it is essentially the forces of production which determine the relations. Therefore adjustments, either of an evolutionary or a revolutionary nature, must occur in the relations of production in order to permit the inevitable growth of the forces of production. This new set of relations should then harness the potential productivity and convert it through the production process into actual output.

Marx's framework, therefore, is of considerable interest precisely because it is abstracted from any specific social form. It can be operationally useful whether one is analysing problems of economic growth and development in feudal, capitalist, socialist or communist societies.

The classical writers, in summary, argued that individuals and their organizations cannot be considered in economic isolation; that representative institutions at national levels are not sufficient to guarantee democracy; and, most importantly, that active participation by individuals in production organizations can improve democracy and stimulate economic growth.

Western Participation Theory

The Western literature on participation is primarily concerned with advocating more worker participation in management, within the framework of modern economic organizations. In this sense this work can be considered an extension of the 'Carnegie' behavioural approach to productivity. The OECD report, *Workers' Participation*, provided the following definition: 'workers' participation in management comprises all the processes whereby workers influence managerial decision-making.' [58] This report, drawing mainly from the experience of France, Germany and the Scandinavian countries, further divides participation into two categories: direct and indirect. Four methods of direct participation are as follows: [59]

(1) Expanding individual workers' responsibilities through redesign of the work organisation, through delegation of managerial function, through flatter organisational structures. Workers themselves make decisions regarding work and/or work conditions which were previously made for them.
(2) Introduction of semi-autonomous groups with considerable responsibility for task execution, ordering of raw materials, quality control etc.
(3) More participative managerial style.
(4) Organising work group meetings for the discussion of problems directly related to production, but also for issues like shift planning, health and safety conditions and vacations.

Direct participation, therefore, involves the individual worker in the execution of his tasks. It is argued that by giving better recognition to a worker's interests and abilities his and hence the organization's performance will improve.

Indirect forms of participation are more familiar and are mainly concerned with labour relations policy. Examples of frequently mentioned alternatives are: (i) shop steward committees; (ii) collective-bargaining procedures; (iii) trades union representation; (iv) shop-floor and department councils; and (v) worker representation on the boards of directors. These indirect mechanisms aim effectively to represent the interests of the workers at higher organizational levels. Typical issues for negotiation with senior management include, for example, introduction of new technologies, closures, lay-offs, plant relocation and expansion plans.

In Western Europe and the United States the issue of indirect participation has predominated. Much less progress has been made in the field of direct participation. As the OECD report suggested:

> When we take *all* managerial decisions in an enterprise as the potential range of decisions which can be influenced by the workers, it becomes increasingly clear that the number of decisions that are influenced by the workers today is only a very small percentage of this potential.[60]

Two counter-arguments are frequently offered by representatives of management in discussions of direct participation. The first argument concerns efficiency. Direct participation, it is often argued, will lower the efficiency of the organization. Yet, as J. Gäbler argues, in order to condemn participation on efficiency grounds, it is not sufficient to prove that equilibrium under direct participation is not Pareto-efficient: 'present market economies are so far away from the utopia of general Pareto-efficiency that it does not really matter whether participation is added to monopolistic market elements, to differences between private and social marginal costs, or state intervention and other factors disturbing the conditions for efficiency'.[61] Rather, Gäbler argues that to condemn direct participation it would be necessary to show that in comparison with the present system it *increases* inefficiency.

A second argument often advanced by managers concerns the question of risk-bearing. It is well known that in various markets in equilibrium, the more an individual participates the more risk he bears. Thus in a market in equilibrium a utility-maximizing individual's propensity to assume risk will depend on his attitude toward risk. It is frequently argued, following this line of reasoning, that many workers, being risk-averse by nature, may desire to have little direct involvement in participation.[62]

The issue of direct participation in Western organizations is a difficult one. Given the present structure of these organizations and the resulting work relations of production, one can reasonably expect slow progress in this field, especially in the absence of convincing empirical evidence and of more robust theoretical analyses. Yet, as the OECD report concluded; 'only a small part of the problems related to workers' participation can be attributed to the attitudes and behavior of either managers or trade unionists; most of the problems are intrinsic in the structure of our organizations. These structural problems are identical under the different economic systems.'[63]

Socialist Self-management Theory

In 1943 Joseph Schumpeter gave a familiar definition of socialism as 'an institutional pattern in which the control over the means of production and over production itself is vested with a central authority – or . . . in which, as a matter of principle, the economic affairs of society belong to the public and not to the private sphere.'[64] Yet, as Włodzimierz Brus has argued 'the thesis of "the leading role of the communist party" and the claim that it represents the general social point of view lead logically to the conclusion that the capacity to take correct decisons lies in narrower and narrower circles of the party leadership.'[65] In recent years a group of Eastern European economists (and other intellectuals) have challenged the orthodox interpretation of socialism and have offered an alternative one.[66]

This definition implicitly draws a distinction between *public* ownership of the means of production on the one hand and *social* ownership on the other hand. This distinction, and the implications for the structure of organizations in a socialist economy which follow from it, have been analysed by several prominent Eastern European writers. In this subsection this distinction will be looked at closely, as it shall provide a framework within which to analyse China's rural organizations.

A reasonable definition of ownership implies 'effective disposition over the object owned by its owner in his interests'.[67] From this definition it follows that social ownership of the means of production would have to meet two criteria: (i) the means of production must be employed in the interests of society; (ii) members of society must have effective disposition over the means of production it owns.[68] By what collective choice mechanism is 'the social interest' to be determined in a socialist country? Revisionist Eastern European writers argue that mere 'nationalisation', followed by absolute determination of the 'social interest' by a small elite cannot possibly meet the criteria that 'society must have effective disposition over the means of production it owns'. Indeed Brus states that:

> a definition of what is and is not in the social interest is impossible – without putting into operation some mechanism for revealing contradictions and reaching solutions which in the nature of things will contain an element of compromise; it is thus impossible without ensuring for society an active role in the process of taking economic decisions. Use of the concept 'the social interest' in a situation where society does not play such a role is in general unfounded, and frequently becomes simply misused to favour the interests of the rulers.[69]

In this view, therefore, a collective choice mechanism must operate in any economy in order to determine what is or is not in the social interest. It is further argued that such a mechanism *must* be democratic: 'under socialism . . . political democratism is an indispensable factor in the objectivity . . . of the process of decision-making; it is thus also an indispensable factor in economic rationality and in the full use of the development potential of society'.[70] A similar view has been offered by Oscar Lange: 'socialist ownership of the means of production involves both the use of the means of production in the interests of society as a whole and effective democratic participation by production and other workers in the management of the means of production'.[71]

The central problem, in the view of these economists, is to create favourable conditions in the economy for promoting the process of social ownership. These conditions can be fostered, in an important way, by the development of a self-management structure within production organizations. Movement toward self-management, according to Brus, means a gradual transfer of disposition over the surplus generated in production to the direct producers: 'this can only mean to postulate the most far-reaching possible decentralisation of economic decisions, which in principle should be taken by self-managing enterprises'.[72]

Economic decisions in any organization can be divided into two categories: technical and social. Technical decisions require expertise, i.e. specific skills and specialized training. In the self-management conception of socialism the role of expertise is chiefly to prepare the ground for social decisions by members of the organization. This is done primarily by technical decisions which eliminate inefficient variants and clearly define the area within which acceptable social solutions can be found. Yet decisions involving the short-term interests of individuals in an organization and the long-term collective interests of the organization (e.g. income distribution or choice of 'time horizons' for investment projects) always have social implications. Such decisions will, therefore, have an important influence on the attitudes of the members of the organizations, thereby affecting their potential for work, their effort discretion, their initiative, etc.

In Brus's view:

> the selection of the optimal variant from a number of possible alternatives arrived at by economic calculation is a political decision. . . . It follows that the optimisation of economic decisions, in the broad sense of the term, embodies not only the system and techniques of economic calculus but also a corresponding political mechanism within which conflicting interests can be clarified and compromises reached, so that the decisions taken in the name of society are as close as possible to real social preferences. It is very important that the alternatives for development strategy should be presented clearly and openly so that they can be publicly discussed.[73]

In the self-managed organization there are two important classes of decision which require democratic procedures to ensure that collective outcomes conform closely to true individual preferences. The first is concerned with income distribution and incentive structures. Income differentials are required as incentives to stimulate productivity. At the same time limits are set by considerations of social justice. Since the idea of justice is a normative one, a self-managed enterprise which has explicit democratic procedures should be able to identify compromise solutions to distributional issues. Such solutions should conform to the concrete conditions of the organization and, if determined democratically, accepted by the workforce as their own decisions, rather than imposed administratively from above.

A second class of decisions in the organization concerns the important problem of the choice of a time horizon for investment plans. This clearly depends on each individual's relative valuation of present versus future consumption. A balance must be determined between the long-term interests of the organization and excessive limitations of current consumption (which may affect adversely labour productivity). As Amartya Sen has argued, this is a vital problem in economic development:

> What is relevant here is not merely the problem of achieving fairness, justice, etc., but also of *making clear* that the choices made have these characteristics when seen from the point of view of the population at large. The difference between success and failure in planning is often closely related to public enthusiasm and co-operation. . . .[74]

By establishing democratic procedures within an organization intertemporal investment and consumption decisions can be reached which more accurately reflect social preferences. If members of the organization perceive such choices to be fair and just, then it is reasonable to expect that more 'enthusiasm and cooperation' will be reflected in more labour and effort expenditure. Moreover, members of the organization can more closely identify with the long-term collective interests of the enterprise.

But it must be pointed out that advocates of self-management socialism emphasize that social ownership of the means of production is a *process*, not a once-and-for-all act. By structuring an organization in a manner which is conducive to democratic decision-making this process can be catalysed. Such an organizational pattern can help to create the conditions in a socialist economy for true social ownership. Yet, as Brus has repeatedly argued, associated changes are necessary at a macroeconomic level.[75] First, a necessary if limited degree of macroeconomic co-ordination in key sectors of the economy must be retained by the central government. Second, a 'regulated' market mechanism (including an efficient price system) must be allowed to operate throughout the economy. Third, democracy must be extended to central levels so that the national leadership is ultimately accountable to the people, and so that a self-managed organization can gain confidence in its own democratic procedures. The importance of these macroeconomic requirements will be discussed in Chapters 8 and 9.

While such changes seem daunting to readers familiar with Soviet-type economies, their advocates remain optimistic. In their view the imperative of sustained economic development (continued growth of the forces of production) will ultimately dictate appropriate changes in the institutional and organizational arrangements. The build-up of pressures in an economy which are reflected in low labour productivity, in high rates of inflation and unemployment and in slow rates of growth should therefore lead eventually to more appropriate structural arrangements within production organizations. For some socialist writers, as for some Western writers, the rearrangement of work relations should give a prominent role to democratic participation in decisions by the members of an organization.

4. CONCLUSION

In this book I shall follow Scott, Kalecki and Brus in interpreting investment in a broad sense, namely as 'a present sacrifice of consumption in the hope of subsequent gain'.[76] Thus investment should be regarded as the cost of shifting an economy from a given position to an improved position. Indeed, if economic growth depends on investment and if investment requires accumulation, then it follows that accumulation is an important precondition for growth. This raises an interesting question: what kind of production organization in a developing country might be successful in promoting savings behaviour by its members? The literature on the social rate of discount suggests an approach to answering this question. Stephen Marglin and Amartya Sen, for example, have argued that under certain conditions the level of market-determined savings may not be socially optimal.[77] There are several reasons for this. First, people in the present generation may not attach sufficient weight to the welfare of future generations. Second, even if the present generation does attach importance to the future, there is an 'externality' involved: each person prefers that others should save more for the sake of future generations. As a result the market determined level of savings may be suboptimal. In Sen's words: 'Given the action of others, each individual is better off not doing the additional unit of saving himself. Hence nobody will, but everyone would have preferred one more unit of saving by each than by none.'[78]

Sen argues that this is just a special case of the general problem in game theory known as the 'prisoner's dilemma'. In this two-person game it is easily shown that through a collective contract each person would be better off than if each had followed a rational 'individualist' strategy. In extending the two-person game to an *n*-person context Sen has called this the 'isolation paradox'.[79] He argues that in the context of savings (and in other contexts) collective action can improve individualistic allocation. This result was first suggested by Rousseau, who drew a distinction between the 'general will' and the collection of 'individual wills'.[80] Although an individual has only one preference-ordering, his behaviour will depend on whether he is acting on his own given the actions of others, or whether he is taking part in a 'social contract', i.e. a collective arrangement.

This issue has also been addressed in the context of an 'assurance' game. William Baumol, for example, argues as follows:

> The individual as a citizen, having his share of local pride, may desire an improvement in the general future state of welfare of the community. If, however, he alone directs his activities in a manner conducive to it, the effects of his action may be quite negligible. . . . Thus neither private interest nor altruism (except if he has grounds for assurance that others, too, will act in a manner designed to promote the future welfare of the community) can rationally lead him to invest in the future, and particularly the distant future, to an extent appropriate from the point of view of the community as a whole.[81]

An important implication of this theoretical literature, therefore, is that collective arrangements in certain contexts can improve upon individualistic arrangements. John Stuart Mill in particular argued long ago that a co-operative production organization would foster work relations which would increase the productivity of labour. This would happen because the workforce would be more willing 'to do the utmost, instead of the least possible, in exchange for their remuneration'.[82]

Mill's contention has been challenged in theoretical studies by Benjamin Ward, Evsey Domar and James Meade *inter alia.*[83] In these studies it is assumed that the co-operative seeks to maximize income per worker. Then, by using standard microeconomic analysis it is shown that the labour-managed firm will result in a negatively-sloped, static supply curve, in excessively capital-intensive investment choices, in high unemployment and in chronic under-investment. Such models have been criticized by Jaroslav Vanek, W. Brus, D. Dubraucić, Joan Robinson, Branco Horvat, R. McCain, Martin Schrenk and others.[84] These critics argue that the results obtained in the models of Ward, Domar and Meade, are a product of the assumptions made, assumptions which are highly unrealistic. The objective function of these models – maximization of income per worker – is very narrow and has been the subject of much criticism. It is argued that this assumption is made in a static framework and is empirically untested. These models were originally based on the Yugoslav self-managed firm. Yet as Schrenk and Ardelan have argued, the Yugoslav self-management system has changed substantially since the 1974 constitution, and thus the reality there conflicts strongly with the organizations that have been modelled by the above writers.[85] In Schrenk's view the complicated structure of these self-managed enterprises and their links with the regional and central government, have not been captured in the models of Ward *et al.* As a result he contends that their assumptions and consequently their results are invalid. Schrenk cites especially the divergence between the predictions of these models and empirical reality in Yugoslavia:

> While the Illyrian model predicts chronic under–investment, no such state of affairs can be observed statistically. In fact the opposite is true: the investment rates (for fixed assets only) in GMP were almost continually above 30 per cent. The fact that the rates were in many years considerably higher than planned, and that 'investment mania' was repeatedly blamed officially as a major inflationary force, adds weight to the point.[86]

In recent years models of labour-managed firms which include dynamic features (e.g. wealth maximization) and considerations of uncertainty have been proposed. Since this literature has been recently surveyed by Alfred Steinherr, only the most important results will be mentioned.[87] Jacques Drèze, for example, assumes that a labour-managed firm seeks to maximize value-added and faces the same production possibilities as a profit-maximizing orthodox firm.[88] He then proves that 'with every labour-management equilibrium one can associate a vector of salaries such that the given allocation, the given prices, and these salaries, together define a competitive equilibrium'.[89] Drèze further proves that, given a suitable redistribution of initial resources, the set of equilibrium allocations in a labour-managed firm is Pareto-efficient. Drèze suggests that Walras had anticipated these results and 'had taken a keen interest in the development of producer co-operatives'.[90] In a statement reminiscent of J. S. Mill, Drèze argues as follows:

> We now have two reasons why the division of future output between labour and capital may fail to bring both groups into agreement about production and investment decisions. First the required division would be hard to define in practice. Second, it would be incompatible with decentralised incentives. We may thus expect the need to reconcile the interests of both groups through some form of participatory decision-making . . . . Tentative as this conclusion may still be, I regard it as providing theoretical justification for the participation of both labour and capital – whether it be publicly or privately owned – in decisions which affect the future of the firm and hence of its workers and capital owners.[91]

In another recent theoretical model of labour management and participation Alfred Steinherr found that 'whatever the objective function of the firm, it requires fairly mild assumptions to make some profit sharing and participation in decision-making always optimal'.[92] He argues that participation in decision-making shares the characteristics of a public good. That is, the optimal level of participation is determined by equality of the sum of the marginal rates of substitution between participation and income with the marginal net cost of participation. In the conclusion of his survey article on the theory of the labour-managed firm Steinherr argues as follows:

> . . . the case for internal decentralisation of decision-making appears thus as relatively strong if optimal democratic processes can be designed and implemented. The literature on labour-managed economies is able to establish the economic viability of labour-management and in several instances the *theoretical* superiority of labour-management over the production of capitalist firms. However, there are also important reasons for regarding these theoretical results as not yet definitive. First, the assumptions underlying past research do not characterise labour-management satisfactorily. For example, the too narrow conception of the objective function of labour-managed firms, giving rise occasionally to odd results, becomes apparent in this survey. Second, there are important 'grey' areas in this field. In particular the dynamic theory is still underdeveloped and future work here could prove fruitful. Another important and largely unanswered question is the one of incentive structures and the internal organisation of labour-managed firms.[93]

An important objective of this book is to explore the potential advantages of co-operative production organizations in the context of rural development. To identify these advantages in operational terms the decisions in an organization shall be divided into two categories: technical and social. Technical decisions require expertise and specialized training. The role of experts is mainly to prepare the ground for social decisions by eliminating inefficient variants and by clearly defining the area within which acceptable social decisions can be found. Social decisions involve a balancing of the short-term interests of individuals with the long-term collective interests of the organization.

If social decisions can be determined by democratic procedures within the organization then such procedures may have an important influence on the attitudes of the members of the organization. The framework for this argument is given in Figure 1.3. In an organization which contains a wide degree of participation in the decision-making process the important link rests with each individual's valuation of the costs and benefits of the democratically determined investment programme and production plans. By participating in these decisions it is postulated that an individual's time horizon can be widened. In this way a closer identification is promoted between individual short-term preferences and the long-term collective interests of the organization. Individuals are perhaps more willing, because of their participation in decisions, to sacrifice present consumption for future consumption. This change in

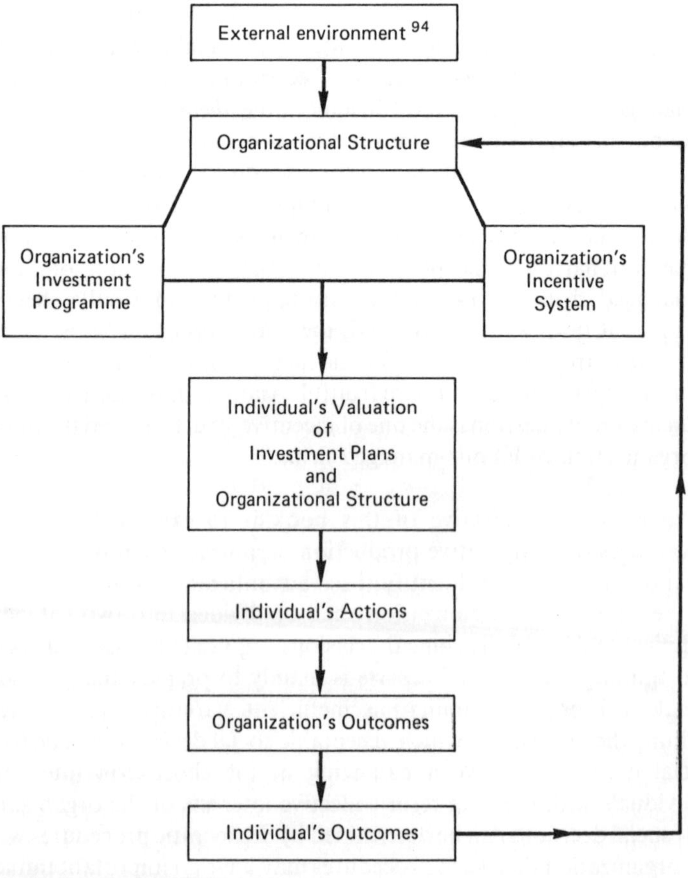

FIGURE 1.3

attitudes, an important requirement in poor countries, should thus lead to a more ambitious investment programme and to better prospects for growth.

The importance of democratic participation in social decisions can be illustrated by considering the following accounting procedures in a co-operative organization. After the organization has sold its output it obtains a gross income. Next the cost of materials and the tax obligations are deducted. This yields a 'surplus' which is then divided between an accumulation component and a distribution (consumption) component. This division – so important for economic growth – necessarily involves social decision-making. A co-operative organization which has explicit democratic procedures for decision-making is perhaps more likely to give a greater weight to the future than would otherwise be the case. In an operational sense this would be reflected in a higher ratio of accumulation to consumption than might be the case in a more orthodox, hierarchical organization. In any particular instance, of course, this ratio would be affected by each individual's valuation of the costs and benefits of the democratically determined investment programme, production plans and incentive arrangements.

There are other aspects of organizational structure which also should play an important part in the process of individual valuation. These aspects include the existing conditions in the country where the organizations are established. These conditions will affect the scale of the organization, which in turn will influence the extent to which the stream of benefits of an investment programme are internalized and captured by the individual. Moreover, if individuals in the organization can reasonably expect permanent membership for themselves and for their children then surely this should affect their inter-temporal decisions.

Suppose, for example, a rural organization decides to construct, over a ten-year period, a comprehensive irrigation scheme. This might require a substantial mobilization of labour and effort-expenditure, particularly during periods of seasonal slack. Even though the stream of benefits from this investment programme might not be realized for many years a family would perhaps be inclined to pay the cost, by undervaluing leisure and current consumption, in order to receive the future benefits for themselves and their children. Moreover, they would be inclined to do so if they participated actively in the formulation of the investment plan, if they believed that these benefits could be internalized within the organization and if they fully expected to remain members of the organization over a very long period.

2 The Emergence of the Rural Organization

The problem of achieving sustained growth and development in poor countries has thus far been considered in theoretical terms. It was suggested in the Introduction that achieving this goal requires, first, a substantial redistribution of land; and, second (and subsequently), the establishment of efficient production organizations which include a wide degree of participation by the members in its plans and decisions. In this chapter and in subsequent chapters the arguments presented previously will be discussed with reference to the organizational arrangements in rural China. This should lend descriptive and empirical concreteness to the arguments.

In Section 1 of this chapter the problem of land redistribution in rural China will be discussed in brief. It will be argued that several crucial economic problems were left unresolved by the redistribution. In order to tackle these problems the government encouraged the setting-up of co-operative organizations in the countryside. These organizations will be analysed briefly in Section 2, making use of the framework developed in the previous chapter.

An important shortcoming remained in the rural economy, however. This was the lack of rural-based light industry to produce both consumer goods for peasants as well as industrial inputs for agriculture. In Section 3 the government's solution to this problem – the creation of a commune organization featuring an industrial sector within them – will be described. In the chapters which follow, these organizations will be analysed.

1. LAND REDISTRIBUTION

Since the publication in 1927 of Mao Zedong's famous paper 'Report on an Investigation of the Peasant Movement in Hunan', land redistribution had always been a cornerstone of the Communist Party's programme.[1] From that time on, Mao and his colleagues steadfastly maintained that social relations and traditional organizations in rural China were the most important obstacles to economic development and growth. They attacked the ever-increasing greed and corruption of landlords and other members of the gentry, as well as the inept management by government officials. They pointed out that much of the surplus extracted and the tax collected by local governments were not returned to agriculture in the way of inputs or services, but were confiscated by local politicians and private armies.

This view of nineteenth- and early twentieth-century China has been well-examined by historians.[2] Many – perhaps most – historians would agree with Robert Ash that, by 1930, the increasing rural impoverishment and agricultural stagnation should be mainly attributed to 'increased inequality in land ownership and growing numbers of landless peasants, increased indebtedness among the peasantry, and neglect of the economic infrastructure'.[3]

Because of data limitations it is difficult to determine the distribution of the ownership of land before 1949. In a recent study published in China Jin Dequn presented data on the distribution of land by household class in rural China in 1934. These data are shown in Table 2.1 and they indicate that poor and landless peasants, who were 70 per cent of the rural population, owned 17 per cent of the land.

The government launched the land-reform programme in 1949 with the objective of changing radically this traditional pattern of ownership. Several years after its completion an official government source asserted that 'after the land reform the poor peasants and middle peasants possessed more than 90 per cent of the total arable land, while the former landlords and rich peasants possessed about 8 per cent of the total arable

TABLE 2.1 *Distribution of Land by Household Class in Rural China, 1934*[a]

	Share of total population	*Per cent of land owned*
Landlords	4	50
Rich peasants	6	18
Middle peasants	20	15
Poor and landless peasants	70	17

[a] These data exclude north-east China.

SOURCE Jin Dequn (1981) p. 63.

land'.[4] Table 2.2 enables one to compare J. L. Buck's survey data for 1929–33 with the results of a large government survey conducted after the reform. This comparison appears to support the government view expressed above and it reveals several other important effects of the land reform. First, the data suggest that nearly 40 per cent of the cultivated land in rural China was redistributed. Second, more than two-thirds of the redistributed land seems to have been taken from landlords and less than one-third from the rich peasants. Less than two-thirds of this redistributed land was given to poor peasant households and more than one-third was given to middle-peasant households. Third, the average crop area owned per household after the redistribution approximately doubled for poor peasants, increased by 17 per cent for middle peasants and decreased by 26 per cent for rich peasants. Perhaps most important, the average cultivated land owned by landlords decreased to one-tenth the amount of land owned before the redistribution. Fourth, the land-redistribution programme also reduced greatly the private renting of land and the private hiring of labour. The share of rental land in cultivated land, for example, declined from 30 per cent to less than 5 per cent.[5] The share of hired labour in total farm labour fell from 15 per cent to minimal proportions.[6]

The redistributive effects of the land reform were, therefore, quite substantial. This success no doubt helped the new government to gain the support of the poor peasants. Indeed, the immediate social implications of the land redistribution were profound: in just a few years

TABLE 2.2 *Some Results of the Land Redistribution Programme by Household Class*

	1929–33			*After land redistribution*		
Class of household	*Share of total house-holds*	*Avge crop area owned (mou)*	*Share of crop area owned*	*Share of total house-holds*	*Avge crop area owned (mou)*	*Share owned of total crop area*
Poor peasant	58.6	6.25	23.5	57.1	12.14	46.8
Middle peasant	29.8	15.81	30.3	35.8	18.53	44.8
Rich peasant	7.7	35.75	17.7	3.6	26.30	6.4
Landlord	3.9	116.10	28.7	2.6	11.98	2.1

SOURCE Compiled from data cited in Peter Schran (1969) pp. 16–24. The data for 1929–33 are from J. L. Buck (1937); the data for after the land reform are from *T'ung-chi Kung-tso*, no. 10 (1957) pp. 31–2.

a centuries-old traditional system of social stratification and power was altered substantially. The old rural gentry, whether in village residence or *in absentia*, lost most of their claims to status, power and land. But while the land reform as a *social* revolution was successful, the economic effects were much less so.

The land-redistribution programme did not overcome three important structural problems in the countryside. First, although the average crop area owned by poor-peasant households approximately doubled as a result of the land redistribution (from 6.25 mou to 12.14 mou) the amount of land still was too small to enable poor-peasant households to produce a marketable surplus. Indeed, Robert Ash argues that in many areas the poor peasants' new holdings were still not large enough for proper subsistence requirements. Ash cites data from a 1952 survey in twenty-four counties of Jiangsu Province in order to demonstrate this.[7] In these counties 33 per cent of the cultivated land was redistributed to 67 per cent of all households. Poor-peasant households, on average, were reallocated 4.9 mou, while middle-peasant households were reallocated, on average, 4.5 mou. The data in Table 2.3 show the output effects of the redistribution in Jiangsu Province by class of household.

TABLE 2.3 *Some Effects of Land Reform in Jiangsu Province by Household Class*

Household class of	*Average size of land owned per capita (mou)*	*Grain output per farm (jin)*	*Caloric content*[a] *per day per capita (calories)*
Poor peasants			
before land reform	0.92	262.2	767.78
after land reform	2.12	604.2	1769.23
Middle peasants			
before land reform	1.89	538.7	1577.29
after land reform	2.97	852.2	2495.28
Rich peasants			
before land reform	n.a.	n.a.	n.a.
after land reform	4.99	1659.2	4858.4

[a] The Chinese Medical Association in 1939 set a figure of 2054 calories per day per capita for a minimum well-balanced diet. See J. L. Buck, O. Dawson, and Y. L. Wu, *Food And Agriculture in Communist China* (Stanford, Calif.: Praeger, 1966) p. 123.

SOURCE 'Report of Land Reform Work in South Kiangsu', *Sunan Ribao*, 1 Jan 1952. Cited in R. Ash (1976b) pp. 528 and 531.

The households of poor peasants were able to increase substantially their output of grain after the redistribution. If one assumes a subsistence requirement of 2000 calories per day, however, these data suggest that, even after the redistribution, the poor-peasant households were not able to achieve this level of consumption. Yet the households of middle peasants were able to produce a small surplus after the redistribution, and the households of rich peasants were able to produce a rather larger surplus.

The inability of the land reform to raise the level of income of poor-peasant households high enough to enable them to produce a marketable surplus is due to one of the 'initial conditions' in China, namely, the income-elastic demand for food grain in the countryside. Because of the initial low level of agricultural productivity in rural China most peasant households after the reform preferred to raise their consumption rather than increase their marketing of grain.

Thus the land-reform programme, while resulting in enhanced consumption by rural households, had paradoxically failed to solve the important problem of the rural–urban marketing of grain. For nearly 60 per cent of the households in rural China the average crop area owned after the reform (12.14 mou) was still not large enough to meet both household subsistence requirements *and* to produce a marketable surplus. The highly unfavourable man–land ratio in rural China was a formidable 'initial condition' which land reform had not yet resolved.

A second important problem that was left unresolved by the land redistribution concerned the distribution of capital in the countryside. That is, although a substantial *land* redistribution had occurred, very little redistribution of tools, animals and farm equipment had taken place. In South Jiangsu Province alone only 33,700 draft animals were redistributed from landlords to 1,663,779 households.[8] Moreover, the situation was aggravated by the slaughter of draft animals by landlords.

A third and perhaps most important problem left unresolved by the land-redistribution programme concerned the need for extensive rural capital construction projects. The 1930s survey of J. L. Buck showed that there was a substantial degree of under-utilised labour in the countryside, particularly during the winter months. The organizational framework which emerged immediately after the reform could no more facilitate the mobilization of these slack resources for rural capital construction than could the traditional organizational arrangements. Yet the long-term prospects for agricultural growth in China (as in other Asian countries) depended, to an important extent, upon the degree to which the under-utilised labour and other slack resources could be mobilized for, say, water-control projects. How could poor-peasant households, which after the reform still owned very small parcels of land, be convinced that the external benefits of such projects could be internalized and captured by their households?

Yet land redistribution should perhaps be seen as a necessary *precondition* for sustained rural development. Indeed, the persistence of rural poverty in many developing countries can be explained, in an important sense, by the political and social relationships which derive from a very unequal distribution of land. If one accepts this argument it may be reasonable to conclude that the land-redistribution programme in China was, on balance, a success. As Franz Schurmann has argued:

> . . . as a social revolution, land reform succeeded in destroying the traditional system of social stratification in the rural areas. The old rural gentry, whether based in the villages or residing in towns, was destroyed. A social element, which had exercised leadership in the village by virtue of its status, its ownership of land, and its access to power had ceased to exist. That class which traditionally had formed a link between local society and the state – the gentry – was wiped out in the process of land reform.[9]

2. THE EARLY CO-OPERATIVES

After the completion of the land redistribution it took the government nine years – from 1953 to 1962 – to establish and to consolidate the commune organization. The decision to establish these organizations was a contentious one within the government. One group thought that the property of the rich peasants should be left intact 'in order to facilitate the early rehabilitation of rural production'.[10] The necessity to procure a marketable surplus from the rich peasants was an important consideration to this group in the government, given the propensity of poor peasants to increase their consumption rather than their marketing of grain. Mao Zedong and his supporters, on the other hand, argued that rural co-operative organizations, in which the households of a village pool and then collectively own their land, could succeed in mobilizing efficiently the under-utilized resources in the countryside. It was argued that this would lead to an increase in internal investment and consequently to increased growth. In essence, this was a debate over short-term strategy, since both 'sides' agreed that the long-term prospects for Chinese agriculture depended upon a technical transformation.

The rapid pace in which the co-operatives were formed (the percentage of all rural households in co-operatives increased from 14 per cent in 1955 to 97 per cent in 1957) suggests that, on this issue, Mao perhaps had a more accurate understanding of conditions in the villages than did some of his colleagues. Moreover, most writers have agreed that the rapid establishment of co-operatives during 1955–7 was not accompanied by the use of coercive methods by the government. Indeed, most available evidence would indicate the contrary: the poor and 'lower-middle' peasants, who composed nearly 70 per cent of the rural population, were quick to join the new co-operatives. Yet how successful were the rural co-operatives in mobilizing slack resources, in increasing internal investment and in promoting agricultural growth during 1954–7? This question will be answered briefly by examining the available data.

Perhaps the most important 'slack resource' in the countryside was labour. The surveys of J. L. Buck from the 1920s and 1930s indicated a considerable seasonal under-employment of labour. Data giving the average and total annual peasant labour days from 1950 to 1957 are shown in Table 2.4. While the average annual number of labour days displayed no tendency to increase during 1950–4, the number of labour days increased by 32 per cent from 1955 to 1957. This is an important empirical finding because it suggests that the co-operative production organization was very successful in mobilizing labour in the countryside.

An important goal of the policies associated with the co-operatives was to encourage the undertaking of capital construction projects in the

TABLE 2.4 *Average and Total Annual Labour Days in Rural China, 1950–7*

Year	*Average annual labour days*	*Total annual labour days (billion days)*
1950	119.0	26.489
1951	119.0	26.835
1952	119.0	27.168
1953	119.0	27.537
1954	119.3	28.155
1955	121.0	29.439
1956	149.0	38.084
1957	159.5	41.518

SOURCE Peter Schran (1969) p. 75.

countryside (e.g. water-control projects) and to increase the intensity of cultivation. Since the data in Table 2.4 indicate that most of the mobilisation of labour occurred from 1955 to 1957, the pattern of utilization of this labour can be determined by examining data on the intensity of cultivation for this period. These data are shown in Table 2.5.[11] The data suggest that during the period when co-operatives were established (1955–7) a substantial increase in the intensity of cultivation was achieved. The amount of irrigated land, for example, increased by 40.5 per cent over the period. A large increase in the multiple cropping index occurred during 1956. The amount of afforested area approximately tripled during 1956, and the percentage of cultivated area sown to improved rice seeds doubled in that year. These data suggest that the co-operative organizations were successful in mobilizing underutilized, conventional factors of production and in promoting internal investment in the countryside.

To what extent did the increased internal investment and the intensification of cropping practices result in increased agricultural growth during 1954–7? Data which give an indication of this growth are shown in Table 2.6. Grain output increased at an average annual rate of 3.8 per cent during the period, an impressive rate of growth. The total value of agricultural production increased at an average annual rate of 4.2 per cent during the period.

TABLE 2.5 *Indicators of the Intensity of Cultivation in Chinese Agriculture, 1954–7*

	1954	*1955*	*1956*	*1957*
1. Multiple cropping index[a]	135.3	137.2	142.3	140.6
2. Cultivated area[b] (1000 mou)	1 640 320	1 652 350	1 677 370	1 677 450
3. Irrigated area[c] (million mou)	340	370	480	520
4. Afforested area[d] (thousand mou)	17 490	25 660	85 850	65 330
5. Per cent of area sown to improved seeds[e]				
Rice	12.0	19.0	41.3	62.9
Wheat	23.5	32.7	58.7	68.7

SOURCE State Statistical Bureau (1960): [a] p. 128; [b] p.128;, [c] pp. 128–30; [d] p.133; [e] p. 131.

TABLE 2.6 *Indicators of Agricultural Growth in Rural China, 1955–7*

	1954	*1955*	*1956*	*1957*
Grain output (million metric tonnes)	160.5	174.45	182.50	185.00
Gross value of total agricultural production (billion yuan at 1952 prices)	51.6	55.54	58.29	60.35

SOURCE State Statistical Bureau (1960) pp. 16, 119.

In a recent study by Tien-Tung Hsueh and Pak-Wai Liu an aggregate agricultural production function for rural China was estimated in order to determine a quantitative relationship between the co-operative organization of production and grain output during the 1952–7 period.[12] Using cross-section data for 1952 and for 1957 they found that the marginal rate of substitution of land for labour rose sharply over the period. Specifically they found that the output elasticity of land was reduced to almost half of what it was in 1952, while the output elasticity of labour increased by 66 per cent.[13] Correspondingly they found that the marginal rate of factor substitution of land for labour increased from 3.437 in 1952 to 10.62 in 1957.[14] Because of the collectivization of production the average peasant put more labour into grain production in 1957 than in 1952. As a result the study found that the average marginal product of labour increased substantially during the period, from 299 jin per capita in 1952 to 531 jin per capita in 1957.[15] In the interpretation of their results Hsueh and Liu suggest that 'the steep rise in the marginal product of labour measured on a per capita basis is directly related to the better utilization of labour in terms of more working days in a year, less slack in the farm season, less idle labour during a workday and possibly more work effort from the peasant labour force'.[16] This study provides strong support for the view that the rural co-operative organization of production was successful in making it possible to employ productively larger amounts of labour.

What happened to the income earned from agricultural production during this period? The data in Table 2.7 show the amount of total consumption increased at an average annual rate of 3.7 per cent from 1953 to 1955 (i.e. the period when individual farming predominated). After most of the rural households had joined co-operatives (1955–7) the amount of total consumption increased at an average annual rate of 1.3 per cent.

TABLE 2.7 *Growth in Accumulation and Consumption in Rural China, 1953–7*

	1953	*1954*	*1955*	*1956*	*1957*
Total consumption (billion yuan at 1952 prices)	33.18	34.66	36.83	39.73	38.30
Average consumption per capita (billion yuan at 1952 prices)	66.9	68.6	71.2	75.2	71.3
Total net accumulation (billion yuan at 1952 prices)	1.29	1.33	1.65	3.13	3.23
Total accumulation / Total consumption	0.039	0.038	0.045	0.079	0.084

SOURCE Peter Schran (1969) pp. 131, 134 and 142.

The trend for total accumulation was quite different. In the 1953–5 period accumulation increased at an average annual rate of 9.3 per cent. However, after the establishment of rural co-operatives (1955–7) the amount of accumulation increased at an *annual* rate of 32 per cent. These data suggest that the establishment of co-operatives in rural China was associated with a substantial decline in the rate of growth of total consumption on the one hand and with a substantial increase in the rate of growth of total accumulation on the other hand. This is reflected in the changes in the accumulation–consumption ratio over the period. Whereas for the 1953–5 period this ratio increased at an annual rate of 5.1 per cent, in the 1955–7 period the ratio increased each year by over five times the earlier rate, i.e. 28.9 per cent.

The strategy to establish co-operation organizations in rural China would thus appear to have been successful in achieving three important goals. First, these organizations were successful in mobilizing under-utilized labour, in achieving a substantial amount of internal investment and in achieving an intensification of cultivation practices. Second, after the co-operatives had been established a modest increase was attained in grain production and in total consumption. This increase is perhaps impressive when it is recalled that some government leaders were worried that a continuation of the process of rural institutional transformation would result in a *decline* in agricultural production. Finally the rural co-operatives were successful in substantially accelerating the rate of accumulation in the countryside.

Management Procedures

In Chapter 1 it was suggested that a self-managed organization which has explicit democratic procedures can reach a compromise over the division of the surplus between accumulation and consumption. Given such democratic procedures, it was argued that decisions to postpone present consumption in favour of greater accumulation would more likely be accepted by members as their own decision, rather than imposed administratively from above. Therefore to what extent did these co-operatives operate on a democratic basis?

The *Model Regulations* of these co-operatives state that 'life in a cooperative should follow the principles of democracy'.[17] Article 6 of the revised regulations reaffirms this as follows:

> The cooperative shall be managed in a democratic way. Leading personnel of the cooperative shall be elected by the members, and important matters of the cooperative shall be discussed and decided upon by members.[18]

According to the *Model Regulations* the highest management body of the co-operative is the general meeting of the members. The *Model Regulations* further recommend that the general meeting convene at least twice per year and that a principal responsibility of the meeting is to 'elect a management committee to run the affairs of the cooperative'.[19] The members also elect a supervisory committee to monitor the decisions of the management committee.[20] The other important responsibilities of the general meeting are as follows:

(1) Adopt and amend the regulations of the cooperative;
(2) Elect or remove from office each year the Chairman and Vice-Chairman of the cooperative, the members of the management committee and the Chairman and members of the supervisory committee;

(3) Approve the valuation of animals, tools etc., turned over to the collective ownership of the cooperative, and the plan for collecting the share fund;
(4) Examine and approve the production plan and the budget drawn up by the management committee;
(5) Approve the proposals for payment and compensation to those engaged in managerial work;
(6) Examine and approve the plan drawn up by the management committee for the distribution of the annual income, and the measures for advance distribution and payment of the income;
(7) Examine and approve the reports of the management and supervisory committees in their work; and
(8) Approve the admission of new members.

A simple majority of the co-operative members constitutes a quorum for the general meeting. Motions concerning items (1) to (6) above require a two-thirds majority to be approved.[21]

According to these documents, at least, the structure of the rural co-operative organizations would seem to include an important degree of participation in decision-making and of democratic practice. There are two democratic features in particular that should be emphasized. First, the members have the right to examine and approve the production and investment plans of the organization. Second, the members have the right to examine and approve the decisions which determine the division of the surplus between consumption and accumulation.

It has been suggested in this section, in summary, that the acceleration in the rate of accumulation in rural China is associated with the structure of the co-operative organization. This theme shall be pursued in the rest of the book.

3. THE TRANSITION TO THE COMMUNE ORGANIZATION

During 1956–7 there was much debate within the government about the need to formulate a long-term strategy for growth. During the previous five-year plan (1953–7) most of the government's investment funds had been allocated to heavy industry. Agriculture was asked 'to pull itself up by its own bootstraps' – largely through the mobilization of slack resources in the countryside. Government leaders became increasingly aware that further rural growth depended upon the availability of modern technical inputs for agriculture. Once the slack resources had been taken up, any further growth would have to derive, for example, from chemical fertilizer, irrigation pumps and high-yielding seeds. It was argued that these and similar industrial inputs for agriculture could be produced in rural areas if light industry could be established there.

The increasing attention given to establishing light industry in the countryside was an important development in the autumn of 1957 and spring of 1958. As suggested above, rural industry had been neglected during the First Five-Year Plan. For 1955–7 the average proportion of economic construction expenditures on rural industry to total economic construction expenditures had been only 9 per cent.[22] Moreover, the proportion of rural industry which produced agricultural inputs was also very small: in 1954 4 per cent; in 1955 5.8 per cent.[23] Speeches and articles by Party leaders paid an increasing amount of attention to the advantages of producing locally the inputs for agriculture, as well as to the processing of raw materials in plants of small scale located near their sources of supply.

The policy of encouraging the development of self-financed local industry was officially promulgated by Liu Shaoqi in his important speech on 5 May 1958. The speech set out the essential elements of the rural development strategy for subsequent years. Liu made the following arguments concerning the advantages of developing local industry:[24]

(1) Fewer investment funds are required. Such funds can be raised from scattered sources in the countryside.
(2) Gestation time is short and outputs are available quickly.
(3) Small-scale industry can be designed and equipped locally, using simple types of equipment 'which are readily available in the localities'.
(4) Small enterprises can be set up over a wide area of the country, and can promote the training of technical personnel as well as balanced development between regions.
(5) The composition of output can be suited to the needs of particular localities and great flexibility can characterise the selection of production processes.
(6) Such plants can be located close to sources of raw materials and markets, thereby reducing transport costs and limiting pressures on existing transport facilities.
(7) An important advantage is the flexible use of local manpower in planned coordination with seasonal cycles of agricultural production.
(8) Establishing a network of rural industry will help reduce rural–urban differentials in the standard of living.

A second development during the autumn of 1957 and winter of 1958 concerned a water-control campaign. The campaign proposed the construction of hundreds of thousands of small and medium-sized irrigation projects financed mainly from local resources. Much attention was devoted to the co-ordination of plans between the different levels of local government and of the co-operatives. Directives were vague, however, and co-ordination proved to be very difficult. On the one hand, provincial and local governments were urged to work out comprehensive plans; while on the other hand co-operatives were asked to work out their plans according to local conditions. The problems of distribution of benefits from projects, of contributions of labour from different co-operatives, of methods of remuneration, of co-ordination of plans for larger projects, etc., proved to be formidable planning obstacles during the campaign. Confusion arose regarding economies of scale for such projects in the matter of size, of finance and efficiency of planning. Several editorials in *People's Daily* complained especially about problems of planning co-ordination. One article stated that

> actual conditions in various localities were extremely complicated and it was impossible to carry out agricultural plans smoothly without heeding the suggestions of peasants and cooperative members. . . . The state agricultural plan and the plans of the cooperatives should be coordinated; in this respect too, there had been shortcomings. The hsien [county] directly controlled the lower level organs; if it could coordinate the higher level plans with local conditions, make suggestions to the higher authorities, and revise inappropriate plans, then many mistakes could be avoided.[25]

Another editorial referred to 'shortcomings in the construction of water construction projects' resulting from the blatant pursuit of speed and quantity.[26] Other Peking publications criticized co-operatives for their pessimism regarding the potential for raising internally the necessary funds for water-control projects. Co-operatives were admonished for 'mistakenly postponing their water conservancy works repair programme . . . on the plea of shortage of funds'.[27]

The difficulties encountered in the water-control projects – especially those relating to appropriate economies of scale for efficient multi-level planning and for accumulation of funds – increased the attractiveness to the government of alternative organizational arrangements, namely, the amalgamation of several co-operatives with the local *hsiang* (township) government. By the Spring and Summer of 1958 the formation of communes had begun, particularly in Henan Province. This movement coincided with the launching of the 'Great Leap Forward'. The policies of the 'Great Leap Forward' were officially announced by Liu Shaoqi on 5 May 1958. The foundation for these policies – the encouragement of rural small-scale industry, the mobilization of off-peak under-employed labour for water-control investment projects, an ideology of self-reliance implied in self-financed rural development – was soundly based in terms of economic rationality. However, a predilection by certain members of the leadership for large scale in crop production and for 'speed and quantity' led to a period of tumult and fluctuation in the countryside. This predilection stemmed from a confusion between optimal size economies of scale for crop production on the one hand, and appropriate financial and planning economies of scale for rural capital construction on the other. This analysis shall be pursued in the next chapter, after describing very briefly in the next section the important institutional features and dramatic fluctuations of the commune organization during the tumultuous 1958–61 period.

4. CONSOLIDATION OF THE COMMUNE ORGANIZATION

In its original form the commune was notable for three important characteristics. First, it was a very large agricultural enterprise, averaging 4000 to 5000 households, although in some sparsely populated areas communes included as many as 10 000 to 20 000 households and composed an entire *hsien* (county).[28] Approximately 740 000 agricultural producer co-operatives were merged into 26 000 communes, with each commune ordinarily corresponding to the size of a *hsiang* (township).[29] A second important feature of the original form of the commune was its system of administration. The commune was a comprehensive unit of government as well as of planning. Many of the duties previously administered by the *hsien* and the *hsiang* were taken over by the commune. Under the commune administration committee departments were set up for agriculture, industry, water conservancy, forestry, animal husbandry, communication, finance, commerce, culture and education, labour allocation, militia, health, planning and scientific research.[30] The commune authority also became the 'main unit of ownership and distribution, with the power to move labour and other resources anywhere within its vast area'.[31] Management decisions regarding crop production was delegated to the 'work brigade', a very large unit which corresponded approximately to the size of a village, although sometimes corresponding in size to several villages (thus resembling in size the "advanced" agricultural producer co-operative). While the large brigade was responsible for daily farming decisions and labour allocation decisions, the commune level fixed production quotas and targets and it co-ordinated rural industrial and capital construction projects.

A third feature of the original communes was its political and ideological aspect. Mass mobilization of labour for construction projects was often accomplished by applying military organization and military terminology. A substantial component of distribution was 'according to need' i.e. a 'free supply' of grain on a per capita basis. 'Ownership by the whole people' was introduced as a step toward communism from the co-operative form of ownership. Private plots, houses, most domestic animals, fishponds, tools for private economic activities (and other 'vestiges of capitalism') became the property of the commune. A 'communist spirit of living' was encouraged through the establishment of mess halls, nurseries and communal handicraft groups.

There are a number of reports of peasant resistance to the policies followed in the original communes. Many peasants were incensed about the arbitrary and commandist attitudes displayed by cadres, particularly concerning output targets, labour allocation methods and the heavy emphasis placed on high rates of accumulation. In a recent book, Jurgen Dömes argued that from October 1958 'peasant resistance assumed in many regions the character of a general, although certainly not co-ordinated movement. The peasants refused to go to work in military formations, contrary to the orders of the cadres'.[32] During November and December 1958 the Chinese provincial press reported riots in no fewer than seven provinces.[33] Thus the attitude of much of the peasantry to the original structure and practices of the commune was a serious threat to the Maoist group in the leadership. At the same time the opposition group, perhaps emboldened by the response of the 'grass roots' to the new communes, pressed for a readjustment of policies and for a more pragmatic approach.

This original concept of the commune did not last long. The Party held a series of conferences from August 1958 to October 1962 in order to determine appropriate readjustment policies. In December 1958 the Party issued a resolution from Wuhan which urged consolidation and warned of succumbing to 'the Utopian dream of skipping the socialist stage and jumping over to the communist stage'.[34] The resolution criticized excessive centralization, the disincentive effects of the 'free-supply' system of distribution 'according to need', 'commandist' tendencies by cadres in labour management, the collectivization of private animals and tools, and the system of communal mess halls. Thus almost as quickly as it had appeared the original structure of the commune was in retreat.

The period of 1959–61 was a particularly difficult one for the government. The disruptions caused by the original communes were exacerbated by extremely bad weather conditions. Ministries in Peking also received grossly inflated statistics during 1959 of the economic performance in the previous year, thereby distorting the true situation in the countryside and making it even more difficult to develop appropriate readjustment policies. The government was particularly concerned about the disruptions to crop production caused by the inefficient allocation of labour for construction projects, by the imbalances and waste which resulted from the 'backyard' steel furnaces and by the damage done to incentives from excessively egalitarian remuneration and distribution schemes. According to Ken Walker:

> the situation in the spring of 1959 was the most serious since 1949 – first because food was scarcer than ever before; second, because the low-level cadres must certainly have been so bewildered, demoralised, and disillusioned that they were incapable of making decisions; and third, because the governments must have lost the support of many peasants who had been activists in the cooperativisation and collectivisation drives.[35]

By 1960 a severe agricultural crisis had emerged. Grain output in 1958 had been 200 million metric tonnes (mmt); in 1959 it had fallen precipitously to 165 mmt; and in 1960 it plummeted further to 143 mmt.[36] Famine conditions prevailed amid reports of widespread hunger and millions of cases of starvation. In November 1960 the Central Committee issued an 'Urgent Directive on Rural Work', comprising '12 Articles'.[37] The directive banned egalitarianism in distribution and admonished the commune leaders for commandist tendencies. Decentralization of responsibility was urged, 'distribution according to work' was to replace the system of 'time wages' and 'free supply', and private plots, family private economic activities and rural free markets were restored.[38] The Ninth Plenary Session of the Eighth Central Committee met in Peking during January 1961. The policy of 'agriculture as the foundation and industry as the leading sector' was set during the Plenum. The Central Committee instructed cadres on the distinction between socialism and communism, especially with respect to the importance of incentives (distribution 'according to work' rather than 'according to need').

In the Spring of 1961 the government issued the 'Draft Regulations Concerning the Rural Communes'.[39] This document banned commandist systems of labour allocation, suspended the mess halls, guaranteed the existence of private plots (to 5 per cent of cultivable land of the commune) and redistributed much of the power and authority of the commune level to the brigade level. An important decentralization trend in the commune organization was thus confirmed. The commune level was responsible for exercising the administrative functions of the original *hsiang* government, for managing its own industrial enterprises, and for the planning and co-ordination of construction projects involving different brigades. While the brigades were responsible for crop management, further decentralization of economic decision-making in agriculture was seriously considered by the government during the rest of 1961. Because of disruptions to agricultural production which resulted from an inefficient allocation of labour to commune-managed projects, a 'contract' relationship was promoted between the higher-level units and the lower-level units within the commune. Moreover, it was thought that the brigade (which comprised approximately 175 households) was an inappropriate scale from which to take daily farming decisions. Such decisions were now thought to be most efficiently taken at a considerably more decentralized level, namely the production team. Teams corresponded to natural neighbourhoods within villages, comprising approximately twenty households.

These conclusions were drawn at the Peitaiho Party Work Conference in August 1962 which preceded the Tenth Plenum in September. The 'Draft Regulations' were revised and issued as the '60 Articles' on agriculture.[40] These '60 Articles' have served as the foundation of rural economic policy up to the present (except for some important revisions since 1978). They contain a detailed description of the scope, organization and scale of the commune. The document sets the production team as the key unit of responsibility in the three-tiered structure. The team was to be the accounting unit and thus responsible for distribution decisions. Teams owned their own land, tools, animals, trees, etc. Among the important clauses in the '60 Articles' concerning the team are the following:[41]

> The labour force within the production teams are at the production team's disposal. The commune or production brigades must consult the members of the production teams concerned if they want to

transfer labour forces from them and, in the absence of their consent, they are not allowed to transfer labour forces from them.

Production teams should make overall arrangements for food crops and industrial crops and for the varieties of food crops and draw up their production plans.

In order to facilitate the organising of production, the production teams may set up fixed or temporary work groups, according to localities, and contract work may be subscribed by period, by season, or by the whole year.

The production team should give rational remuneration to its members according to the quality and quantity of labour performed, and egalitarianism should be avoided. . . . The production team should gradually introduce the system of fixed labour quotas and exercise control over such quotas. Work under this category must be given work points as required by the fixed quota system. . . . When fixing the labour quota, it is necessary to fix a rational standard for work points, as dictated by the technical level required by different types of labour, the intensity of such labour, and the importance of such labour in the process of production.

The production team must practise the system of democratic management of the team, and bring to the full the activism of making commune members the masters. All important things such as the teams' production [plans] and income distribution must be decided through discussion at a general meeting of commune members, and not by cadres. Before any decision is reached, opinions of the commune members should be solicited, and several different plans submitted to them, with details of each plan clearly explained to them, before any decision is reached after full deliberation at a general meeting of commune members.

The commune members' general meeting of the production team should be held periodically, at least once a month. It may also be called as required by the needs of production and work assignment and as demanded by the commune members. . . . The chief of the production team, the accountant, the control committee members should all be elected by the commune members' general meeting; their tenure of office is one year but it may be extended when re-elected . . . these officials, when found incompetent, may be dismissed at any time by the commune members' general meeting.

One can see from these regulations that most of the farm management, labour allocation and distribution decisions were meant to be taken at the level of the production team. Moreover, this process of decision-making was to have conformed to democratic principles. The remuneration and distribution guidelines provided for material and personal incentives. While most of the crop production decisions fell within the purview of the production team, the commune and brigade levels shared responsibility for the management of industrial production and for the planning and co-ordination of capital construction projects.

Thus by the autumn of 1962 the commune's scale, structure and function had changed considerably from its original form. The number of communes had increased from 26 000 to 74 000, a reduction in average size of approximately two-thirds.[42] G. William Skinner has noted that this consolidated commune structure has preserved the important spatial and marketing relationships between the town and the village which were typical of traditional rural China.[43] Indeed, the similarities between the efficiency of traditional patterns of organization and the post-1962 commune system are striking: the production team corresponds approximately to the traditional neighbourhood; the production brigade with the natural village; and the commune level with the marketing town. Yet an important innovation of the post-1962 system of organization lay in the economic functions of the brigade level and the commune level. By making them responsible for capital construction and industrial production an efficient planning and accumulation scale was determined and brought into use in the countryside. This pattern of organization remained intact until the 1980s (see Chapter 8 for a discussion of the recent reforms).

3 Analysis of the Rural Organization

In this chapter two important aspects of the rural organizations will be analysed. First I will discuss the problems of incentives and organization that arose in the early attempts to establish an efficient structure for the commune. Next an important source of disagreement among leading members of the government concerning an appropriate scale for crop production will be identified. Finally I will discuss the relationship between certain external effects and the structure of the organization.

1. DISECONOMIES OF LARGE SCALE IN CROP PRODUCTION

In Chapter 2 some of the original features of the commune organization were briefly criticized. There is little doubt that, taken together, many of these original features had a disruptive effect on incentives and on agricultural production. One feature in particular ought to be analysed rather more carefully, because (unlike, say, communal mess halls) it is deeply rooted in Marxist–Leninist ideology.

It was noted in Chapter 2 that the original commune was in part an amalgamation of agricultural producers' co-operatives both in structure and in function. The very large unit which emerged during 1958 and 1959 was characterized by a high degree of centralization of economic decisions, not only for the organization of rural capital construction projects and of industrial production, but also for crop production. This predilection for large scale in both industry and agriculture can be traced to the writings of Marx and Engels, and found throughout the writings of Kautsky, Trotsky, Lenin, Stalin and Mao Zedong. In these writings agriculture is treated analytically in a manner similar to industry. The equating of the two processes is strained because of the fundamental differences in the characteristics of agriculture and of industry. These differences were well-recognized by Adam Smith:

> Not only the art of the farmer, the general direction of the operations of husbandry, but many inferior branches of country labour, require much more skill and experience than the greater part of mechanics trades. The man who works upon brass and iron works with instruments and upon materials of which the temper is nearly always the same, or very nearly the same. But the man who plows the ground with a team of horses or oxen, works with instruments of which the health, strength, and temper are very different upon different occasions. The condition of materials upon which he works is as variable as that of the instruments which he works with, and both require to be managed with judgement and discretion.[1]

While industry is continuous in time, concentrated in space and monotonous in activity, agriculture is intermittent in time, dispersed in space and multifarious in activity.[2] Land can be used for many purposes. Moreover, unlike industry, agriculture is constrained by natural phenomena, variations in which often require quick, 'on-the-spot' decisions. Unlike industry the dispersion in space of most agricultural operations makes centralized supervision difficult, and therefore is most efficiently served by an extremely decentralized management structure. Yet Marx, perhaps unduly influenced by the expansion of tenant farming in nineteenth-century England, neglected to consider in his analysis the multi-operational character of agriculture. He argued that the internal logic of agricultural development would lead to the evolution of very large enterprises, just as in industry.[3] The peasant would be replaced by the wage-labourer, a process facilitated by the production of agricultural machinery. Just as large industrial enterprises could be efficient in capitalist terms, so, he argued, could a large scale in agriculture also be efficient.

Engels, too, insisted upon the superiority of large-scale farming. He did this despite the fact that the small farmers in Europe weathered more successfully than the large the 'agrarian crisis' of the late nineteenth century which resulted from a dramatic fall in grain prices.[4] In 1894 Engels argued that, upon confiscation, the estates of landlords should be immediately organized for large-scale farming and placed 'under the control of the community'.[5] The publication of Kautsky's book *The Agrarian Question* in 1899 continued this ideological legacy. In this work (which was praised by Lenin) Kautsky argued that capitalism was creating the conditions 'for socialisation of agricultural production, which must originate through the rule of the proletariat as certainly as the socialisation of industry with which it will merge to form a higher unity'.[6]

In 1906 Trotsky published an important book entitled *The Permanent Revolution*. This book was influential because it challenged an important aspect of orthodox Marxism, namely, that a socialist revolution would first occur in advanced, industrial countries. Trotsky argued that, on the contrary, it would be possible 'for the workers to come to power in an economically backward country sooner than in an advanced country'.[7] Yet Trotsky did not challenge the orthodox view of institutional transformation in agriculture. He suggested that a revolutionary government 'must adopt the tactics of permanent revolution . . . and go over to more and more radical social reforms'.[8] He developed his argument as follows:

> The first thing the proletarian regime must deal with on coming into power is the solution of the agrarian question, with which the fate of vast masses of the population . . . is bound up. In the solution of this question, as in all others, the proletariat will be guided by the fundamental aim of its economic policy, i.e. to command as large as possible a field in which to carry out the organisation of the economy. . . .[9]

Although Lenin had on occasion supported the orthodox Marxist view regarding the superiority of large-scale farming[10] he was forced for political reasons temporarily to alter his view. In order to ensure rural support for a Bolshevik government he advocated distribution of the large estates to the peasantry. However some large estates were nevertheless converted to large state farms.[11] Stalin and his successors have continued this preference for large agricultural enterprises.

There is early evidence of Mao's acceptance of the orthodox Marxist–Leninist advocacy of large-scale farming. In his 1943 speech entitled 'Get Organised' he wrote:

> Among the peasant masses a system of individual economy has prevailed for thousands of years, with each family or household forming a productive unit. This scattered, individual form of production is the economic foundation of feudal rule and keeps the peasants in feudal poverty. The only way to change it is gradual collectivisation and the only way to bring about collectivisation, according to Lenin, is through cooperatives in the border region, but at present these are only of the rudimentary type and must go through several stages of development before they can become cooperatives of the Soviet type known as collective farms.[12]

While the Yanan period provided Mao with experience of the beneficent effects of co-operatives it also may have been the initial source of confusion between the appropriate scale for crop production on the one hand and for rural industrial production and capital construction on the other. In the chapter on co-operatives in his 1942 book *Economic and Financial Problems* Mao concluded by arguing that:

> Enlarging the scope of cooperative undertakings should not be limited to consumption alone but should include production, transport, credit, and so forth. This is an inevitable trend in cooperative development henceforth. That is to say, we must run comprehensive cooperatives.[13]

One can see from this quotation the seeds of the commune which emerged in 1958. Yet the confusion in the early commune between size economies of scale in crop production and financial and planning economies of scale in construction and in industrial production perhaps resulted from Mao's determination to establish 'cooperatives of the Soviet type known as collective farms'. Indeed, Mao re-emphasized this determination in his important July 1955 speech 'On the Cooperative Transformation of Agriculture'. In the speech he argued as follows:

> . . . some of our comrades have not given any thought to the connection between the following two facts, namely, that heavy industry, the most important branch of socialist industrialisation, produces for agricultural use tractors and other farm machinery, chemical fertilizer, modern means of transport, oil, electric power, etc. and that all these things can be used, or used extensively, only on the basis of an agriculture where large-scale co-operative farming prevails.[14]

Yet owing to the vastly different 'initial conditions' of Chinese agriculture the optimal scale for farming is inconsistent with the large Soviet-type collective organization and management. Chinese agriculture resembles horticulture in character. It is marked by an intensive, irrigation-dominated pattern of farming, typical of many Asian countries. Chinese-type irrigation involves a multitude of variegated tasks such as inter-tillage, weeding and harrowing. These operations do not lend themselves well to centralized management and to centralized decision-making. But neither were the 'initial conditions' of Chinese agriculture appropriately suited to family farming. Indeed, the extremely unfavourable man–land ratio in traditional rural China often gave rise to temporary forms of co-operation between households. Labour-service exchange and collective cultivation were practised and are well-documented by historians.[15] Small groups of households often related and living in the same neighbourhood within a village, frequently co-operated to stagger planting dates and to contribute labour during the different harvest periods. Such co-operative activities have been noted in other Asian countries with similiar 'initial conditions' as China.[16]

The 'mutual aid teams' which flourished from 1953 to 1955 were based on the sharing of land, labour and tools by small groups of families (often six to ten families). Indeed, during this period, when between 40 to 60 per cent of all rural households were organized in mutual aid teams, grain production increased at an average annual rate of 3.8 per cent.[17]

The 'elementary' agricultural producers' co-operatives represented only a slight enlargement in the scale of crop production. These co-operatives had an average membership of twenty-seven households in 1955, and usually conformed to the size of a neighbourhood within a village.[18] The amalgamation of a half-dozen or more neighbouring 'elementary' cooperatives into an 'advanced' co-operative represented a substantial enlargement in scale. By 1957, there were, on average, 157 households per 'advanced' co-operative.

Yet the most important consideration concerning the efficient organization of crop production is not the absolute size of the co-operative organization, but rather its structure. That is, given the nature and conditions of agriculture in China, one would expect that an extremely decentralized organization of crop production would produce the best results. In this way small groups of families who perhaps live in the same neighbourhood, and who may be related, can take their own daily decisions concerning crop production.

Soon after the formation of the 'advanced' agricultural producer co-operatives the crop management diseconomies of this larger scale became evident to some leading members of the Party. A directive of the Central Committee and State Council in September 1956 criticized the 'commandist' tendencies of some rural cadres and called for the rectification of such shortcomings. The directive stated further that:

> Agricultural production differs from industrial production. A greater proportion of agricultural production is self-supporting in nature and is at the same time dependent on natural and

> geographical conditions. Agricultural producer cooperatives are not State enterprises, but are managed under a collective system or partial collective system. Therefore we cannot draw up agricultural production plans as we draw up industrial production plans. While mapping out such plans, the habits of the local peasants in cultivating certain particular crops or engaging in particular types of sideline production should be continued.[19]

The directive further urged that large, inefficient co-operatives ought to be divided where appropriate:

> . . . the scale of an agricultural cooperative is of importance in its organisation and construction. . . . In regard to large cooperatives, all those that can be operated properly should be maintained. Those which are inefficient in production, causing a majority of the cooperative members to demand a division of the cooperative should be so divided in a suitable manner.[20]

It seems likely that a division of opinion among the leadership emerged during 1956 and 1957 over the issue of the choice of optimal scale for crop production. Although it is difficult to speculate on the membership of factions in this (and other) disputes, the evidence would indicate that Deng Zuwei, the director of the Rural Works Department of the Central Committee and Chen Yun, a leading member of the Central Committee, were opposed to the tendency toward a larger scale. In his speech at the Third Plenum of the Eighth Party Congress meeting in September and October 1957, Deng Zuwei stated that:

> In the past many agricultural producer cooperative cadres misunderstood collective labour. There were serious wastages of labour resulting from the use of methods such as 'banging the gong and all get together to go down to the fields'; 'let's work like a hive of bees'; 'squad, brigade attack'. These methods have to be overcome.[21]

Six days before the convocation of the controversial Third Plenary Session, the Central Committee published two directives on improving the efficiency of co-operatives. Among the arguments in these directives were the following:

> It appears from past years' experience that in the majority of cases, 'one village-one cooperative' would be a suitable

arrangement . . . but some cooperative farms which have grown to large and unwieldy proportions should be properly readjusted according to the demands of the masses, either by reducing their size or by retaining the form of united cooperatives, in which case the team can operate on their own acount. Each production team, basic production unit of a cooperative, should preferably comprise twenty households in general but may embrace more or less than this number according to local characteristics. Too big size will make management unwieldy. . . . [22]

. . . agricultural production is scattered and is restricted by natural conditions, and consequently, is characterised by a regional character and a seasonal character. Because of this and the manual operations that still characterise agricultural production, a certain initiative and flexibility must be maintained in production administration. Thus, a correct combination of the unified management and centralised leadership of the cooperatives with the development of the initiative and flexibility of the production teams in production administration becomes the basic principle for directing the agricultural producer cooperatives' administration of production . . . production teams are the basic units of a cooperative to organise labour power and manage agricultural production.[23]

The size of a cooperative and production team has much to do with the administration of agricultural production. Agriculture has its characteristics and the level of technique and management of agricultural production is low. As a result of practice in the past years, it has been proved that big cooperatives and big teams are generally not suited to present production conditions. . . . The proper size of a production team is about 20 households living close to each other. . . . Once the size of the cooperative farm and production team is fixed, an announcement should be made that there will be no change for the next ten years.[24]

These directives were remarkable for several reasons. First, they were published under the name of the Central Committee, indicating that they had considerable support among the leadership. Second, the arguments put forward in these documents showed a perceptive understanding of an appropriate scale for crop production and for farm management well-suited to Chinese 'initial conditions'. Third, in arguing that larger units were not conducive to efficiency in Chinese agricultural production, the directives offered a refutation of the orthodox Marxist–Leninist predilection for large-scale farming.

Fourth, in urging a 'correct combination of the unified management and centralised leadership of the cooperatives with the development of the initiative and flexibility of the production team', the directives drew an important distinction between crop production economies of scale and financial and planning economies of scale. Yet even more remarkable than the content of these directives was their immediate obsolescence. After the close of the controversial enlarged Third Plenum in October 1957 the policy of the Central Committee suddenly changed and the commune movement began to gather momentum, culminating in the formation of the very large communes in the Spring and Summer of 1958.

2. THE IMPORTANCE OF INCENTIVE ARRANGEMENTS IN THE COMMUNE ORGANIZATION

In the previous section it was suggested that an important reason for the inefficiency of the large scale of the communes in the 1958 and 1960 period was the nature of the incentive arrangements operating within them. This is consistent with the view, expressed in Chapter 1, that an important determinant of the productivity and efficiency of an organization is the nature of the incentive system which operates within it. Recent developments in two distinct areas of economic theory lend support to this view. The first is the recent economics of information literature and in particular the problems associated with team production. The second are recent extensions in the theory of collective production. This literature will be discussed very briefly in order to derive some insights for our analysis of the structure of the commune organization.

In Chapter 1 it was argued that each member of an organization has an important discretionary variable: his output of effort. Yet most employment contracts are incomplete in the sense that the level of individual effort expended cannot be explicitly stipulated in the contract. Hence an asymmetry of information exists: individuals know what level of effort they are providing, while employers do not have complete information about this discretionary variable. The problem is particularly evident in team production, where it is difficult and therefore costly to define or determine each individual's contribution to team output. Since the output yielded by a team is not the sum of separable outputs of each of its members, the management of the organization faces a screening problem. Another problem for management, associated with screening and the nature of team production, is the prevention of 'free-rider' abuse by individuals (also known as effort-shirking). This problem arises because of potential conflicts of interest within the organization.

Some of the characteristics of team production, of the asymmetry of information, and of 'free-rider' abuse have been captured in theoretical models in the recent literature. Joseph Stiglitz, for example, has argued that an important aspect of information is the property of 'nonconvexity'.[25] That is, the value of a given amount of information increases with the frequency of its use. He concludes that 'it can be shown that, in general, it does not pay to acquire just a little bit of information: a little information has negative net value, i.e. the costs always exceed the benefits. Thus it does not pay to monitor just a little; it either pays not to monitor at all, or to monitor at a finite level.'[26] This is an important result for the discussion here. The piece-rate system of remuneration which operated in the co-operatives suggests that the costs of finite monitoring in crop production would be substantial when large numbers of people are involved. The daily performance of each farm worker had to be evaluated and the appropriate number of workpoints assigned by management cadres. As suggested above, however, agriculture is dispersed in space, is subject to variations in weather, is discontinuous in time, etc. These conditions make it highly unlikely that, in the case of large numbers of agricultural works, the management of the organization could effectively 'monitor at a finite level'. Yet the efficient operation of a daily piece-rate system of remuneration requires a substantial amount of monitoring. Thus for large agricultural groups the organization is likely to be caught in the costly 'middle ground' between 'not monitoring at all' and monitoring effectively 'at a finite level'.

The larger the set of labour inputs about which performance information is collected within the organization, the greater the costs of collecting information. Thus the larger the organization the more difficult and costly are efforts to monitor performance. To counter this problem Roy Radner, Joseph Stiglitz, Armen Alchian and Harold Demsetz, Oliver Williamson and others have suggested that a large organization should be decentralized and specialized in order to reduce these costs.[27] Recent empirical research in industrial economics suggests that organizations which are structured in a decentralized way achieve better performance.[28]

For reasons discussed above, it is likely that in 1957 the efficiency of the rural co-operatives would have been improved through a decentralization of structure and of decision-making. The opposite tendency, reflected in the developments during 1957–60, led to a marked decline in agricultural production. By 1962, however, the consolidated organization that emerged was characterized by a substantial degree of decentralization in its structure. Indeed the post-1962 commune organization was still a very large organization: the financial and planning economies of scale associated with industrial production and rural capital construction required, for reasons of efficiency, a large scale. But the efficiency requirements of agriculture are quite different. This was recognized by the 'opposition' group in the leadership during 1957–62 and they eventually succeeded in convincing their colleagues to encourage some decentralization in the levels of decision-making and in the management of crop production.

The '60 Articles' document published in 1962 recommended that crop-production decisions be taken by production teams. Indeed, even within a production team crop-management decisions could be further decentralized to the level of small work groups (e.g. 4–6 households). These groups or households could sign contracts with the team for delivery of a fixed output at a future date. The production decisions would then be made by the members of the group and consequently the management cadres of the production team would no longer have to monitor individual effort 'at a finite level'. The 'job responsibility and contract system', moreover, stipulated that bonuses could be paid for overfulfilment of the contract.

The advantages of such a contract system of remuneration in agriculture have been well-explained by Joseph Stiglitz. He argues as follows:

> . . . incentives are a problem mainly because of difficulties in monitoring individuals' inputs and outputs. . . . Thus the magnitude of this problem depends on how we organise the production process . . . if we hired workers to pick weeds, and paid them by the weight of weeds picked, they would pick the largest weeds, not necessarily the ones which would most likely interfere with the growth of the vegetables; if we hire workers to grow vegetables, and pay them in proportion to their output of vegetables, they will pick the correct weeds.[29]

One result of Stiglitz's model, in which it is assumed that the effort of an individual cannot be costlessly or directly monitored, is that an equilibrium contract would entail a piece rate in addition to a time rate. The 'job-contract and responsibility system' operating at the level of the work group or household within the production team in the commune contained elements of both piece rate and time rate. If such a system had been implemented within the communes after 1958 there are sound economic reasons to believe that it would have promoted efficiency in agricultural production.

Yet the remuneration systems that operated in the early communes not only involved a cumbersome and costly degree of monitoring of individual tasks, but also rewarded 'need' to a larger extent than 'work'. The theoretical literature on labour allocation in co-operative production can offer some useful insights concerning such 'mixed' incentive systems.[30]

The standard labour allocation model in this literature assumes that a household allocates its time between the collective sector, the private sector and leisure in such a way as to maximize its utility. It does so by equalizing its expected marginal utility of time in each activity. While a household earns the full output of their labour in the private sector, their earnings from the collective sector, however, depend not only on their own labour, but also on the labour input of other households. Thus, in considering the potential benefits of labour allocation and effort-discretion in the collective sector the household will have to weigh the effects of its own decisions on the behaviour of other households and vice versa. (This is sometimes called 'cohesion', 'sympathy', or 'elasticity of labour allocation'.)

By formal analysis it can be shown that when distribution is 'according to need', individual labour allocation to the collective sector will be suboptimal, unless the degree of interaction of household labour allocation decisions is high, or unless the household weighs the incomes of other households heavily in its own utility function.[31] Amartya Sen has demonstrated that in cases where there is not 'perfect sympathy' among households (i.e. households do not attach, on average, equal weight to the utility of their neighbours), then there will be some combination of 'distribution according to work', and 'distribution according to needs' which will provide optimal incentives.[32] Louis Putterman and Dennis Chinn have demonstrated in recent papers that the collective remuneration system which will provide optimal incentives will depend, to an important extent, on the *size* of the group. Specifically, they argue that decisions to allocate labour to the collective sector will depend in part on the 'cohesion' between households in the work group. The smaller the size of the work group the larger will be 'team cohesion', and the larger will be the ratio of collective sector labour to private sector labour. Putterman also adds that the costs of monitoring will:

reduce the attractiveness of collective but not private labour, as we may state that improvements in the quality or reductions in the cost of monitoring labour input in the collective sector will increase the ratio of collective to private work, *ceteris paribus*. If the quality of work-monitoring may be supposed to decrease as the size of the work group rises, this will provide another reason why the relative collectivity of labour falls with increasing group size.[33]

There are, in summary, good theoretical and practical reasons why the Marxist–Leninist–Maoist predilection for large scale in crop production can be damaging to the structure of incentives facing households. First, the characteristics of agriculture are not conducive to large-scale management of crop production. Second, the costs of enforcing labour contracts will increase with the size of the group. The asymmetry (and other properties) of information in team production suggests that specialization within an organization will lead to the most efficient results. Third, the theoretical models discussed above suggest that in a collective organization with an active private sector, the amount and intensity of labour allocated to the collective sector varies inversely with the size of the work group. Moreover, small work groups improve 'cohesion' within the team and consequently enable some 'optimal' combination of distribution 'according to work' and 'according to need' to be found.

3. EXTERNAL EFFECTS AND THE COMMUNE STRUCTURE

An important goal of the rural development strategy was the stimulation of self-financed investment in the rural sector. Such investment had been difficult to induce because of the low level of productivity and other 'initial conditions' in the countryside. I shall argue here that the post-1962 commune structure has encouraged self-financed investment because of certain external effects.

It has been recognized since Adam Smith that the propensity to invest is limited by the size of the market. The commune structure enlarges the market in both a microeconomic sense (intra-commune) and a macroeconomic sense (inter-commune and commune-state). The microeconomic case will be considered first.

In many developing countries the divergence between the private marginal product of labour and capital and their social marginal products often inhibits entrepreneurs from undertaking rural construction projects. The construction of a road or a water-control project, for example, may yield benefits which cannot be captured solely by the investor. The commune structure contributes substantially to the internalization of the external benefits of such projects. By combining the financial resources and the planning skills of a dozen co-operatives and by employing labour to a point where its marginal product was equal to its opportunity cost and hence perhaps only just greater than zero, many more projects could be undertaken. An important planning and management function at the commune level and the brigade level consisted in ensuring that the stream of benefits of each project were proportional to each subunit's labour and financial inputs, and that current agricultural production was not disrupted during the construction period. The streams of benefits which flowed to participating teams and brigades had an external effect in raising a unit's accumulation–consumption ratio. It is much easier to persuade peasants to alter their inter-temporal valuations in favour of savings if the benefits of such savings shortly become visible to them. Moreover, if a commune planned a water-control programme, for example, the establishment of a small plant to produce the required tools involved less risk: the market for its output was guaranteed. By undertaking a wide range of projects, and by establishing enterprises for the production of inputs for agriculture, the commune created its own markets and thereby stimulated internal investment and economic growth.

A further important external effect within the commune involved the reduction of overhead capital costs which obtain from locating the capital construction projects within a relatively short distance from the households of the participating labour force. This organizational pattern minimizes the 'leakage'. That is, in the process of mobilizing the off-peak seasonally underemployed labour for infrastructural projects, potential saving can be converted into actual saving if the mobilized labour force make no extra claims on the current consumption fund. If the commune found it necessary to construct housing facilities or other amenity overheads, or if it had to absorb the costs of feeding the labour force, then 'leakage' occurs. Actual savings will be substantially less than potential savings. The commune structure permitted the conversion of 'labour into capital' while minimizing such outlays because of the rationality of its scale. Moreover, the workpoints system (in which team workers who are seconded to commune-level or brigade-level construction projects are paid in team workpoints) prevented the seconded worker from making any additional claims upon either the team's consumption fund or the funds of higher levels. Furthermore, by increasing investment without increasing consumption claims the commune structure alleviated inflationary pressures in the rural economy. Thus the opportunity cost of the mobilized labour force was near zero for the team, the commune and the country as a whole.

In the macroeconomic sense external effects were equally as important. The industrial growth which took place during the First Plan period created a transport network and a procurement and supply system for materials. These networks and systems were an important precondition for the later expansion of provincial and county-level industrial enterprises. The rural industrial construction which took place during the Great Leap Forward, although marked by poor planning and by inefficiency, did have certain advantages when viewed in the light of external effects. Schumpeter has conceived of an 'initial burst' of creative entrepreneurial investment which 'in the first instance' invariably 'spell disturbances [and] losses'.[34] He argued, nevertheless, that such a 'frontal attack' stimulates a wave of new applications of capital over a wide range of industries. The provincial industrial activity which took place during the Great Leap Forward widened the market at the local level and thus helped to stimulate investment at the commune level. The American small-scale industry delegation commented in their report that

> . . . the industrial aspects of the Great Leap of the 1958–60 can be viewed as a premature effort to link large and small-scale industry which, despite its failure, achieved further consolidation of existing handicraft production, established some enterprises, and provided industrial training and experience which has contributed to the subsequent success of small-scale plants.[35]

A network for forward and backward linkages was thus established by the strategy of rural industrialization, which represented an important enlargement of the commune's external markets. The improvement in transport networks, an important consequence of rural industrial growth, creates new investment opportunities for the commune. A commune enterprise's costs of procuring supplies or of delivering products can be decreased, thereby making profitable many processes of production. The establishment of a machine-tools plant at county level, for example, may induce a near-by enterprise to invest in a small plant which can subcontract with the county plant for component parts.

4. CONCLUSION

In Chapter 2 I discussed the circumstances which led the government to formulate a comprehensive rural development strategy. An important consideration was the need to promote labour-intensive light industrial production in the countryside. In order to do so, the government decided to change the structure of the rural co-operative organizations. In effect the government sought to introduce an 'industrial sector' into the agricultural co-operatives. Yet there was considerable disagreement among the leadership concerning the appropriate structure for such a 'mini-economy'. In this chapter it was argued that this disagreement arose from confusion between the appropriate scale for the management of crop production and the need for large economies of scale in finance and in planning for rural industrial production and capital construction projects. This confusion led to a substantial fluctuation in the structure of the rural organization from 1957 to 1962 (and, as will be seen, from 1979 to the present).

It was also suggested in this chapter that the confusion among the leadership concerning the optimal scale for the management of crop production reflected an orthodox interpretation by Mao Zedong and his supporters of the Marxist–Leninist view which favoured a large scale in agriculture. It was argued that this orthodox view is fundamentally flawed since it represents a misunderstanding of the characteristics of agricultural production. An important feature of agriculture is the necessity for a decentralized pattern of decision-making in the daily management of crop production. It has been argued that, for reasons of incentives, crop production is most efficient when it is managed by very small groups which have considerable autonomy in daily decision-making. Indeed, recent theoretical discussions in the economics literature support this view. The asymmetry of information associated with incomplete employments contracts, and the high costs of monitoring an individual's daily performance suggest that small groups or individual households, working under contract for specified outputs, are perhaps the best way to organize agricultural production in rural China.

Yet these considerations were largely ignored by the government during 1958–60. Crop production was managed on the basis of an extremely large scale and the remuneration system placed emphasis on distribution 'according to need' rather than 'according to work'. As a result the efficiency of the incentive system was reduced and grain production declined substantially during the period.

The poor performance of agriculture from 1959 to 1960 led to a reassessment within the government of the structure of the commune organization. By 1962 this structure was finally consolidated and it changed little until after 1978. The commune now includes a decentralized system of decision-making in crop production, based on the scale of 'elementary' producer co-operatives. This unit is called the 'production team' and it corresponds closely to a neighbourhood of a traditional village. Even within the team, however, decisions can be further decentralized to work groups, which correspond closely to the 'mutual aid teams' (of, say, four to eight families) which existed during 1953–5. These groups, or indeed individual households, can make their own daily production and labour allocation decisions and can work on a contract basis with the team for fixed outputs. The post-1978 policy changes will be discussed in Chapter 9 (e.g. contracts between the production team and individual households).

The flexibility of the consolidated commune organization was evident from the fact that a large scale was maintained for industrial production and for rural capital construction. These activities have been managed at the commune and brigade levels. This enabled the organization to capture the substantial economies of scale in finance and in planning. The implications of this structure for the dynamic processes of economic growth and of income distribution will be analysed in greater detail in Chapters 4 to 7.

An important attribute of the commune organization has been its provision of a basic level of health and education. Health clinics and primary and secondary schools were provided by most communes and were often administered at the brigade level. As such, the commune organization can be interpreted as an institutional framework which provided 'basic needs' in the Chinese countryside. In 1983–4 these duties were taken over by new township and village committees (see Chapter 8).

Some writers justify basic needs expenditures only in terms of welfare. Hollis Chenery and Montek Ahluwalia, for example, draw a distinction between the provision of rural welfare and the need for capital formation.[36] Recent evidence, however, indicates that such a conflict is empirically misleading.[37] While Paul Streeten, Irma Adelman and Cynthia Morris, Keith Griffin and others[38] have argued that a complementary relationship can exist between expenditures on basic needs and productivity there is recent evidence which suggests that even these writers may have under-estimated the empirical validity of their arguments. Dennis Wheeler, for example, makes use of a recently published set of 'social indicators' by the World Bank to analyse the relationship between output and indicators of health, nutrition and education. He obtains 'consistent and relatively efficient parameter estimates' from large samples of countries in Africa, Asia and Latin America.[39] The study concludes that changes in the physical quality of life appear to have an empirically strong effect on productivity in poor countries. A recent survey by M. Lockeed, D. Jameson and L. Lau suggests that primary education has positive effects on farmer productivity.[40] The evidence which they review suggests that education is likely to increase the productivity of farmers if complementary efforts are made to provide basic rural infrastructural development and technological change. Given such a 'modernizing' environment they suggest that four years of schooling is capable of increasing the output of traditional farmers, *ceteris paribus*, by as much as 10 per cent per year.[41]

The results of these studies are important for an analysis of China's rural organizations. These studies indicate a substantial source of self-financed growth: the provision of basic health and education. It is perhaps more accurate, therefore, to think of such low-cost sources of growth as investments in human capital.

The expenditures on health and welfare in the commune organization are drawn from the 'public welfare fund'. The written constitution of the commune (the '60 Articles') stipulates clearly the manner in which these expenditures are to be determined:

> A certain amount for the public welfare fund may be deducted from the total income of the production team each year . . . decisions may be reached after serious deliberation at a general meeting of commune members. The way the public welfare fund is used must be discussed and decided at a general meeting of the commune members and in no case may be determined by a minority of cadres.[42]

The document contains similar guidelines for the process by which the amount of accumulation funds and distribution funds are to be determined. Article 35, for example, states that:

> Decisions on the amount of public accumulation funds to be deducted each year by the production team must be reached through serious discussion at a general meeting of commune members. . . . How the public accumulation fund is to be used may be decided upon through discussion at a general meeting of commune members and it must not be determined by a minority of cadres.[43]

These guidelines give an indication of the important degree to which democratic principles were expected to operate in the communes. The government, in formulating these guidelines, was apparently concerned to ensure that 'the scope of various commune organisations should be democratically determined by commune members'.[44] Commune members had the right to elect each year the members of the administrative and control committees of the commune 'by secret ballot after full deliberations'.[45] The regulations continue to encourage today an important degree of participation in the determination of the production and investment plans of the organization and in the process by which the surplus is divided between accumulation and distribution components.

A primary concern of this book is to suggest that a rural co-operative organization, which is structured in a decentralized and democratic way, can affect the attitudes of its members. That is, the willingness of its members to pay 'the cost of change' by 'sacrificing the present for the future' may be increased. This, in turn, would be reflected in a higher level of investment and in a higher ratio of accumulation to distribution than would otherwise have been politically feasible. Since this argument concerning the relationship between organizational structure and economic growth is a microeconomic one it should be useful to turn in the next two chapters to empirical case-studies of growth in rural communes which I have visited.

4 A Case-Study of Rural Agricultural Growth

The pattern of agricultural production in Asia depends on the control of water. By control of water one means both its supply (irrigation) and its partial elimination (flood control and drainage). The object is to ensure that water in a crop field is available at the appropriate time and level. When water is controlled in this way agriculture can be freed from the fluctuations of nature and controlled mainly through the efforts of man. The essentially 'hydraulic' nature of Asian agriculture contrasts sharply with other regions of the world.

Shigeru Ishikawa has studied the relationship between water control and productivity in Asia. His empirical studies were undertaken for eleven Asian countries.[1] The results corroborate the role of water control as a 'shift variable'. In summarizing his results for Taiwan, South Korea and Japan he argues:

> The above observations indicate that, in Taiwan and Korea, a rise in productivity from the level of contemporary India and many other South and Southeast Asian countries to that of the early Meiji era [in Japan] was accompained, first, by a mild improvement of traditional irrigation and, then, by a drastic expansion of technologically superior irrigation works. In this period, irrigation clearly played the role of the leading input . . . . Thus the experience of Taiwan and South Korea, together with that of Japan, seems to indicate that the technology pattern of productivity increase in Asian agriculture is broadly the same, both in the past and in the present. . . . The fundamental requirements of the productivity rise are, first, control of water and, then, technological innovation centring around the introduction of high-yielding varieties with high fertilizer response.[2]

In the case of Taiwan and Japan in particular, the central governments played an active role in the provision of investment capital. Yet such flows of funds from the industrial sector or from the state budget were constrained in China by the priorities for industrial growth and expansion. The Chinese strategy has involved the substitution of minor, locally financed projects, in which off-peak, seasonally under-employed labour participated actively in the construction work. The co-operative and later the commune provided the organizational framework for these efforts. In order to illustrate these arguments this chapter will look closely at one commune's investment plan and its empirical results.

1. WU GONG COMMUNE[3]

Wu Gong People's Commune is located in Hebei Province on the North China plain. This is primarily a grain-producing region of China, in which wheat, maize, sorghum and millet are the major crops. Cotton and oilseeds are other important crops. The commune itself was composed of ten production brigades and thirty-six production teams. The total population at the time we visited it in 1979 was 16 500. The total labour force was 7200 of whom 6058 were involved in agricultural production. The commune covered an area of twenty-four square kilometers (36 000 mou), of which 34 873 were under cultivation.

During our visit we concentrated our research efforts on one brigade of the commune (also called Wu Gong). Since the empirical analysis which follows in the next Section covers the progress of agricultural production in this brigade it is useful briefly to review the history of Wu Gong Brigade.

Wu Gong Production Brigade

Before liberation Wu Gong village comprised 4000 mou of land, most of which was owned by five resident landlords. This land supported 290 households, of whom most were landless agricultural workers. During the winter of 1947–8 the landlords' land was seized and then divided between the remaining peasant families in proportion to the size of household. Although most of the families farmed their own land, by 1951 a small co-operative had been established comprising twenty-five poor families. The co-operative achieved good results in agricultural production and by 1953 most of the other households had joined voluntarily. In 1955 a decision was taken to collectivize completely and the co-operative was divided into ten production teams. Each team farmed the land it owned. Table 4.1 shows the rapid pace of agricultural collectivization at Wu Gong Brigade.

TABLE 4.1 *The Pace of Collectivization of Agriculture in Wu Gong Brigade, 1947–55*

Year	*Total area cultivated (mou)*	*Collectively cultivated area (mou)*	*Percentage of cultivated land farmed collectively*
1947	4850	123	2.5
1948	4850	183	3.8
1949	4850	187	3.8
1950	4850	179	3.7
1951	4850	219	4.5
1952	4850	285	5.9
1953	4840	3093	64.0
1954	4840	4271	88.2
1955	4840	4829	99.8

During 1959 the Wu Gong People's Commune was formed as a result of an amalgamation of neighbouring co-operatives.

The Wu Gong Co-operative was renamed the Wu Gong Production Brigade. The ten production teams of the co-operative were combined into three approximately equal-sized production teams under the brigade. At that time the brigade numbered 126 households and comprised 1774 people. The structure of the brigade has remained the same (as of 1979) although the population has grown. In 1978 the brigade numbered 664 households, with a total population of 2573. The labour force now numbers 1197, of whom 987 are involved in agricultural production. When one visits Wu Gong Commune it soon becomes clear that neither the commune nor Wu Gong Brigade are 'typical' of other communes in the province. Indeed, the data clearly show that the per capita income of the commune in 1978 was well above the provincial mean (see Chapter 7). Yet this does not affect the general significance of the argument since only the *process* of agricultural growth over time at Wu Gong will be analysed here. It will be argued that this growth was achieved through an efficient mobilization of resources, through a strong emphasis on investment and through insightful decision-making.

2. AGRICULTURAL GROWTH AT WU GONG BRIGADE

In this section the immediate or most direct sources of growth in agricultural production at Wu Gong Brigade from 1953 to 1978 will be analysed. The objective, however, is to determine *why* that growth occurred. It will be argued that the organizational rearrangements which took place during the 1950s at Wu Gong played a very important part in explaining this growth. Since Wu Gong is located in a predominantly grain-producing area of China the analysis will be focused on the growth in grain production.

In Figure 4.1 the growth in grain output at Wu Gong from 1953 to 1978 has been plotted. Upon inspection one can see that the trend rate of growth of grain production for the sub-period 1968–78 is rather faster than the corresponding rate of growth for the sub-period 1953–68. The causes of this shift in trend will be examined closely. First, however, it is important to determine the sources of this growth over the entire period.

There are two possible explanations for the growth in grain production at Wu Gong: (i) an expansion in the area of land under cultivation, or (ii) an increase in the productivity of existing land or some combination of (i) and (ii). From Table 4.2, one can rule out an expansion of cultivated land as a possible explanation. Indeed the data in column 1 indicate that the area of cultivated land for grain declined by

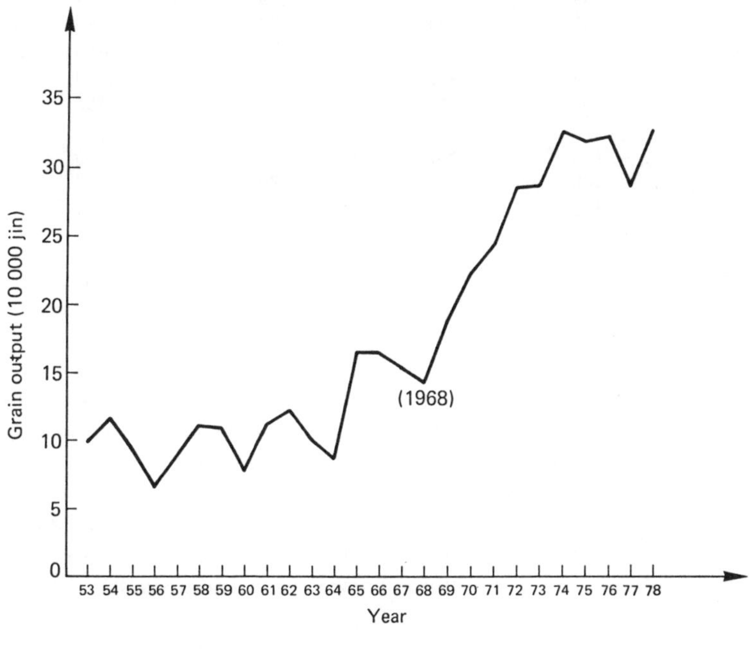

FIGURE 4.1 *Grain Production at Wu Gong Brigade, 1953–78*

TABLE 4.2 *Growth in Cultivated Area and in Grain Yields at Wu Gong Brigade, 1953–78*

	(1) Cultivated area (mou)	(2) Total grain yield in (jin per mou)	(3) Summer harvest grain yield (jin per mou)	(4) Autumn harvest grain yield (jin per mou)
1953	3400	210	150	230
1954	3340	253	180	281
1955	3101	198	205	195
1956	2261	124	234	81
1957	2772	195	152	217
1958	2998	258	187	292
1959	2492	323	267	342
1960	2258	235	430	166
1961	2296	334	215	378
1962	2600	355	231	399
1963	2300	285	356	255
1964	2100	210	161	247
1965	2100	476	304	573
1966	2020	454	352	523
1967	2349	370	298	419
1968	2232	381	223	480
1969	2531	439	378	475
1970	2404	495	478	510
1971	2300	486	485	488
1972	2470	563	615	508
1973	2410	582	562	605
1974	2400	664	680	647
1975	2370	667	728	601
1976	2350	664	741	582
1977	2450	559	600	517
1978	2450	664	825	497

nearly a third over the entire period. It is clear therefore that the considerable growth in foodgrain production over the period must be explained by an increase in the productivity of existing land.

From the data in column 2 of Table 4.2 it is evident that a substantial growth in grain yields occurred during the period; the yield for all grains more than tripled from 1953 to 1978. If, however, one disaggregates the data in column 2 into an autumn harvest yield and a summer harvest yield a clearer picture emerges. This disaggregated data have been plotted below in Figures 4.2 and 4.3 respectively. These data reveal a very different pattern of growth in the post-1968 period of autumn and

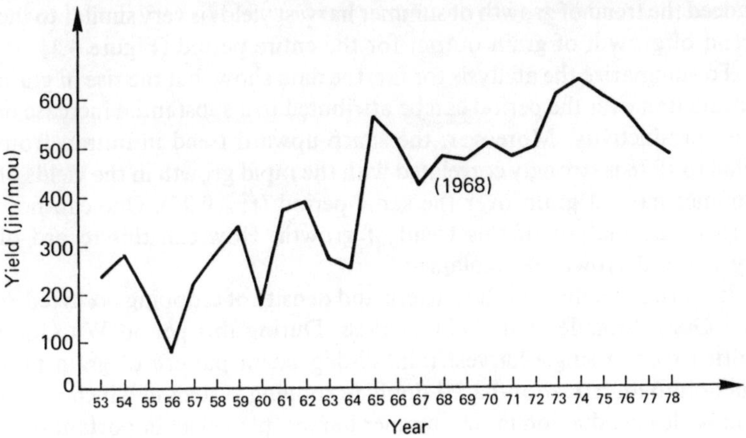

FIGURE 4.2 *Growth of Autumn Harvest Grain Yield, Wu Gong Brigade, 1953–78*

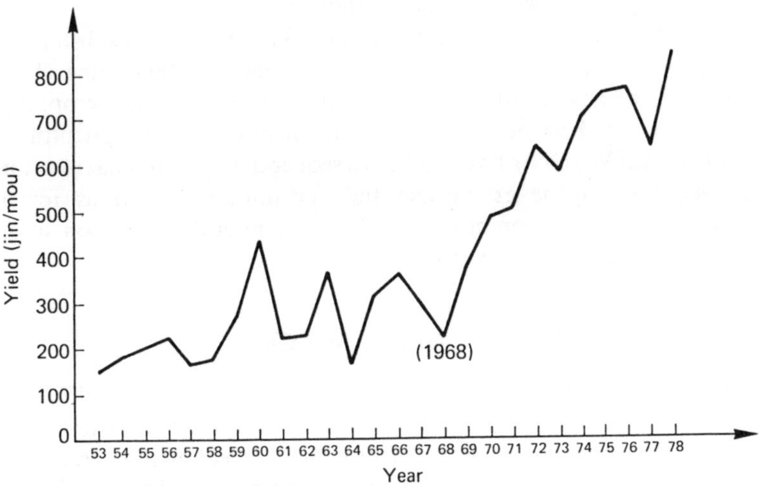

FIGURE 4.3 *Growth of Summer Harvest Grain Yield, Wu Gong Brigade, 1953–78*

summer harvest yields. Autumn harvest yields for example have shown little or no tendency to increase since the middle 1960s. Summer harvest yields on the other hand, while displaying little growth in the pre-1968 period, have since grown by 9.2 per cent a year – a very sharp increase.

Indeed the trend of growth of summer harvest yields is very similar to the trend of growth of grain output for the entire period (Figure 4.1).

To summarize the analysis for far, the data show that the rise in grain production over the period can be attributed to a substantial increase in land productivity. Moreover, the sharp upward trend in output from 1968 to 1978 is strongly correlated with the rapid growth in the yields of summer harvest grain over the same period ($r^2 = 0.95$). One can now turn to an analysis of this trend of growth. How can this record of agricultural growth be explained?

Important changes in the pattern and density of cropping occurred at Wu Gong Brigade from 1953 to 1968. During this period Wu Gong shifted from a single-harvest rainfall-dependent pattern of grain production to an irrigation-based double-cropping system in which wheat and barley production in the summer harvest played an important role. Table 4.3 presents data which depict this change in the density and pattern of crop production. Between 1953 and 1971 the multiple-cropping index increased from 1.35 to approximately 2.0. Moreover from the late 1960s to 1978 the data in column 5 show that the area sown to summer grain expanded considerably.

These data indicate that during the late 1960s there was a substantial expansion of the area sown to the high-yield summer grains. This expansion coincided with the establishment of a double-cropping system in the brigade. It is evident, therefore, that agricultural production at Wu Gong has exhibited a sequential pattern. That is, prior to 1968 the brigade established the appropriate conditions for a productive double-cropping system. The most important component of this system will now be examined.

The Importance of Water Control at Wu Gong

The most effective way of raising productivity in Asian agriculture is, first, control of water and, subsequently, the introduction of technical inputs. This sequential pattern of growth has been demonstrated in empirical studies of Asian agricultural growth by a number of writers.[4] Agricultural growth at Wu Gong is no exception to this pattern. Indeed from 1953 to 1969, Wu Gong Brigade carefully planned and constructed a comprehensive irrigation system. Each production team was responsible for mobilizing its members during slack periods to dig wells, ditches, canals, etc., for a brigade-wide water-control system. The progress of this investment programme can be inferred clearly from the data plotted in Figure 4.4.

TABLE 4.3 *Changes in Grain Cropping Density and Patterns, Wu Gong Brigade, 1953–78*

	(1) *Cultivated area for all grains (mou)*	(2) *Sown area all grains (mou)*	(3) *Multiple[a] cropping index*	(4) *Sown area autumn grains (mou)*	(5) *Sown area summer grains (mou)*
1953	3400	4600	1.35	3400	1200
1954	3340	4640	1.39	3340	1300
1955	3101	4415	1.42	3101	1314
1956	2261	5089	2.25	3675	1414
1957	2772	4269	1.54	2772	1497
1958	2998	4416	1.48	2998	1428
1959	2492	3313	1.34	2492	821
1960	2258	3058	1.35	2258	800
1961	2296	3144	1.34	2296	850
1962	2600	3532	1.36	2600	932
1963	2300	3300	1.43	2300	1000
1964	2100	3700	1.76	2100	1600
1965	2100	3250	1.54	2100	1600
1966	2020	3420	1.69	2020	1400
1967	2349	3857	1.64	2349	1508
1968	2232	3589	1.60	2232	1357
1969	2531	4012	1.58	2531	1481
1970	2404	4438	1.84	2334	2104
1971	2300	4751	2.06	2300	2451
1972	2450	4856	1.98	2352	2504
1973	2410	4746	1.97	2211	2535
1974	2400	4793	2.00	2273	2520
1975	2370	4571	1.93	2201	2370
1976	2350	4707	2.00	2277	2430
1977	2450	4900	2.00	2400	2500
1978	2450	4900	2.00	2400	2500

[a] The multiple-cropping index is the ratio of the sown area for all grains (column 2) to the cultivated area for all grains (column 1).

From 1944 to 1953 very little progress in water control had been achieved at Wu Gong. After the establishment of a collective organization in Wu Gong, however, under-employed labour was effectively mobilized for water-control construction work. This work began in 1953 and was completed in 1969. The organizational framework provided by the co-operative and later the commune enabled the members of the organization to establish a foundation for the rapid growth in agricultural production from 1969.

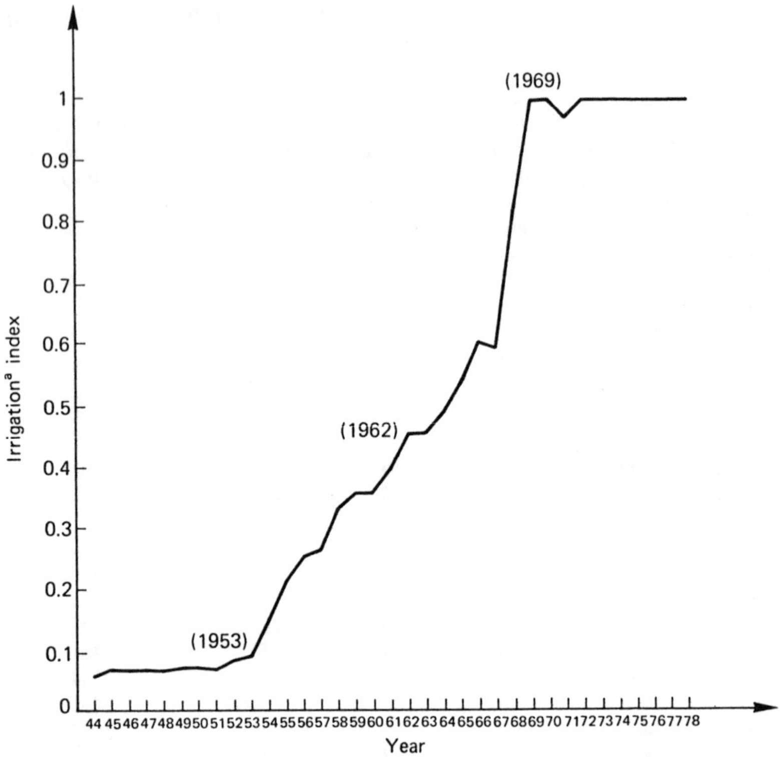

FIGURE 4.4 *The Pace of Water-control Construction at Wu Gong Brigade, 1944–78*

[a] The irrigation index is the ratio of irrigated area to the total area of cultivated land.

It is likely that the establishment of a comprehensive water-control system during 1953–69 enabled the brigade to change substantially their pattern of cropping. To test this proposition I have regressed the ratio of sown area of summer grains to the sown area of autumn grains (SAR) on the ratio of the total irrigated area to the total area of cultivated land (IR). The regression covered the 1953–78 period and the results are reported in the equation below:

$$(1)\ \mathbf{SAR} = 0.169 + 0.81\ \mathbf{IR};$$
$$(9.78)$$

$r^2 = 0.78$, and the t-statistic is shown in brackets.

The equation suggests that the change in the pattern of cropping at Wu Gong is statistically significantly correlated with the change in the extent of irrigation.

A clearer picture of the change in the cropping pattern from 1953 to 1978 at Wu Gong can be seen from Figure 4.5. The figure displays the change over time in the ratio of the sown area of summer grains to the sown area of autumn grains. Upon inspection one can see that there have been two discrete shifts in the pattern of cropping over the period. To display the relationship between these shifts and the extent of irrigation I have included in the figure three different levels of irrigation.

The most significant change in the cropping pattern occured in response to the change from I_2 to I_3. Indeed the area sown to summer grains increased by nearly 70 per cent from 1969 to 1978, whereas from 1953 to 1969 this total area displayed only a slight upward trend.

Asian agriculture is also marked by an important complementarity in inputs for production. That is, growth is an interactive process. The introduction of chemical fertilizer and high-yielding seeds achieve their

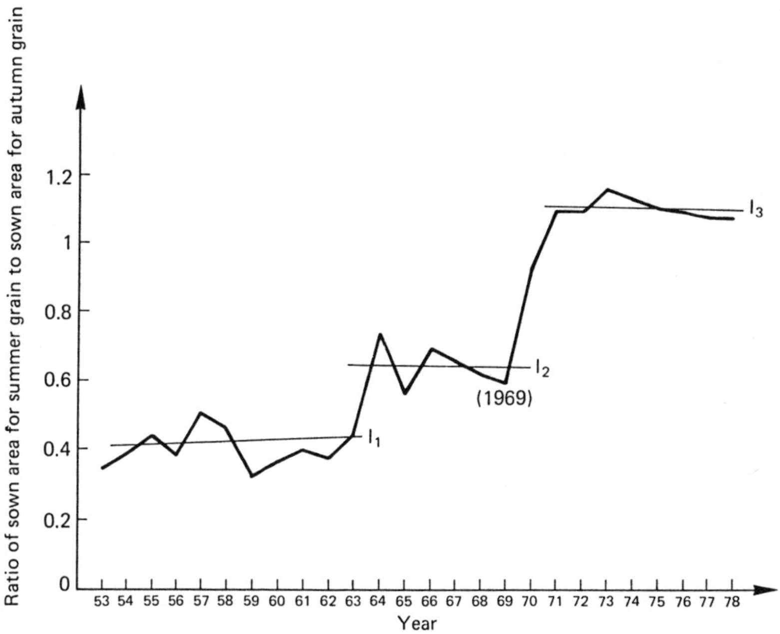

FIGURE 4.5 *Changes in Cropping Pattern at Wu Gong Brigade, 1953–78*

best response, for example, when combined with appropriate amounts of water. Data on procurement and application of technical inputs at Wu Gong confirm that members of the brigade were well aware of this interactive and complementary pattern of Asian agricultural growth. This can be seen from the data plotted in Figures 4.6 and 4.7. In Figure 4.6 the increase in the quantity of nutrient available as fertilizer in agricultural production at Wu Gong has been plotted. From 1953 to 1970 the available nutrient was organic. The brigade did not even begin to purchase chemical fertilizer until after 1970. Between 1970 and 1978 the total amount of available nutrient increased by 154 per cent. Since the rate of growth of organic fertilizer remained nearly constant over this later period most of this increase is attributable to the substantial purchases of chemical fertilizer from 1971 to 1978.

In Figure 4.7 the data illustrate a similar decision to postpone procurement of water-control machinery and equipment until the irrigation system had been completed. Moreover, the brigade did not begin to purchase other farm equipment such as threshers until after

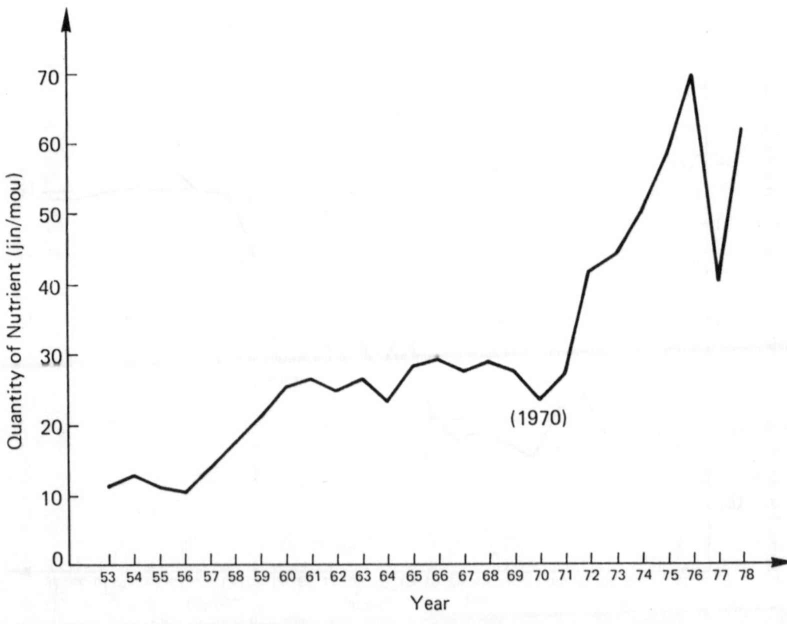

FIGURE 4.6 *Application of Fertilizer at Wu Gong Brigade, 1951–78*

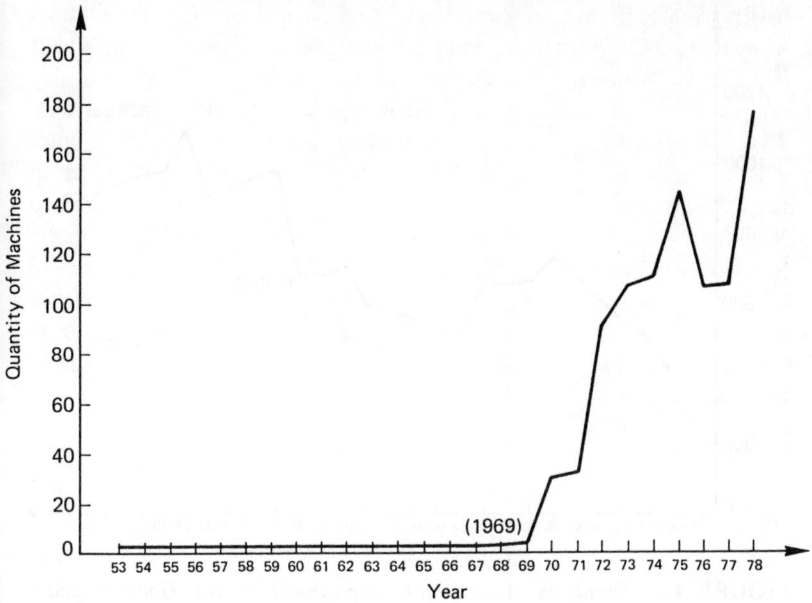

FIGURE 4.7 *Growth of Stock of Powered Water-control Equipment at Wu Gong Brigade, 1953–78*

1970. From 1970 to 1978 Wu Gong purchased 9 tractors, 4 planting machines, 7 threshers and approximately 100 crop-dusting machines.

Thus the substantial increase in the growth rate of grain production at Wu Gong after 1969 can be attributed, first, to a mobilization of labour for the construction of a comprehensive irrigation system, and, second, to the subsequent introduction of technical inputs. The complementary effects of water and these technical inputs played an important part in enabling the members of the brigade to alter the cropping pattern after 1969 in favour of high-yield summer crops. It is precisely such summer crops as wheat and barley which are very responsive to the availability of water and the application of technical inputs. Moreover, with the establishment of a double-cropping system at Wu Gong by 1969, the demand for agricultural labour was increased. This can be seen in Figure 4.8 below. These data show that, after 1969, agricultural production at Wu Gong absorbed considerable amounts of additional labour. The establishment of the water-control system permitted a substantial increase in the multiple-cropping ratio. As a result, cropping practices were intensified, which in turn increased the demand for agricultural labour.

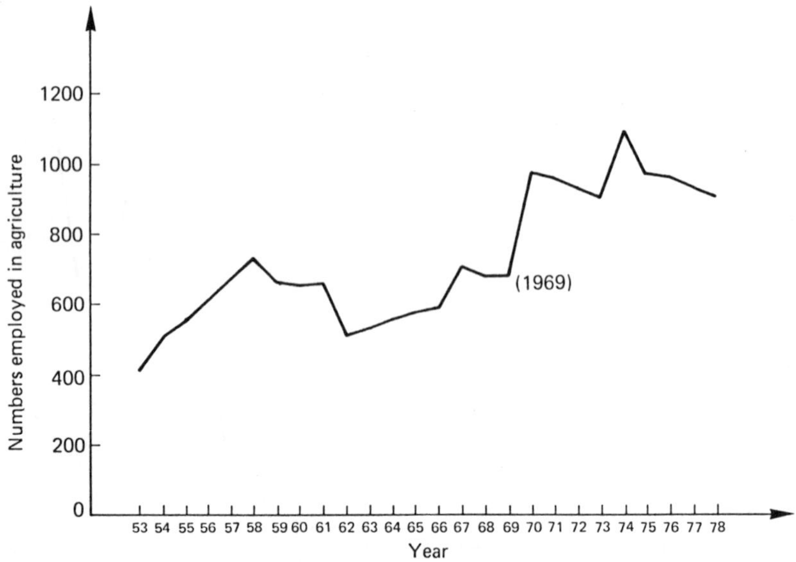

FIGURE 4.8 *Trends in Agricultural Employment at Wu Gong Brigade, 1953–78*

3. STATISTICAL ANALYSIS

Looking at the period as a whole from 1953 to 1978 the growth in agricultural production at Wu Gong Brigade has been quite impressive. A clearer picture emerges, however, if one divides the twenty-six years into two sub-periods, namely 1953–69 and 1969–78. Whereas for the sub-period 1953–69 the average annual rate of growth of grain output was 2.5 per cent, for the later sub-period 1969–78 the average annual growth rate was 12.5 per cent. It has been argued that the rapid growth of grain output and of summer grain yields after 1969 should be attributed to the shift to a double-cropping system, to changes in the cropping pattern and to the introduction of modern inputs. It has been emphasized, however, that these changes were made possible by the construction of a comprehensive irrigation system at Wu Gong. The framework provided by the collective organization of production enabled the members of the brigade to mobilize under-utilized labour during slack seasons and to co-ordinate their efforts in the construction of the water-control system.

The importance of irrigation in this record of agricultural growth can also be demonstrated by multiple regression analysis.[5] For the entire period 1953–78 total grain yield (TGY) was regressed on (i) an index of labour availability per mou of sown land (LA); (ii) an index of total fertilizer nutrient per sown mou of land (TF); and (iii) the ratio of irrigated land to the total cultivated land (IR). This regression yielded the following equation:

$$(2)\ \text{TGY} = \underset{}{45.86} + \underset{(0.5193)}{0.8698}\ \text{LA} + \underset{(4.576)}{5.112}\ \text{TF} + \underset{(4.259)}{259.5}\ \text{IR};$$

$r^2 = 0.90$, and the t-statistics are shown in brackets.

The overall fit of the equation is good. Although the coefficient for labour availability is not significantly different from zero, the coefficients for fertilizer and irrigation are significant at the 1 per cent level. Moreover, the equation implies that if all of the land is irrigated nearly 260 jin per mou of yield can be attributed to the irrigation input.

Yet the story of agricultural growth at Wu Gong is more clearly understood by considering separately the two sub-periods: a period from 1953 to 1969 when 'traditional' methods of cultivation were used and the later period 1964–78 when 'modern' practices were adopted. Regressions have been run for each sub-period. For the traditional period total grain yield (TGY) was again the dependent variable. The independent variables were also the same: (i) an index of labour availability per sown mou of land (LA); (ii) an index of fertilizer per sown mou of land (TF); and (iii) the irrigation ratio (IR). Equation 3 gives the results:

$$(3)\ \text{TGY} = 92.3 - \underset{(-0.6197)}{1.654}\ \text{LA} + \underset{(2.112)}{10.85}\ \text{TF} + \underset{(1.017)}{116.3}\ \text{IR};$$

$r^2 = 0.69$, and the t-statistics are shown in brackets.

Although the overall fit of the equation is moderately good it is the regression coefficients that are most revealing. The large coefficient for irrigation would appear to confirm its importance in determining yields during the 1953–69 period, but the coefficient is not statistically significant. The coefficient for fertilizer, however, is significant at the 5 per cent level and it is the availability of this input which was important in raising agricultural productivity during the traditional period. The coefficient for labour is again not significantly different from zero. This indicates that variations in labour input had no effect on yields when traditional methods of cultivation were used. This is perhaps not too surprising a result.

The irrigation system was completed at Wu Gong in 1968. Subsequently the brigade began to use substantial quantities of modern inputs for agricultural production. The most important of these inputs for which data are available are chemical fertilizers and water-control equipment. Thus it was postulated that after 1968 total grain yields depend primarily upon irrigation technology, applications of chemical fertilizer and the amount of labour employed. To test this hypothesis a multiple regression was run covering the period 1969–78. The equation produced a rather different picture from the equation covering the earlier, 'traditional' period. Since all of the cultivated land was under irrigation by 1969 an index of irrigation equipment expressed in units of horsepower (IE) was substituted for the irrigation index as the 'irrigation variable'. Then for the fertilizer variable an index of chemical fertilizer application per sown mou of land (CHF) was used. The index of labour availability (LA) remained the same. Equation 4 below gives the results of the regression:

$$(4)\ \text{TGY} = 191.8 + \underset{(5.125)}{5.084}\ \text{LA} + 3.128\ \text{CHF} + \underset{(4.185)}{0.689}\ \text{IE};$$

$r^2 = 0.98$, and the t-statistics are shown in brackets.

The overall fit of the equation is very good and all of the coefficients are statistically significant at the 1 per cent level. The most important difference between this equation and equation 3 for the traditional period is the coefficient for labour. Whereas in the traditional period this coefficient was not statistically significantly different from zero, in the modern period the coefficient for labour is large and highly significant. This suggests that the shift to double cropping permitted by the establishment of the irrigation system substantially raised the average and marginal productivity of labour above that which prevailed when traditional technology was used. This is an important result, for it indicates that technological change in agricultural production at Wu Gong has been labour-augmenting, in the sense that it has made it possible productively to employ larger amounts of labour.

Another important result of this analysis concerns the stability of yields. The pattern of the stability of yields over time at Wu Gong can be determined by illustrating in a graph the difference between actual yield and the yield predicted by the regression equations. That is, we have plotted in Figure 4.9 the time series of residuals as a proportion of the fitted values. The data for the period 1953–68 were generated from equation 3, and the data for the period 1969–78 are from equation 4.

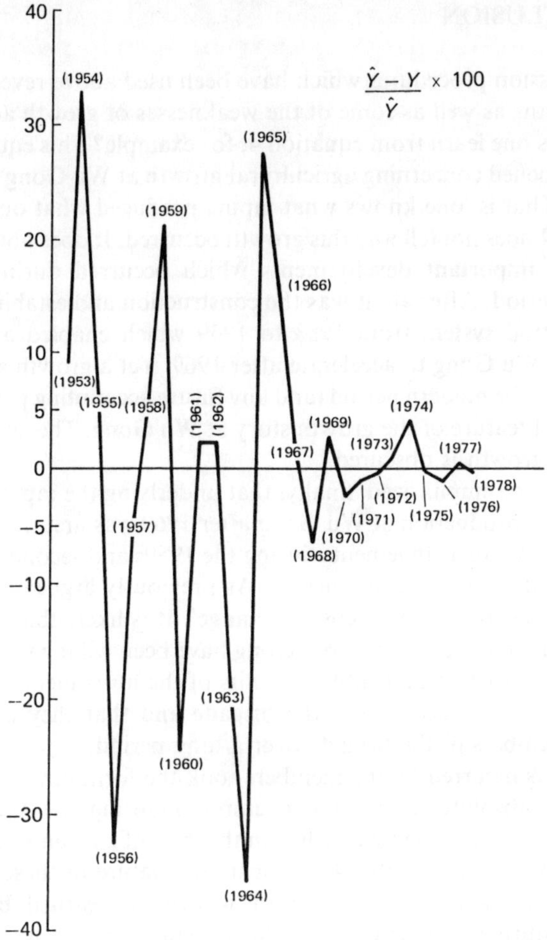

FIGURE 4.9 *Stabilization of Grain Yields at Wu Gong Brigade, 1953–78*

Upon inspection of Figure 4.9 it is evident that the year-to-year fluctuations in yields were reduced considerably in the modern period. Clearly, improved control of water played an important part in reducing the dependency of grain yields on variations in the weather. The shift to double-cropping and the rapid introduction of technical inputs in the modern period had important stabilizing effects. Thus the construction of the irrigation system at Wu Gong not only helped to raise grain yields substantially, but also to stabilize them.

4. CONCLUSION

The regression procedures which have been used above reveal some of the strengths as well as some of the weaknesses of growth accounting. What does one learn from equation 4, for example? This equation tells what happened concerning agricultural growth at Wu Gong from 1969 to 1978. That is, one knows what inputs produced what outputs. But equation 4 does not tell *why* this growth occurred. It does not reveal the extremely important developments which occurred during the traditional period. After all, it was the construction and establishment of the irrigation system from 1953 to 1969 which enabled agricultural growth at Wu Gong to accelerate after 1969. Yet a growth accounting exercise for the modern period (and any future accounting period) hides this central feature of the growth story at Wu Gong. The 'experienced' nature of growth is obscured.

It should be emphasized, finally, that underlying the rapid growth in agricultural production at Wu Gong after 1969 was first the important organizational rearrangements during the 1950s and second the investment in water-control construction. As previously argued, investment should be regarded as the 'cost of change'. It is likely that among the reasons why the members of Wu Gong have been willing to incur these costs are their belief that future benefits of the investment programme would be internalized within the brigade and that they expected to remain members of the brigade over a long period.

The costs incurred by the members took the form not so much of a decline in absolute levels of consumption during the years of the investment programme as a decline in the level of consumption per day of work. The data in Table 4.4 indicate the nature of these 'costs'.

These data show the number of workpoints earned by brigade members during three years when the investment programme was well

TABLE 4.4 *Workpoint Claims at Wu Gong Brigade, 1963–5*

	1963	*1964*	*1965*
Team 1	68 490	67 797	85 296
Team 2	59 338	61 782	83 306
Team 3	77 500	87 369	102 238
Total	205 328	216 948	270 840
Rural labour force (persons)	650	680	680

under way, namely, 1963, 1964 and 1965.[6] Each workpoint entitled the earner to claim the value of the workpoint each year from a fixed stock of grain available for distribution.

During the period 1963–5 grain output increased by 58 per cent and the amount of grain marketed increased by 136 per cent. Moreover, the amount of grain available for distribution to members of the brigade increased by 16 per cent and consumption per capita increased by 10 per cent. However during this period labour was mobilized during slack seasons in large scale to construct the irrigation system. In consequence the total number of workpoints increased by 32 per cent (the size of the rural labour force increased by only 4.6 per cent). As a result the amount of leisure decreased and the value of a workpoint in terms of grain declined by 12 per cent over the period. Thus during the three-year investment period payment per work day declined. The commune organization was successful, therefore, in increasing significantly the amount of grain sold while substantially restricting the amount of grain consumed and reducing the consumption value of a workpoint.

The empirical findings in this chapter are consistent with the view that the structure of this collective organization played an important part in promoting a 'sacrifice of the present for the future'. The data indicate that there was an increase in the quantity of work, accompanied by a decline in the level of consumption per workpoint. As a consequence of these developments a comprehensive irrigation system was built and an acceleration in the rate of growth of agricultural output was achieved. Thus, the institutional rearrangements and the structure of the new organization of production, 'explain' in an important sense the record of agricultural growth at Wu Gong.

5 A Case-Study of Rural Industrial Growth

What is the best way for production organizations in rural China to finance their own expansion? In this chapter it is argued that commune industry can be the 'engine of growth' in the rural sector. Like the previous chapter the arguments will be illustrated through a case-study analysis of rural industrial growth. In Section 1 the communes which will constitute the empirical case study will be described. In Section 2 the data collected there will be analysed and in Section 3 conclusions are drawn from the statistical analysis.

1. COMMUNE BACKGROUND

Cheng Dong Commune is located in Jia Ding County in the Shanghai Municipality.[1] This is a wealthy area of China, possessing a remarkable inland waterway system. Its advanced level of development is immediately obvious to the visitor. However, Cheng Dong is an 'average' commune in the area in terms of both per capita production and distribution. The commune has a thriving agricultural sector, in which yields are extremely high and grain is triple-cropped. Yet it is the relatively advanced level of industrial production which differentiates this region of rural China from most other regions.

The commune covers a total area of 28 square kilometers and has a population of 25 626 of whom 16 000 are part of the labour force. The commune is composed of 17 brigades and 150 production teams. Over 90 per cent of its cultivated land is irrigated, and the sown area is approximately 61 490 mou. Cropping patterns reflect this intensity of cultivation. There are two rice crops per year, one wheat crop and one cotton crop. Garlic and onions are also raised.

The industrial sector of the commune is well-developed at both commune level and brigade level. At commune level the most important industrial enterprises are an agricultural machine-repair factory, a bicycle-spokes factory, a towel factory, a plastics factory, a bamboo factory, a spare-parts factory, a lemon-processing factory and a tractor station. There is also, at commune level, a capital construction unit and a waterway transport unit.

Brigade industry is also well-developed. Indeed at brigade level there are over 96 different industrial enterprises. These include hardware, metal-processing, tractor production and repair, textiles spare parts, a foundry, a mill and grain and fodder-processing. Many of these enterprises have contracts to provide component parts for state-owned enterprises at county level and to procure materials from other state enterprises.

The history of the commune is not unusal. Before liberation over 80 per cent of the cultivated land was owned by a very small number of landlords and rich peasants. Land redistribution occurred at Cheng Dong in 1950–1. By 1953 three hundred mutual aid teams had been formed, and by the following year the first agricultural producer co-operatives had been formed. By 1955 eighty co-operatives had been established, and in the next two years they were combined into twelve 'advanced' agricultural producer cooperatives. These twelve 'advanced' co-operatives were amalgamated into the Cheng Dong People's Commune in September 1958. The final structure of the commune was set in 1962 and has changed little until recently (see Chapter 8).

Another commune considered in this chapter is Wu Gong Commune in Hebei Province. The industrial sector at Wu Gong is less developed than at Cheng Dong Commune in the Shanghai region. At commune level there is a hardware workshop, a flour-milling plant, a pharmaceutical plant, a metal-casting enterprise, a brick kiln, a machinery repair shop and an insulating materials enterprise. At brigade level there is a flax rope-making enterprise, a farm tools repair shop, a string-making plant, a rubber workshop and an enterprise producing plastic strips for binding.

2. EMPIRICAL DISCUSSION

In this section the importance of industrial production in the process of commune economic growth will be demonstrated empirically. This will be done by analysing time-series data from two communes – Cheng Dong Commune in the Shanghai Municipality and Wu Gong Commune in Hebei Province. This analysis will involve a disaggregation of each commune's financial accounts. Such a disaggregation should reveal the process of growth in the commune, and should enabled one to identify a very important part of that process, namely, the division of the available surplus between accumulation and distribution. It will be argued that the structure of the commune, which includes a wide degree of participation by its members in planning and decision-making, can promote a high rate of investment. By closely identifying the interests of the individual with the social interests of the organization the time-horizon for intertemporal decisions is extended, thereby raising the accumulation–distribution ratio above what it might otherwise have been. The industrial sector of the commune plays a vital role in this process.

Cheng Dong Commune

In Table 5.1 data are presented on the sources of income at Cheng Dong for 1972 to 1978.[2] During this period income grew rapidly, at an average annual rate of 17.5 per cent. Most of this growth can be attributed to the industrial sector: commune industrial income grew at an average annual rate of 33.2 per cent, and industrial income generated by brigade-level enterprises grew at an average annual rate of 16.5 per cent. By contrast agricultural income (team level) grew at an average annual rate of 4.1 per cent.[3] The process of structural change at Cheng Dong can be seen clearly from this table. In 1972, for example, industrial production generated 52 per cent of total commune income. By 1978 this proportion had increased to approximately 75 per cent.

The next stage in the disaggregation of the commune accounts is to deduct from income the value of expenditures on the materials used in production. These data are provided in Table 5.2. This table indicates an important difference between the two sectors in the rate of growth of material costs. Team-level agricultural expenditure increased only slightly over the period; indeed, by 1978 agricultural expenditure comprised only 14.7 per cent of total material costs. Expenditure on industrial materials, on the other hand, has grown rapidly. The average annual growth of material costs for commune industry, for example, was 31.5 per cent. The corresponding annual growth rate for brigade industry over the same period was 18.2 per cent.

The rapid increase in material costs for commune and brigade industries is not surprising. Industrial production requires large investments in fixed capital. Moreover, raw material costs per unit of output in industrial activities are expected to be much higher when compared with agricultural activities. One would expect, therefore, to see a decline in the

TABLE 5.1 *Sources of Income at Cheng Dong Commune, 1972–8*

unit = 10 000 yuan

	1972	*1973*	*1974*	*1975*	*1976*	*1977*	*1978*
Total income	1194.5	1865.8	1981.0	2075.0	2165.5	2426.5	2663.0
of which:							
Commune industry	373.6	956.4	1040.9	1050.0	997.4	1179.8	1243.1
Percentage of total income	31.3	51.3	52.5	50.6	46.1	48.6	46.7
Brigade industry	248.2	329.4	371.7	432.1	550.7	519.9	535.0
Percentage of total income	20.7	17.7	18.8	20.8	25.4	21.4	20.1
Production teams	572.6	580.1	569.3	593.8	617.3	494.9	619.4
Percentage of total income	48.0	31.0	28.7	28.6	28.5	20.0	23.2
Transitional brigades[4]	–	–	–	–	–	231.9	265.5
Percentage of total income						9.6	10.0

TABLE 5.2 *Sources of Expenditure at Cheng Dong Commune, 1972–8*

unit = 10 000 yuan

	1972	*1973*	*1974*	*1975*	*1976*	*1977*	*1978*
Total expenditure	568.7	1137.6	1128.6	1124.4	1138.4	1344.6	1381.4
of which:							
Commune industry	244.6	764.8	710.6	684.7	651.4	783.6	784.3
Percentage of total expenditure	43.0	67.3	63.0	60.9	57.2	58.2	56.8
Brigade industry	123.3	157.7	197.4	219.2	264.1	264.0	281.0
Percentage of total expenditure	21.7	13.9	17.5	19.5	23.2	19.7	20.3
Production teams	200.8	214.1	220.5	220.6	222.9	176.4	202.9
Percentage of total expenditure	35.3	18.8	19.5	19.6	19.6	13.1	14.7
Transitional brigades	–	–	–	–	–	120.6	113.2
Percentage of total expenditure						9.0	8.2

productivity of material expenditure in commune industry as structural change occurs. Since the marginal returns to industrial investment have been adequate the commune has continued to expand its industrial sector.

After paying for the materials used in production each enterprise must also pay a tax to the state. This tax liability, for team agricultural production and for brigade-level and commune-level industrial production, is a very small proportion of income. The data indicate an average liability of approximately 5 per cent of gross income, with annual variations from 0 to 10 per cent.

The next stage in the disaggregation of the commune's accounts, after tax is paid, yields a residual which shall be called the 'surplus'. The surplus is particularly important for this analysis because it is this surplus which must be divided between accumulation and distribution. The data in Table 5.3 show the sources of surplus at Cheng Dong for the period 1972–8.

The aggregate surplus has grown rapidly over the period, nearly doubling from 1972 to 1978. A disaggregation of the surplus is very revealing, however: over three-quarters of the growth in the total surplus can be attributed to the growth in the surplus generated by industrial production. Indeed, while the surplus from agricultural production has

TABLE 5.3 *Sources of Surplus at Cheng Dong Commune, 1972–8*
unit = 10 000 yuan

	1972	*1973*	*1974*	*1975*	*1976*	*1977*	*1978*
Total surplus	580.3	690.0	681.4	822.0	898.7	928.8	1088.7
of which:							
Commune industry	117.2	190.5	194.7	273.8	261.6	300.7	348.8
Percentage of total	20.2	27.6	28.6	33.3	29.1	32.4	32.0
Brigade industry	121.1	163.3	165.7	202.5	270.4	232.9	212.6
Percentage of total	20.9	23.7	24.3	24.6	30.1	25.1	19.5
Team activities	342.2	336.2	320.9	345.6	366.7	295.1	393.1
Percentage of total	59.0	48.7	47.1	42.0	40.8	31.7	36.1
Transitional brigades	–	–	–	–	–	100.1	134.3
Percentage of total	–	–	–	–	–	10.7	12.3
Total industrial surplus	283.3	253.8	360.4	476.3	532.0	583.6	628.4
Percentage of total surplus	41.1	51.3	52.9	57.9	59.2	62.8	57.7

remained high in absolute terms it has grown at an average annual rate of only 2.1 per cent. The surplus from industrial production, on the other hand, has grown at an average annual rate of 24.4 per cent. Within the industrial sector of the commune the surplus generated by the larger enterprises at commune level has grown most rapidly, i.e. at an average annual rate of 28.2 per cent.

These data reveal, therefore, an important aspect of the commune economy, namely the capacity of the industrial sector to generate a large surplus. Moreover, the industrial enterprises have managed to increase their share of the total surplus each year despite the rapid rise in their expenditure on raw materials. At Cheng Dong the proportion of industrial surplus in the total surplus has grown from 41 per cent in 1972 to nearly 58 per cent by 1978.

The contribution of industrial production to commune growth, however, will depend not on the surplus *per se*, but on the proportion of that surplus that can be allocated to accumulation. That is, the surplus must be divided between an accumulation component and a distribution component. This division involves making *social* decisions. Such decisions involve a balancing of the short-term interests of individuals with the long-term interests of the organization. These decisions will have an important influence on the attitudes of the members of the organization, thereby affecting their potential for work, their effort-discretion, their initiative, etc. In Chapter 1 it was argued that a self-managed organization which has explicit democratic procedures can reach a compromise over the division of the surplus between accumulation and distribution. If such a compromise can be determined democratically it may be more likely to be accepted by the workforce as their own decision rather than imposed administratively from above.

The results of the decisions concerning the division of the surplus between distribution and accumulation at Cheng Dong during 1972–8 are reported in Tables 5.4 and 5.5. In Table 5.4 the data show that the total amount allocated to distribution has grown steadily over the period. In this table, a row for per capita distribution has been added in order to normalise for population growth.

From 1972 to 1975 the proportion of the surplus distribution per capita displays no upward trend. From 1976 to 1978, however, the amount of distributed per capita did grow substantially. Table 5.4 also shows clearly that the team level has a large share of the distributional component, although this proportion has declined steadily, from 67 per cent in 1972 to 48 per cent in 1978. This is not surprising. In 1975, for example, over 70 per cent of the labour force in the commune was

TABLE 5.4 *Distribution by Source at Cheng Dong Commune, 1972–8*

unit = 10 000 yuan

	1972	*1973*	*1974*	*1975*	*1976*	*1977*	*1978*
Total distribution	439.8	462.4	454.0	510.0	515.3	515.3	649.4
Average per capita (yuan)	178.8	185.4	175.8	185.3	185.3	201.0	261.0
of which:							
Commune industry	71.8	81.5	77.5	88.1	90.2	93.8	121.0
Percentage of total	16.5	17.6	17.1	18.1	17.7	18.2	18.6
Brigade industry	72.01	83.6	88.3	93.2	103.9	92.3	124.6
Percentage of total	16.4	18.2	19.4	19.2	20.4	17.9	19.2
Team activities	295.9	297.1	288.2	304.4	316.0	259.7	317.2
Percentage of total	67.3	64.2	63.5	62.7	61.9	50.4	48.3
Transitional brigades	–	–	–	–	–	69.5	86.7
Percentage of total	–	–	–	–	–	13.5	13.4

engaged in agricultural production; by 1978 this proportion had declined to approximately 55 per cent.

Yet the most important aspect of Table 5.4 is perhaps the relatively low rate of growth of distribution per capita given the rate of growth of the surplus over the same period. From 1972 to 1977, for example, distribution per capita increased at an average annual rate of 2.1 per cent. These data suggest that the members of Cheng Dong have 'sacrificed the present for the future' by accepting a low rate of growth of distributed income over the period.

The magnitude of this 'sacrifice' is reflected in the data presented in Table 5.5. These data show the amount and proportion of the surplus that has been allocated to accumulation at Cheng Dong from 1972 to

TABLE 5.5 *Accumulation by Source at Cheng Dong Commune, 1972–8*

unit = 10 000 yuan

	1972	*1973*	*1974*	*1975*	*1976*	*1977*	*1978*
Total accumulation	140.5	227.6	227.4	336.3	388.6	413.5	439.3
of which:							
Commune industry	45.4	109.0	117.2	185.7	171.4	206.9	227.8
Percentage of total	32.2	48.3	51.5	55.2	44.1	50.0	52.0
Brigade industry	49.1	79.5	77.4	109.3	166.5	140.6	88.0
Percentage of total	34.8	34.9	34.0	32.5	43.0	43.0	20.0
Team activities	46.3	39.1	32.7	41.2	50.7	35.4	75.9
Percentage of total	33.0	16.8	14.5	12.2	13.1	8.6	17.3
Transitional brigades	–	–	–	–	–	30.6	47.6
Percentage of total	–	–	–	–	–	7.4	10.8

1978. The total amount of accumulation has grown rapidly over the period at an average annual rate of 30.5 per cent. Once again disaggregation by sector is very revealing; about 90 per cent of the growth in accumulation can be attributed to accumulation in the industrial sector. The average annual rate of growth of accumulation for commune-level industry was 57 per cent; for brigade-level industry the corresponding figure was 31 per cent; and for team-level agriculture the annual rate was 9 per cent. By 1978 approximately three-quarters of the total accumulation of the brigade was derived from industrial production.

The accumulation potential of the industrial sector can be identified more clearly by analysing the differences in the rates of accumulation between the two sectors (where rate of accumulation refers to the ratio of accumulation to surplus). These ratios have been calculated for each sector and are presented in Table 5.6. For the entire commune economy the rate of accumulation has increased substantially from 24 per cent in 1972 to 40 per cent in 1978 (row 1). A more revealing picture can be obtained, however, by disaggregating, and then by considering the rate of accumulation within each sector. These ratios are given in rows 3, 5, and 7 and 11 of Table 5.6. For most of the period less than 15 per cent of the agricultural surplus was accumulated (row 7). In the industrial sector, on the other hand, over half of the surplus generated by that sector was accumulated in each year after 1972 (row 11). At Cheng Dong the industrial sector therefore has clearly served as the 'engine of accumulation'.

It has been suggested above that the 'costs' of achieving such high rates of industrial accumulation are borne by the members of the organization. They are in effect sacrificing present distribution for higher future distribution. This should be reflected in high accumulation–distribution ratios. In Table 5.7 these ratios are shown in Cheng Dong for 1972 to 1978.

These data suggest that the industrial sector of the commune has achieved a steady increase in the accumulation–distribution ratio from 1972 to 1977. During the same period the agricultural sector was unable to increase its corresponding ratio. It is interesting to note, however, that in 1978 the production teams did manage to increase substantially their ratio of accumulation to distribution. Yet in that year the members of the commune clearly decided to allocate a larger share of the total surplus to distribution (row 1 in Table 5.6). Thus in 1978 the industrial enterprises increased the share of distribution from their own respective surpluses. As a result there was a 30 per cent increase in per capita

TABLE 5.6 *Rates of Accumulation by Source at Cheng Dong Commune, 1972–8*

Row	*Ratio*	*1972*	*1973*	*1974*	*1975*	*1976*	*1977*	*1978*
1	Total accumulation/total surplus	0.24	0.33	0.33	0.41	0.43	0.44	0.40
2	Commune industry accumulation/total surplus	0.08	0.16	0.17	0.23	0.19	0.22	0.21
3	Commune industry accumulation/commune surplus	0.39	0.57	0.60	0.68	0.65	0.69	0.65
4	Brigade industry accumulation/total surplus	0.08	0.11	0.11	0.13	0.18	0.15	0.08
5	Brigade industry accumulation/brigade surplus	0.40	0.49	0.47	0.54	0.61	0.60	0.41
6	Team accumulation/total surplus	0.08	0.05	0.05	0.05	0.056	0.04	0.07
7	Team accumulation/team surplus	0.13	0.12	0.10	0.12	0.14	0.12	0.19
8	Transitional brigade accumulation/total surplus	–	–	–	–	–	0.03	0.04
9	Transitional brigade accumulation/transitional brigade surplus	–	–	–	–	–	0.30	0.35
10	Total industrial accumulation/total surplus	0.16	0.27	0.28	0.36	0.38	0.39	0.32
11	Total industrial accumulation/total industrial surplus	0.40	0.53	0.54	0.62	0.63	0.62	0.54

TABLE 5.7 *Accumulation–Distribution Ratios at Cheng Dong Commune, 1972–8*

Ratio	*1972*	*1973*	*1974*	*1975*	*1976*	*1977*	*1978*
Commune industry accumulation / Commune industry distribution	0.63	1.34	1.51	2.11	1.90	2.21	1.88
Brigade industry accumulation / Brigade industry distribution	0.68	0.95	0.88	1.17	1.60	1.52	0.70
Team level accumulation / Team level distribution	0.15	0.13	0.11	0.13	0.16	0.14	0.24
Total commune accumulation / Total commune distribution	0.32	0.49	0.50	0.69	0.76	0.80	0.67

distribution at Cheng Dong in 1978, financed largely from industrial surpluses.

The empirical analysis of Cheng Dong's financial accounts has revealed two important aspects of the commune economy. First, expansion of industrial activity would seem to be essential in generating the surplus necessary to finance economic growth. Indeed, given a development strategy which demands that the rural sector 'self-finance' its own sustained development this would suggest that the growth of the commune industrial sector is indispensable. Second, while the industrial sector displays a considerable potential for accumulation (when compared with agriculture) it is important to remember that the achievement of such high rates of accumulation depend upon the willingness of the members of the organization to incur the 'costs of change' by restricting the proportion of the distributed component in the division of the surplus.

It may be recalled that Cheng Dong Commune lies in a wealthy region of China, not least because the area around Shanghai had a high level of industrialization for many years. There is a possibility, therefore, that the analysis of industrial production in the commune may have been biased. Therefore a commune in a predominantly agricultural region of China shall now be considered.

Wu Gong Commune

The available data from Wu Gong do not allow one to make the detailed disaggregation of the financial accounts that was possible for Cheng Dong. Nevertheless, an analysis of the aggregated accounts for selected years should enable one to determine the role of industrial production in the accumulation process at Wu Gong. In Table 5.8 a summary of the financial accounts for selected years from 1961 to 1978 is provided. Gross income increased substantially over the period, at an average annual rate of 31.8 per cent. The sectoral composition of this income changed dramatically from 1972 to 1978. In 1972 79 per cent of this income derived from agricultural production and 12 per cent came from industrial production. By 1978 agriculture's share in commune income had decreased to 42 per cent, while industry's share had increased to 45 per cent. Structural change at Wu Gong, therefore, has in recent years occurred very rapidly. As the share of industrial income in total commune income has increased rapidly so has the size of the surplus. Unfortunately one cannot determine the sectoral sources of the surplus, but it is very likely that industrial production contributed the largest share in the growth of this surplus. The amount of the surplus distributed per capita to commune members increased steadily from 1972 to 1978 at an average annual rate of 8.8 per cent. The amount of the surplus allocated to accumulation, however, increased at three times this annual rate, viz. 27 per cent. For the entire period 1962–78 the rate of accumulation was raised from 10 per cent in 1962 to 33 per cent in 1978. The 'sacrifice of the present for the future' by members of the commune can be seen from the steady rise in the accumulation–distribution ratio. This ratio increased from 0.11 in 1961 to nearly 0.50 in 1978.

A similar aggregation of accounts from Wu Gong Brigade in Wu Gong Commune is given for selected years 1966–78 in Table 5.9. Gross income rose very rapidly over the period, at an average annual rate of 35 per cent. The sectoral composition of this income changed remarkably at Wu Gong Brigade in only a four-year period. In 1975, for example, agricultural income accounted for 73 per cent of commune income. By 1978 this share had decreased to 29 per cent. Over the same period the share of industrial income in total commune income increased rapidly from 20 per cent in 1975 to 61 per cent in 1978. During this four-year period of rapid structural change in the economy of the brigade, the size of the surplus increased at an average annual rate of 11 per cent. For the previous four-year period, 1972–5, the surplus grew at a much slower rate per year, viz. 3.6 per cent. Thus, the rapid industrialisation in the Brigade from 1975 to 1978 is associated with a three-fold increase in the rate of growth of the surplus. Moreover during this period of rapid structural change (1975–8) the share of the surplus allocated to accumulation by brigade members increased at an average annual rate of 41 per cent. For the same period the corresponding share of the

TABLE 5.8 *Aggregated Financial Accounts of Wu Gong Commune, Hebei Province, for Selected Years, 1961–78*
unit = 10 000 yuan

	1961	*1966*	*1972*	*1975*	*1977*	*1978*
Gross income	89.2	101.9	201.8	308.8	489.05	599.5
of which:						
Agriculture	n.a.	n.a.	160.5 (79.5)	206.4 (66.9)	206.7 (42.2)	250.9 (41.9)
Industry	n.a.	n.a.	24.5 (12.1)	77.2 (25.0)	195.1 (40.0)	268.1 (44.7)
Surplus						
of which:						
Distribution	56.8	61.4	106.3	117.4	142.6	178
Distribution per capita	44.7	42.8	69.1	74.6	89.8	111.8
Accumulation	6.4	9.7	30.1	63.1	55.4	87.6
Ratios						
Accumulation/surplus	0.10	0.14	0.22	0.35	0.28	0.33
Accumulation/distribution	0.11	0.16	0.28	0.54	0.39	0.49

NOTE Percentages of total gross income are shown in parentheses.

TABLE 5.9 *Aggregated Financial Accounts of Wu Gong Brigade, Hebei Province, for Selected Years, 1966–78*

unit = 10 000 yuan

	1966	*1972*	*1975*	*1978*
Gross income	309 000	578 815	746 667	1 712 685
of which:				
Agriculture	n.a.	424 327 (73.3)	547 157 (73.2)	502 370 (29.3)
Industry	n.a.	60 800 (10.5)	151 759 (20.3)	1 046 742 (61.1)
Surplus	212 300	419 621	480 000	692 142
of which:				
Distribution	192 000	327 650	401 294	484 017
Distribution per capita	87.7	131.7	157.5	188.8
Accumulation	20 300	91 971	78 706	208 125
Ratios				
Accumulation/surplus	0.09	0.22	0.16	0.30
Accumulation/distribution	0.10	0.28	0.20	0.43

NOTE Percentages of total gross income shown in parentheses.

surplus allocated for distribution increased at an annual rate of 5 per cent. The importance attached to accumulation by brigade members is also reflected in the change in the rate of accumulation. This rate nearly doubled during the 1975–8 period from 16 to 30 per cent.

The data from Wu Gong Commune corroborate the general trends identified in the previous analysis of Cheng Dong Commune. First, structural change towards industry has occurred with economic development, and this industrial growth has generated a large share of the surplus and the accumulation. Second, the members of the commune have been willing to accept a small increase in the amount of the surplus available for distribution in favour of high rates of accumulation.

It would be interesting to see if such trends can be identified at larger levels of the economy. In Table 5.10 a similar aggregation of financial accounts for all the rural communes in Hebei Province is presented. As mentioned, this is a predominantly agricultural province, and the distributed income per capita is below the national average. These data include over 3600 rural communes and nearly 45 million people. The data show that the process of structural change, given by the changing sectoral composition of income, is not nearly as advanced in the province as a whole as in Wu Gong Commune. Nevertheless the share of industrial income in total commune income has more than doubled from 1970 to 1978. Moreover, for the same period the surplus has grown at an average annual rate of 13.6 per cent. The amount of surplus distributed per capita increased at an average annual rate of 3 per cent from 1970 to 1978, while the amount of surplus accumulated per capita increased by over three times this rate per year for the same period.

It is likely that the increase in the rate of accumulation in the province (from 12 per cent in 1965 to 21 per cent in 1977) was associated with the expansion of industrial production within the communes during this period. If this is so the data in Table 5.10 add further support to the proposition that commune industry is the 'engine of growth' in the rural economy.

Data showing the aggregated financial accounts of Jia Ding County in the Shanghai Municipality for selected years, 1958–78, are also available. This county contains nineteen communes, of which Cheng Dong Commune is one. A summary of these accounts is given in Table 5.11. It is important to note that the data include only the accounts of the 243 brigades and 2322 teams in the county. Thus, commune-level industry is excluded from the table.

The rapid expansion of industrial activity within the communes of the county can be seen clearly from the table. In 1965, for example, brigade

TABLE 5.10 *Selected Financial Data and Ratios for All Communes, Hebei Province, for Selected Years, 1962–78*

unit = 10 000 yuan

	1962	*1965*	*1970*	*1973*	*1977*	*1978*
Gross income	246 570	309 706	276 598	483 810	584 758	705 869
of which:						
Agriculture	196 842 (79.8)	237 982 (76.8)	230 071 (83.1)	364 250 (75.2)	348 314 (64.7)	456 922 (64.7)
Industry	32 627 (13.2)	31 584 (10.1)	35 539 (12.8)	65 659 (13.5)	134 842 (23.1)	185 231 (26.2)
Surplus	160 725	214 759	188 478	319 859	333 654	419 636
of which:						
Distribution	149 022	188 985	161 674	261 645	265 054	339 129
Accumulation	11 703	25 774	26 904	58 214	68 600	80 507
Population	3 528	3 677	2 718	4 284	4 444	4 477.4
Distribution per capita (yuan)	42.2	51.4	59.5	61.1	59.6	75.7
Accumulation per capita (yuan)	3.3	7.0	9.9	13.6	15.4	18.0
Ratios						
Accumulation per capita / Distribution per capita	0.08	0.14	0.17	0.22	0.26	0.24
Accumulation/surplus	0.07	0.12	0.14	0.18	0.21	0.19
Distribution/surplus	0.93	0.88	0.86	0.82	0.79	0.81

NOTES 1. The unreported residual in the composition of gross income includes mainly fishing, forestry and animal husbandry.
2. Percentages are shown in parantheses.

SOURCE Interview with Wu Cheng, Deputy Head of the People's Commune Section of the Office of Agriculture, Hebei Provincial Government, 14 June 1979.

TABLE 5.11 *Aggregated Financial Accounts, Jia Ding County, Shanghai Municipality, 1978*
(brigades and teams only)
unit = million yuan

	1958	%	*1965*	%	*1976*	%	*1978*	%
Gross income	42.7		99.7		191.5		233.2	
of which:								
Agriculture	39.5	92.5	82.2	82.4	107.3	56.0	110.6	47.4
Industry	3.2	7.5	17.5	17.5	84.2	44.0	122.5	52.6
Surplus	22.6		63.8		99.8		123.6	
of which:								
Distribution	19.4		52.1		70.4		91.2	
per capita	69		152		189		243	
Accumulation	3.2		11.7		29.4		32.4	
Ratios								
Accumulative/surplus	0.14		0.18		0.29		0.26	
Accumulation/distribution	0.16		0.22		0.42		0.35	

industry accounted for 17.5 per cent of gross income; by 1978 this proportion had grown to 42.6 per cent of gross income. From 1965 to 1978 agricultural income increased at an average annual rate of 2.5 per cent, whereas brigade industrial income increased at an average annual rate of 42.8 per cent. From 1965 to 1976 the rate of accumulation increased from 18 per cent to 29 per cent and the accumulation–distribution ratio nearly doubled from 0.22 to 0.42. Moreover, during the period of rapid expansion of brigade-level industry (1965–78) the amount of the surplus allocated to accumulation increased at an average annual rate of 12.6 per cent, while the amount of the surplus allocated to distribution increased at a corresponding annual rate of 5.3 per cent.

Thus, the available macroeconomic data from Hebei Province and from Jia Ding County lend further support to the conclusions reached in the analysis of Cheng Dong Commune and Wu Gong Commune. Expansion of the industrial sector within the commune would seem to be important in assuring a substantial growth in the surplus and in the rate of accumulation.

3. CONCLUSION

In Section 2 it was argued that an expansion of industrial production in the commune is usually associated with an increase in the rate of growth of the surplus. The data show that the commune organization has allocated a very large share of the surplus to accumulation rather than to distribution. This indicates that the members of the commune have sacrificed present consumption for future consumption, i.e. they have paid the 'cost of change'. Why should members of a commune organization be willing to do this? In this section an answer to this important question will be suggested.

In Section 2 no attempt was made to disaggregate and then to analyse the accumulation accounts. Unfortunately only limited cross-section data on the accumulation accounts at Cheng Dong Commune are available. Analysis of these data should, however, enable one to suggest how the pattern of investment might have affected the weights of the arguments in individual utility functions. Of particular interest are the weights attached to the present value of future consumption. An increase in this coefficient, for example, should result in a decrease in the weight attached to leisure or an increase in the weight attached to effort, or some combination of these.

In Table 5.12 data are presented on the investment programme at Cheng Dong Commune for 1975. Before discussing these data I should point out that *ex-ante* accumulation in the commune does not usually equal *ex-post* physical investment. The investment plans for the year are determined in advance after discussion by members. Each level places their accumulation in a fund from which their investment expenditures are drawn. At the end of the year, therefore, the total amount spent on investment may be slightly less or slightly more than the total amount accumulated. In 1975, for example, commune-level investment was slightly less than commune accumulation, while brigade-level and team-level investments were slightly more than their respective accumulation.

From these data the importance of industrial accumulation in the commune investment programme can be seen clearly. Indeed, 83.3 per cent of total investment in the commune in 1975 was financed from industrial accumulation. Moreover, the industrial sector of the commune financed entirely the aid given to poor teams, the contributions to cultural, educational and health programmes in the commune, and the administrative expenses incurred at all levels. Perhaps most surprising is the fact that nearly 43 per cent of investment from industrial accumulation was allocated to the agricultural sector.

The vital role of industrial accumulation in financing agricultural investment can be seen more clearly in Table 5.13. Accumulation from industrial production, for example, has financed 95 per cent of the investment in roads and bridges, 92 per cent of the investment in the

TABLE 5.12 *Investment Programme at Cheng Dong Commune by Source, 1975*

	(1) *Commune level*	%	(2) *Brigade level*	%	(3) *Total industrial investment*	%	(4) *Team* ***level***	%
Total investment	147.9	–	123.2	–	271.1	–	54.3	–
of which:								
Agriculture	62.9	42.5	52.8	42.8	115.7	42.7	54.3	100
of which:								
roads and bridges	10.2	6.9	0.97	0.8	11.2	4.1	0.6	1.1
irrigation and drainage	4.8	3.2	9.5	7.7	14.3	5.2	1.2	2.2
farm machinery	1.0	.7	31.6	25.6	32.6	12.0	20.4	37.6
aid to poor teams	6.3	4.3	1.8	1.5	8.1	3.0	–	–
contribution to circulating funds for lower units	40	27.0	5.1	4.1	45.1	16.1		
New construction	–	–	–	–	–	–	24.8	45.7
other	0.6	0.4	3.8	3.0	4.4	1.6	7.3	13.3
Industrial	77.8	52.6	50.7	41.1	128.5	47.4	–	–
of which:								
new construction	40.8	27.6	17.7	14.4	58.5	21.6	–	–
new machinery	7.3	4.9	33.0	26.9	40.4	14.9	–	–
other	29.7	27.0	–	–	29.7	10.9	–	–
Public Welfare Fund (culture health, education)	1.3	0.9	3.6	2.9	4.9	1.8	–	–
Administration	2.4	1.6	4.7	3.8	7.1	2.6	–	–
Housing	–	–	2.7	2.2	2.7	1.	–	–
Miscellaneous	3.5	2.4	8.6	7.0	12.1	4.4	–	–

TABLE 5.13 *Agricultural Investment Programme at Cheng Dong Commune by Sectoral Source, 1975*

unit = 10 000 yuan

Activity	*Amount of investment*	*Proportion financed from industrial accumulation*	*Proportion financed from team level accumulation*
Total agriculture	170	68.1	31.9
of which:			
Roads and bridges	11.8	95	5
Irrigation and drainage	15.5	92.2	7.8
Farm machinery	53.0	61.5	38.5
Aid to poor teams	8.1	100	–
New construction	24.8	–	100
Contribution to circulating fund for lower units	45.1	100	–
Other	11.7	37.6	62.4

water-control system, and over 60 per cent of the investment in farm machinery. Moreover, the industrial sector makes a large contribution each year to the working capital fund for teams, from which, for example, the purchases of chemical fertilizers and other technical inputs can be financed. The industrial sector therefore is not just the 'engine of accumulation' in the commune: it also makes a very important contribution toward the modernization of agriculture and the promotion of agricultural growth.

These data indicate that the structure of the commune organization has enabled an important share of the benefits of one sector (industry) to be captured by the other sector (agriculture). In 1975 at Cheng Dong, for example, more than 70 per cent of the labour force was employed in agriculture at the team level. The structure and the scale of the commune thus played an important part in the internalization of the 'externalities' from industrial production.

The empirical analysis in Section 2 indicated that commune members have sacrificed the present for the future. This tendency was evident from the steady increase in the accumulation–distribution ratios that were observed. This reflects a widening of individual time-horizons and is likely to result in an increase in the weight attached to the present value of future consumption, and perhaps in an increase in the quantity and intensity of the input of labour.

It is possible, however, that the observed rise in the accumulation–distribution ratios were due not to voluntary decisions to sacrifice present for future consumption, but to coercion. As discussed in Chapter 2 there is evidence that in some communes cadres used 'commandist' tactics to increase the relative share of accumulation in the accounts. To the extent that this occurred in the communes studied the interpretation of the data in this chapter would have to be qualified. I have found from my research, however, that the use of such tactics was not pervasive in the countryside, and indeed 'commandism' often met with considerable resistance by the peasantry.[5]

The investment programme at Cheng Dong in 1975 indicates, finally, that there is a considerable degree of *social* control over the surplus generated in production for the direct benefit of the commune members. The structure of the commune organization and the degree of social ownership within it have encouraged a sacrifice of the present by its members in order to receive future benefits for their children and for themselves.

6 The Private Sector in the Rural Organization

In the previous two chapters the process of agricultural and industrial growth in several rural organizations has been discussed. Yet many economic activities take place not in the collective sector of the organization, but in the private sector. In this chapter, therefore, the discussion will be broadened to include the important contribution of private production to economic growth in the countryside.

In the major rural policy document published by the government during 1961–2 – called the '60 Articles' – regulations for private production within the commune organization were clearly defined. Indeed, for several years thereafter, many households vigorously pursued private production as an adjunct to collective production. By 1964–6, however, the Maoist group in the government began to attack the private sector as a 'tail of capitalism' – a tail which ought to be chopped off. The private sector was seen by this group as a threat to the promotion of socialism in the countryside. Despite the existence of the '60 Articles' document they effectively succeeded in curtailing its operation for more than ten years. (The policies of the 1966–76 period will be analysed in some detail in Chapter 8.)

By 1978 the 'opposition' group in the government had consolidated their position after the death of Mao and the fall of the 'Gang of Four'. This opposition group led by the same men (e.g. Deng Xiaoping, Bo Yibo, Chen Yun) who opposed the large-scale commune movement in 1957–9, who succeeded in consolidating the commune organisation in 1961–2 and who were instrumental in composing the '60 Articles' regulations. In December 1978 the government published a revised '60 Articles' which not only reiterated the legitimacy of private production in rural China, but also stressed its importance by extending its size and scope.

In Section 1 of the chapter a description of the scope and composition of the private sector in the countryside will be given. In Section 2 an empirical estimation of the size of the private sector and of its contribution to total household income will be provided. Although the relationship between private activity and the distribution of income will be considered in detail in the next chapter, this section will also anticipate the discussion there: the data suggest that private economic activity may be relatively more important in poor regions than in rich regions. In the concluding section recent policy towards the private sector and some empirical results from those policies will be considered.

1. THE SCOPE AND COMPOSITION OF THE PRIVATE SECTOR

The private sector in rural China consists of a large number of economic activities. The most important are the private plots, animal husbandry, afforestation and horticulture, handicraft and other 'cottage' industries, and the marketing of the outputs from these activities. The government uses a variety of mechanisms actively to encourage private production. In this section these activities will be described and some empirical material will be presented.

The Private Plot

The commune allocates individual plots of land to each household 'for their own use on a permanent basis'.[1] Both the 1962 and the 1978 '60 Articles' state that 'private land will usually account for five to seven per cent of the cultivated land owned by the production teams'.[2] In a 1965 study of ten communes the share of land allocated to private plots ranged from 5 to 9.3 per cent; and from 3 to 11 per cent in a study of seven communes in the early 1970s.[3] However, there is currently room for a flexible interpretation of the regulation. The '60 Articles' also state that 'in localities with forested hills or barren slopes, land may be allocated to commune members for their own use as needs and customs of the masses may be; once such land is allocated, it will also be kept for private farming on a permanent basis'.[4] Because of government encouragement for local initiative there has been an expansion of the area of land allocated to the private plot. For example, in July 1980, the Ningxia Hui Autonomous Regional CCP Committee declared that a commune member may retain a maximum of 12 per cent of team land as private plot.[5] A recent editorial in *People's Daily* urged that considera-tion be given to 'local situations in order properly to expand family plots and fodder plots, with the maximum area of both plots set at 15 per cent of the total farmland of the production team'.[6] In Henan Province a decision was recently made to 'designate hilly land for private use by isolated households'.[7]

The size of the plot per household varies between communes according to local allocation rules. In the two studies cited earlier the largest average size of individual plots was six to seven times larger than the lowest average. It is likely that local allocation rules depend mainly on man–land ratios. In Hebei Province, for example, the allocation rule is 0.1 mou per capita; in the more densely populated Guangdong Province the allocation rule is 0.05 mou per capita; in the Shanghai Municipality the rule is 0.085 mou per capita.[8]

There does not seem to be a uniform production pattern on the private plots; local marketing conditions and individual household needs are the most likely determinants of what is grown. Vegetable production is common, especially in communes near towns and cities. Field observers have also noted a variety of other crops such as sugarcane, grain, peanuts, sweet potatoes, etc. Cropping decisions are made by the household; production teams are encouraged to provide families with some inputs. A March 1980 Hebei Provincial Party Committee document stated that 'private plots should be run by commune members themselves. Commune members may grow whatever they like. Production teams should supply commune members with adequate water and fertiliser for their private plots.'[9] In addition to land allocated to the private plot the '60 Articles' document also makes provision for the private reclamation of wasteland. The document states that 'the amount of such land in general may be equal to that of private land allocated for each member'.[10]

Animal Husbandry

Zhang Pinghua, First Vice-Minister of the State Agricultural Commission remarked in September 1979 that 'animal husbandry might become the predominant sector in China's agriculture in future'.[11] There is no doubt that the government is attaching increasing importance to animal husbandry, if one is to judge from recent official statements. The private sector figures prominently in this respect; pork is the chief source of meat in China and the vast majority of pigs are owned privately. Moreover, the state has provided the private animal husbandry sector with an extraordinary amount of economic and material encouragement in order to foster its development and expansion. Official policy for the private animal sector is stated clearly in the 1978 '60 Articles': 'Commune members may raise pigs, sheep, chickens, ducks, rabbits and geese; households which measure up to the requirements may raise dairy cows or beef cattle.'[12]

A state subsidy for private pig-raising is explicitly stipulated in Article 51 of the 1978 '60 Articles':

> It is important to continue to encourage the families of commune members to raise pigs, and to develop pig-breeding energetically . . . the breeding of pigs and sheep by commune members should be subsidised collectively by the state by providing a certain amount of feed. When purchasing pigs from the producers, the state should sell them feed as encouragement to continue raising.[13]

The state uses a variety of mechanisms to encourage pig production, such as increases in state procurement prices, feed and fertilizer subsidies, allocation of land for fodder production and the provision of free clinics for disease prevention and medical treatment. In Guangdong Province, for example, for each pig delivered to the state, a household is allowed to purchase 30 jin of rice and small amounts of chemical fertilizer at subsidized prices; coupons to buy processed meat are also exchanged.[14] Moreover, for each pig raised by the household, 0.03 mou of land is allocated for fodder (in addition to the private plot allocation). A team can also award workpoints for the delivery of pig manure.[15] In Anhui Province a state foodstuffs company has set up clinics staffed with full-time veterinarians to innoculate pigs against plague.[16] Fodder crushers and mixers also are made available to families. For poor areas the state gives financial assistance 'when individual commune members have difficulty in raising large livestock such as pigs and sheep'.[17] In the Ningzia Hui Autonomous Region the state provides families who raise oxen and sheep with forage grass and feed lots.[18]

Private Afforestation

The State Council issued a directive in March 1980 calling attention to the alarming state of afforestation in China. Only 12.7 per cent of China's land is covered with trees, ranking the country 120th out of the 160 countries in the world in percentage of afforested national territory. The policies promulgated by the State Council give encouragement to the private sector to contribute to China's forestry programme. The directive delcared:

> The peasants are encouraged to plant trees in and around their courtyards, or in places designated for tree planting by their production teams. Private plots may be allotted to peasants for growing trees or grass in places where there is too much wasteland or there are too many barren hills which cause an acute shortage of firewood . . . trees planted by peasants and the forestry products from them are private property. The owners are permitted to sell them in rural markets.[19]

This directive revised the 1978 '60 Articles' which makes reference only to the planting of fruit trees and bamboo around commune members' houses. Since its publication a number of provincial directives have been issued encouraging implementation of this policy. For example, a 'Forum on Production Development in Mountainous and Old Revolutionary Base Areas' was held in June 1980 by the Inner Mongolian Autonomous Region. Five declarations were made:[20]

(1) Remove all restriction on the number of privately owned animals.

(2) Actively encourage and support commune members to carry out afforestation.

(3) Communes and brigades may allow their members to have a certain amount of sandy land, mountainous land and wasteland for planting trees and forage crops. All income earned from these endeavours should belong to the commune members themselves and the ownership by the commune members of these lands should be ensured.

(4) Commune members should be encouraged to enclose pastures in pastoral areas and allowed to plant trees, grass, vegetables and millet. They should also be allowed to set up hay-cutting workshops.

(5) Commune members have the right to market freely the products produced in their sideline agricultural and livestock production. The products may be sold to the state and may be sold by negotiating prices at rural markets. All retailers and peddlers of these commodities may conduct their sales from house to house.

Other Private Economic Activity

At the household level the '60 Articles' permit a wide variety of 'sideline' activities, e.g. knitting, embroidery, grass and wood-gathering, sericulture, apiculture, herb-collecting, fishing and hunting. The factor endowments of a particular area determine which of these activities are adopted by households. There are also other private activities which have received emphasis in the press, such as individual trading by artisans and craftsmen. In the summer of 1980 the Economic Research Institute of the Chinese Academy of Social Science held a series of discussions on the subject of the 'individual economy', along with the Institute of Marxism–Leninism–Mao Zedong Thought. New China News Agency reported that:

> A number of participants agreed that the individual economy may exist and develop to some extent to enliven the market and supplement the people's requirements. . . . It was stated that the municipality of Shanghai and Liaoning Province had over 100,000 individual traders and artisans. The economists pointed out that China's many trades still depended on manual labour. Repairs and services were areas required to ease the lives of people and could not be undertaken completely by the state and collective economy. Under such conditions, the individual economy would exist not only at present but in the future too.[21]

A similar article in *Workers Daily* called for 'individual undertakings which do not exploit others, to supplement the socialist economy'.[22] In Guangdong Province the response to this policy was rapid: by May 1980 the provincial government had issued 53 220 private business licences.[23] Most of these businesses involve repair services, grinding of knives, mending of cooking-pots, repairing of umbrellas and furniture, haircutting, dressmaking, waste recovery, catering and selling of local products. Skilled workers in production teams are allowed to become self-employed, but on a contract basis with the team. Rural craftsmen such as carpenters, bricklayers, blacksmiths, stone-cutters, leather workers, masons and seamstresses will often travel to near-by villages and render services to teams or households in return for cash. According to the terms of the contract with the craftsman's team, a fixed proportion of his income could be handed over to the team (e.g. 20 per cent).

Rural Markets

Rural markets have been a prominent feature of the Chinese countryside for thousands of years. G. William Skinner has argued that the commune organization has preserved an ancient pattern of location in which a remarkable equidistant spatial relationship between village and market can be described in terms of a hexagonal model.[24] The proximity of each village to the market-place determines the ease with which each household can sell their surplus output in the market, usually during early mornings and evenings. The 1962 '60 Ariticles' recognized the importance of these markets: 'After the State Purchase Quota is fulfilled as prescribed by contract and aside from any specific restrictions imposed by the state, the remaining products may be sent to the rural markets for sale by the commune members.'[25] The number of these locations was estimated at 40 000 in 1961 and in aggregate they handled about 25 per cent of the total trade in agricultural and sideline products.[26] These markets came under attack during the 1966–76 period and attempts were made to ban them or bring them under state control.[27] The 1978 '60 Articles', however, reaffirmed the right of rural markets to exist. Article 32 states:

> Rural trade fairs are a necessary adjunct to a socialist commerce. Commune members have the right to market in the trade fairs, making up what one lacks by what another has in surplus. No unit or individual is allowed to meddle with these fairs. Commune members are also permitted to sell and buy small amounts of oil-bearing crops through the trade fairs after they have provided what the state requisitions.[28]

The necessity for rural markets, aside from their importance as a source of supplementary cash income for households, lies in their marketing efficiency. The state marketing system would encounter severe inefficiencies were it to attempt to handle all commodities with a marketable surplus. Rural markets are a convenient institutional arrangement for making supply adjustments, correcting imbalances and for giving the state some indication of the relative strength of supply and demand and thereby enabling prices to be determined efficiently. The Peking Radio Service's 'Lectures on the Commune' argued that

> Some products are perishable. They would be a problem for state shops and supply and marketing cooperatives were they to procure such products. Therefore such products have to be sold at rural fairs . . . it is impossible for state shops and supply and marketing cooperatives to supply all that commune members need and to procure all that they want to sell. That is why rural trade fairs are needed.[29]

Between December 1978 and June 1979 more than 30 000 rural fairs opened, as well as a number of 'country fairs opening in 20 cities'.[30] By May 1981 this number had increased to 40 800 of which nearly 3000 are located in cities.[31] During 1980 transactions in these markets amounted to 23 500 million yuan, a 28 per cent increase from 1979, and accounted for 8.4 per cent of all retail sales in China.[32]

Rural markets tend to be more numerous in mountainous areas where a more diversified economy usually exists. Moreover, the costs of state marketing services tends to be very high in these areas. Rural markets also are important in county towns and areas around cities where demand is high from workers in the industrial sector. Clearly households which have ready access to county towns or urban areas are at an advantage. Proximity to such lucrative markets would thus be an important determinant of household behaviour toward this segment of the private sector.

Most markets commence on specified days in early morning. They are thriving and bustling affairs with a quite remarkable diversity of commodities on offer. In a visit to a market in Jia Ding County, Shanghai Municipality, in June 1979 I found the following animal products to be on sale: eggs, rabbit, duck, eel, crab, assorted other fish, chickens, turtles, portions of pig and shrimp. Vegetables for sale included cabbage, green beans, potatoes, aubergine, squash, greens, tomatoes, onions, bamboo shoots and peppers. In discussion with Management Committee officials at this market it was learnt that there are no restrictions on what can be sold, with the exception of cotton (an important industrial crop), garlic (for export only), oil-bearing crops and collective grain. Private grain, however, may be sold. All incomes, prices and quantities have to be reported by all agents to the market manager. A market management group from the local branch of the Provincial Bureau of Agricultural Trade enforces these regulations and attempts to check speculative activity. Price surveys are conducted every few months to keep the state informed of market conditions and to exchange information with neighbouring counties and thereby check speculation. Investigations are carried out regularly when speculative activity is suspected. Production teams and individual households are allowed to sell surplus commodities in the market provided all state delivery quotas have been met. Teams usually designate a representative to act on their behalf in the market. Prices for most commodities in the market were slightly higher than state prices for the same commodities. Under 'normal' circumstances this price differential could be regarded as the (opportunity) cost to the household of selling in a rural market rather than directly to the state or to the collective. In 'abnormal' circumstances, i.e. when price differentials increase, the state is given useful information on which to alter its own prices.

2. EMPIRICAL ESTIMATES OF PRIVATE ECONOMIC ACTIVITY AT THE HOUSEHOLD LEVEL

Private economic activity is important in supplementing total agricultural production and household income. But just how important is it? One study published in 1978 in *Guangming Ribao* did estimate that in 1977 about 25 per cent of the total value of state purchases of agricultural and sideline products was from private production.[33] This study unfortunately ignored the value of exchange between households.

An impression, however, can be obtained from a sampling of a small number of households which I visited in three different regions of China in 1979.[34] Four households were interviewed at two different communes in Hebei Province, three households in Jia Ding County, Shanghai Municipality, and two households in the north of Guangdong Province. Data from these interviews are shown in Tables 6.1 and 6.2. A number of observations can be made from a glance at these tables. First, private plots in the two communes in Hebei Province were collectivized in the sense that they were farmed collectively although the output was distributed directly to households (Table 6.1). Second, pig-raising is an extraordinarily important part of the household economy, often accounting for more than half of private sector income (Table 6.2). Third, the direct consumption of vegetables and meat raised in the private sector makes a significant contribution to the quality and variety of a household's diet.

Given the limited number of households in the sample and the differences between the regions it is difficult to draw any definite conclusions. It is possible, however, to state the range and average obtained in the sample and compare these results with other estimates from Western and Chinese sources. The sample yields a range of 16 to 47 per cent of household income derived from private economic activity and an average of 30 per cent. Is this a reasonable estimate? Burki and Deleyne have published estimates of an average of 19 and 15 per cent respectively for the middle 1960s, and in three separate studies, Etienne, Rawski, and Whyte and Parrish have estimated 20 per cent for the middle and late 1970s.[35] Crook has given a much lower estimate of an average of 5–10 per cent for the middle 1970s.[36]

TABLE 6.1 *Basic Data From Nine Rural Households, 1979*

Household	1	2	3	4	5	6	7	8	9
Commune	Wu Gong	Wu Gong	Qie Ma	Qie Ma	Cheng Dong	Cheng Dong	Cheng Dong	Tang Tang	Tang Tang
Size of family	3	4	7	7	4	4	4	7	4
Income per head (yuan)	318.3	138.4	120.7	147.8	330.5	408.7	405.7	97.9	123.7
Total income (yuan)	955	553.5	845	1035	1322	1635	1623	685.1	495
Distributed collective income (yuan)	800	363	400	800	1100	1050	1123	410	263
Remittances from workers in state enterprises (yuan)	0	0	300	0	0	0	0	0	0
Private sector income (yuan)	155	190.5	145	235	222	585	500	275.1	231.8
Private sector income as a percentage of total income	16	34	17	29	17	36	31	40	47

NOTE: Wu Gong and Qie Ma Communes are in Hebei Province, Cheng Dong Commune is in Shanghai Municipality and Tang Tang is in Guangdong Province.

TABLE 6.2 *The Composition of Private Sector Income in Yuan, 1979*

Households	1	2	3	4	5	6	7	8	9
Income from private plots	collectivized	collectivized	collectivized	collectivized	136	200	140	88.5	61.64
of which, cash income	–	–	–	–	0	0	35	0	
Income from pigs	70	148	95	190	0	260	341	154	164
of which, cash income	70	98	0	0	0	260	341	154	164
Income from poultry	85	42.5	50	45	86	75	19	32.6	6.12
of which, cash income	0	0	10	18	0	0	0	0	3.06
Other income	0	0	0	0	0	50	0	0	0
Total private sector income	135	190.5	145	235	222	585	500	275.1	231.8

The evidence would indicate that these Western estimates, if used as a description of the recent situation, are perhaps a bit low. This conclusion is strengthened by data published recently in China. These data are shown in Table 6.3 and give an empirical indication of the important contribution of private production to rural economic growth. The table reports the results of six rural household surveys conducted by provincial statistical bureaux and of two similar surveys conducted by the central government. The data show that the relative importance of the private sector increased considerably from 1978 to 1980. This reflects the effects of the rural economic policies which were formulated at the Third Plenum in December 1978 (see the discussion of these policies in Section 3). One national survey (survey b in Table 6.3) shows that the increase in private income from 1978 to 1979 accounted for 42 per cent of the increase in total income per head in that year.

Perhaps the most striking observation from Table 6.3 is that the data for five provinces and one autonomous region show that the private sector, on average, accounted for 41.5 per cent of total household income in 1980. Moreover, these data suggest a rapid increase from 1979 to 1980 in the income earned from private activity. In Guizhou Province, for example, the increase in private income from 1979 to 1980 accounted for 68 per cent of the increase in total income per head in that year, and in Yunnan Province the increase in private income from 1979 to 1980 accounted for 74 per cent of the increase in total income per head.

The data in Tables 6.1 and 6.3 also allow one to anticipate the analysis in Chapter 7 concerning the relationship between private economic activity and the distribution of income. These data suggest that the private sector is *relatively* more important in poor than in rich regions. The data in Table 6.1 show, for example, that the households where the private sector accounted for the largest proportion of total household income came from Tang Tang, a commune in the poorest of the three regions of China that I visited. In 1979 the distributed collective income per head in these two households was 58.5 yuan and 65.9 yuan respectively. In the same year the average distributed collective income per head for all rural China was 102 yuan. The proportion of private sector income in total income for these two households was 40 and 47 per cent respectively, while the national average proportion of private income in total income in 1979 was 27.5 per cent.

While these data are only suggestive a clearer picture of the relative importance of private activity in poor regions can be seen from the data in Table 6.3. Two of the provinces listed in the table were well below the average distributed collective income in 1979, namely, Guizhou

TABLE 6.3 *Selected Data on Sectoral Composition of Household Income per Head in Selected Regions of Rural China, 1978–80*

Survey	*National*[a]	*National*[b]		*Guizhou*[c]		*Inner Mongolia*[d]	*Jilin*[e]	*Liaoning*[f]	*Shandong*[g]	*Yunnan*[h]	
Year	*1978*	*1978*	*1979*	*1979*	*1980*	*1980*	*1980*	*1980*	*1980*	*1979*	*1980*
Income per head (yuan)	133.57	133.6	160.2	148.2	189.5	217.3	244.8	273	n.a.	120.6	147.1
Distributed collective income per head (yuan)	89.53	87.1	102	87.2	100.5	130.5	122.5	152	n.a.	71.4	77.4
Private sector income per head (yuan)	35.79	32.9	44	61	89	86.8	102.4	84	n.a.	50	69.7
Other sources[i] of income per head (yuan)	9.25	13.6	14.2	–	–	–	19.9	37	n.a.	–	–
Private sector income as a percentage of total income	26	24.8	27.5	41	47	40	42	31	42	41	47

Sources and Notes

Survey

[a] State Statistical Bureau, *China's Statistical Yearbook* (Beijing, 1983). Cited in Keith Griffin (ed.) *Institutional Reform and Economic Development in the Chinese Countryside* (London: Macmillan, 1984) p. 306.

[b] Survey conducted by the State Statistical Bureau of 10 282 households in twenty-three provinces, municipalities and autonomous regions. NCNA, 2 Jan 1981, p. 5.

[c] Guizhou Provincial Statistical Bureau Survey of 690 households in twenty-three counties, special areas and districts. Data for 1979 is derived. Guiyang, Guizhou Provincial Service, 24 Mar 1981, in *SWB*, FE/W1134/A/pp. 2–3, 20 May 1981.

[d] Survey conducted among fourteen communes in Zhangian Banner, Yilin Gol League. This is a livestock-rearing area (like most of Inner Mongolia) and the data refer to herdsmen. Hohot, Inner Mongolia Regional Service, 20 Apr 1981, in *SWB*, FE/W1134/A/p. 3, 20 May 1981.

[e] Provincial survey of 330 households in twelve counties and municipalities. Changchun, Jilin Provincial Service, 4 May 1981, in *SWB*, FE/W1134/A/pp. 3–4, 20 May 1981.

[f] Liaoning Provincial Statistical Bureau Survey of 500 households from fifty communes in eighteen counties. Shenyang, Liaoning Provincial Service, 28 Mar 1981, in *SWB*, FE/W1134/A/p. 4, 20 May 1981.

[g] No information is given on survey methodology. NCNA, Chinese Service 21 Apr 1981, in *SWB*, FE/W1134/A/p. 5, 20 May 1981.

[h] Yunnan Provincial Statistical Bureau Survey of 610 commune households in twenty-eight counties. Data for 1979 are derived. Kunming, Yunnan Provincial Service, 28 Mar 1981, in *SWB*, FE/W1134/A/p. 5, 20 May 1981.

[i] 'Other sources of income' refer mainly to remittances from other family members who may be employed in state enterprises outside the commune or by the military etc.

Province (87.2 yuan) and Yunnan Province (71.4 yuan). Yet in each of these provinces in that year private sector income per head accounted for 41 per cent of total income per head compared to the national average of 27.5 per cent. This suggests an inverse relationship, at the regional level, between the level of distributed collective income per head and the proportion of private income in total income. Private production in poor regions, therefore, may have a diminishing effect on regional differences in the distribution of income. Or, put another way, without a relatively more active private sector in these poorer regions, the differences in the distribution of income between regions would perhaps be greater than they are.

Another important observation from Table 6.3 concerns the contribution of private activity to the economic growth of the poorer provinces. Nationally, the private sector accounted for 42 per cent of the growth of per capita rural income from 1978 to 1979 (survey b). Yet in Guizhou Province and Yunnun Province private economic activity accounted for 68 per cent and 74 per cent respectively of the growth of income per head, 1979–80. This interesting result adds support to the argument that the private sector may help to alleviate regional disparities in the distribution of income.

3. RECENT DEVELOPMENTS IN POLICY AND PRACTICE, 1978–84

The data and analysis presented in this chapter suggest that the commune organization ought to be understood as a four-tiered structure. At the fourth tier – the household – a thriving private sector operates as an adjunct to the collective sector of the other three tiers (commune, brigade and team levels). Private economic activity can make an important contribution to the household diet, to household income and to alleviating supply and marketing problems in the countryside.

Calling private economic activity ‘small freedoms’, a January 1980 editorial in *Sichuan Daily* emphasized the most important benefits of the private sector as follows:

> Commune members should make use of their professional skills and leisure time to enjoy small freedoms. They can thus turn scattered plots of unused land, and odd items of material resources into social wealth required by the state. People’s commune members should

> make use of their leisure time to cultivate their private plots and pursue household sideline occupations, sell surplus portions of their agricultural and sideline products in fairs and markets, help supply each other's needs and increase their income in addition to the distribution by the collective.[37]

This article, published in one of the most influential provincial newspapers, gives a good indication of the recent policy position of the government towards private production.

Perhaps paradoxically an important consideration for the government in encouraging the private sector was the pressing need to supplement the income of poor households in poor regions. At an important December 1979 conference of County CCP Committee Secretaries in Sichuan Province, for example, the participants called for more flexibility in the handling of economic affairs in relatively poor regions of the country. They argued that peasants in these regions should be 'allowed more room for manoeuvre in enjoying "small freedoms" [i.e. private activities]'.[38] A similar conference was held in Jilin Province by financial and trade department directors in order to 'help poor rural brigades develop production, increase their income, and transform their backward state'.[39] They recommended that local government officials explicitly help poor team members to develop private household activities such as 'planting, or breeding, gathering and weaving.'[40] A key editorial published in *People's Daily* argued that private economic activity

> can put auxiliary labour to use and, moreover, it is an effective way to absorb surplus rural labour . . . it can increase peasant income. In localities where commune members' income is low due to an underdeveloped collective economy, the developing of family sideline production and family plot production is a particularly effective way to solve people's livelihood problems and set their minds at rest.[41]

Yet the government currently sees the private sector not just as a means to help poor households supplement their income. Private economic activity, it is increasingly argued, is seen as an ideologically acceptable means of improving the efficiency of the rural economy. A recent document of the Central Committee stated, for example, that:

> In the struggle for agricultural modernization, we should rely more on the peasants and bring their enthusiasm into full play. . . . A

> diversified economy developed by communes and brigades is a socialist economy. The commune members' small plots or livestock tended for personal needs, their household sideline production, and village trade fairs are all auxiliary or supplementary elements of the socialist economy, and no one should criticize or ban them on ground that they are a reflection of capitalist economy. . . . While ensuring the consolidation and development of the collective economy, the peasants should be encouraged and helped to engage in domestic side occupations, increase their income, and stimulate the rural economy.[42]

Far from seeing private economic activity as a threat to socialism in the countryside, then, the government argues almost daily (in statements like the one above) that such activities are a 'necessary adjunct' to a socialist countryside.

Have these recent policies had a significant effect on household incomes in rural China? In Table 6.4 data is presented which allows one to compare the proportion of private income in total per capita income from 1978 (when the policies were first actively promoted) to 1982.

In 1978 private income accounted for 26 per cent of total income per capita; by 1982 private income had significantly increased its share to 38 per cent. Indeed private income grew at more than three times the rate of collective income over the period. Approximately half of the growth in

TABLE 6.4 *Sectoral Composition of Household Income per Head for Rural China, 1978–82*

	1978[a]	*1979*[b]	*1982*[c]
Total net income per head (yuan)	133.57	160.2	270.11
of which:			
distributed collective income per head (yuan)	89.53	102	140.12
private sector income per head (yuan)	35.79	44	102.8
other sources[d] of income per head (yuan)	9.25	14.2	27.19
Private sector income as percentage of total income per head	26	27.5	38

SOURCE [a] State Statistical Bureau, *China's Statistical Yearbook* (Beijing, 1983) op. cit.
[b] State Statistical Bureau, NCNA, 2 Jan 1981, op. cit.
[c] *Beijing Review*, 28 May 1984, p. 18.
[d] 'other sources of income' refer mainly to remittances from other family members who may be employed in state enterprises outside the commune or by the military, etc.

per capita income in rural China from 1978 to 1982 derived from private economic activity.

While these data are aggregated for all of rural China it may be useful to look at corresponding figures for provincial levels. Data for three provinces are given in Table 6.5.

The data show that the private sector in these provinces is relatively more important than the national average for 1982 (38 per cent). The data may also indicate the trend for the next few years. This is because all three provinces in the table have recently served as experimental 'laboratories' for new policies. In these provinces banks and extension agencies have been encouraged to provide loans and technical advice to households for private production; marketing organizations have supplied help to households in marketing their privately produced products; and new guidelines on labour allocation allow some members of households to work *full time* in the private sector, provided one member engages actively in collective production.[43]

These practices have spread rapidly throughout rural China in 1982–4 (see Chapter 8). It seems likely that for other provinces the proportion of private income in total income will approach the 1982 shares for Sichuan, Shaanxi and Hubei Provinces. Indeed the recent reforms in rural China have blurred the distinctions between the private sector and the collective sector. The essence of the reforms is that crop production has been decentralized to the level of the household, while rural small-scale industries continue to be run as co-operative organizations. Since crop production occurs mainly at the household level the distinction between the collectively owned land farmed on a contract basis by a household on the one hand and the household's own private plot on the other hand becomes one of semantics, if not of philosophy.

Perhaps not surprisingly in 1983 the provincial branches of the State Statistical Bureau in their rural household surveys stopped publishing

TABLE 6.5 *The Private Sector in Three Provinces, 1982*

Province	*Total net income per capita (yuan)*	*Private sector income as percentage of total*
Sichuan	183	53.6
Shaanxi	218	41
Hubei	286	51.4

SOURCE K. Griffin (ed.) (1984) op. cit., epilogue table 3; and chap. 8, table 13. The data for Sichuan are for 1981.

data which distinguished between net income in the collective and in the private sectors. This does not mean that rural China's economy is no longer composed of two sectors – collective and private. The collective sector is alive and well and making an important contribution to growth and development. It may mean however, that quantitative estimates of private output and income derived from sales or consumption of private output may have lost some of their meaning.

China's rural organizations, in summary, have shown exceptional flexibility. In recent years a fourth tier – the household – has become the hub of crop production, and, increasingly, of a wide range of private production. Some of these activities are traditional household pursuits (e.g. pig-raising, vegetable-raising and handicrafts, etc.). Others, however, are quite new forms of entrepreneurial activity (e.g. setting up private carpentry or house construction businesses).

It is hard to escape the conclusion, then, that within China's rural organizations a thriving private sector co-exists with the collective sector. Although the value of output from private production as a proportion of the gross value of agricultural output is only 20–25 per cent the proportion of total household income from private activity is close to 40 per cent. On present trends it is likely that these proportions will steadily increase in coming years. This has raised the spectre of ideological disquiet among the left in China as well as among the left in the West.

Yet the diet and the incomes of tens of millions of peasant households in rural China have been significantly improved through private production. In an important sense it is the flexibility of the rural organizations, and the policies which operate within them, which have facilitated private production. There are good reasons, moreover, to believe that within the rural organization private economic activity helps to reduce inequality. This will be discussed in the next chapter.

7 The Distribution of Rural Income

Development economists ought to be just as concerned with the *pattern* of growth as with the rate of growth. What has happened to income distribution in rural China? Just as it has been argued previously that the structure of the commune organization has promoted both agricultural and industrial growth in the countryside, so I shall argue in this chapter that the structure of the commune has promoted a narrowing, over time, in the distribution of rural income.

In Section 1 cross-section data on distributed collective income in rural China will be analysed. These data should give a clear indication of the recent pattern of income distribution in the Chinese countryside. In Section 2 an important relationship between the structure of the commune organization and the dynamics of the distribution of income shall be discussed. Section 3 will tackle a serious omission in the analysis in the first two sections, namely the relationship between income earned in the private sector and rural income distribution. In Section 4 the effects of recent reforms on the distribution of income will be considered.

1. THE DISTRIBUTION OF COLLECTIVE INCOME IN RURAL CHINA

All Rural China

During 1979 the Ministry of Agriculture conducted several surveys of the distribution of rural collective income. The first covered approximately five million 'accounting units' in the countryside, and thus refer almost exclusively to production teams. The results of the survey are presented in Table 7.1 (column A). The data show income intervals for the five million collective units. These data indicate a low level of inequality in the countryside. Only 27.3 per cent of the collective units, for example, have an average distributed collective income per head below 50 yuan, while only 24.8 per cent of the units have an average distributed collective income per head of more than 100 yuan.

This pattern of collective income distribution can also be seen from the results of the second survey (column B in Table 7.1). This survey covered 339 'typical' brigades in the countryside and included approximately 466 000 people. The data show that only 8.8 per cent of the brigades have an average distributed collective income per head of less than 50 yuan, while less than 24 per cent of the brigades in the sample have an average distributed collective income per head of more than 150 yuan.

These data indicate that the degree of inequality in collective income per head among the rural accounting units in China is low. In Survey A, for example, only 8.2. per cent of the units have a distributed collective income per head of less than 40 yuan, while only 2.3 per cent have a distributed collective income of more than 300 yuan. Yet these data do suggest a rather large *range* of distributed collective income at the extremes, say, 1:10. Moreover, it should be remembered that these surveys refer only to collective income per head of aggregated units (e.g. production teams). In the final section of the chapter it will be suggested that there are reasons to expect the gap between the richest and poorest to be considerably wider when considering the distribution of collective income among individual households.

China is a very large and diverse country. It is perhaps more useful, therefore, to look closely at the distribution of collective income per head within selected regions.[1]

TABLE 7.1 *Per Capita Distribution of Rural Collective Income in China, 1979*

	A[a]		*B*[b]
Per capita income (yuan)	*Percentage of 5 040 000 'accounting units'*	*Per capita income (yuan)*	*Percentage of 339 'typical' production brigades*
0–40	8.2	0–50	8.8
41–50	19.1		
51–69	29.8	51–150	67.8
69–100	18.2		
100–150	17.2	151–200	17.9
		201–250	3.5
150–300	5.3	251–300	0.9
Over 300	2.3	over 300	1.5

SOURCES [a] *Beijing Review*, 19 Jan 1981.
[b] *Nongye Jingji Wenti*, Sep 1980, pp. 28–31.
Both surveys are cited in E. B. Vermeer (1982) p. 14.

Hebei Province

Hebei Province lies on the North China plain. It is a predominantly grain-producing region. The province is very large, covering an area of approximately 190 000 square kilometres. It is also very populous: in 1978 the rural population was 44.8 million, of whom 17 million were in the labour force. The province, then, is larger than many developing countries (e.g. Thailand or the Philippines).

In 1978 the distributed collective income per capita in Hebei was 75.7 yuan. This places the province below the national average for distributed collective income in that year of 87.1 yuan.[2] In Table 7.2 data are reported on the distribution of per capita income in Hebei for 1978.

These data show income intervals for the 247 788 production teams in the province and for the 148 counties. The data indicate a low level of inequality in the distribution of collective income among the production teams in the province. Only 11.5 per cent of the counties in the province, for example, have an average distributed collective income per head of less than 50 yuan, while only 12.0 per cent of the counties have an average distributed collective income per head of more than 100 yuan. If one assumes an average, say, of 1600 production teams per county, then it is likely that the poorest teams (i.e. those in 0–40 yuan per capita range) are distributed more or less randomly throughout the province and are not clustered in the poorest counties. This implies that differences in regional geography and in climate cannot explain the observed inequality in the province.

The data available from the smaller units in the province can now be examined. In Table 7.3 the distribution of collective income per head are shown from two communes in the province, namely, Wu Gong and Qie Ma Communes. For each commune the data are given for brigade level

TABLE 7.2 *Per Capita Collective Income in Hebei Province, 1978*

Per capita income (yuan)	*No. of production teams*	*Percentage of teams*	*No. of counties*	*Percentage of counties*
0–40	34 331	13.9	2	1.4
41–50	35 009	14.1	15	10.1
51–60	34 937	14.0	19	12.8
61–80	58 663	23.7	54	36.4
81–100	42 253	17.1	39	26.4
101–150	36 569	14.8	17	11.5
more than 150	6 056	2.4	2	1.4

TABLE 7.3 *The Distribution of Collective Income per head in two Communes in Hebei, 1978*
(yuan)

Brigade	*Wu Gong Commune Hebei*	*Qie Ma Commune Hebei*
1	188.00	123.00
2	127.00	104.00
3	112.80	102.00
4	98.00	100.00
5	95.00	99.00
6	84.00	92.00
7	83.00	87.00
8	72.00	86.40
9	66.50	8.100
10	66.00	
Average brigade income per head	111.80	99.93
Ratio of highest to lowest income	2.85	1.52
Total population	16 565	19 466

only. One way of describing the level of inequality within each commune is by the ratio of highest income to lowest income. In Wu Gong Commune this ratio is 2.85 and in Qie Ma Commune the ratio is considerably lower, viz. 1.52. The richest brigade in Wu Gong Commune is the Wu Gong Brigade. If one omits this 'model' brigade, the ratio of highest income to lowest income falls to 1.92. Moreover, most of the remaining brigades fall within one standard deviation of the recalculated mean (89.4) yuan.

The level of inequality in Wu Gong Commune can be seen more clearly in Table 7.4.

This table displays the distribution of collective income per head among the thirty-six production teams in the commune for 1978. Nearly 60 per cent of all the teams in the commune fall within the 60–100 yuan range, and nearly 90 per cent of all the teams fall within the 60–150 yuan range. This is a narrow band and it indicates a low level of inequality among the teams of the commune.

TABLE 7.4 *The Distribution of Collective Income Among the thirty-six Production Teams of Wu Gong Commune, 1978*

Brigade	*Number of teams*	*Per capita income (yuan)* 50–60	60–80	80–100	100–150	Over 150
Wu Gong	3					3
Zhou Chun	5		1		4	
Guan Zhuang	3		2		1	
Dong Song	2		2			
Yang Zhuang	4		1	1	2	
Wang Qiao	4			3	1	
Song Qiao	3	1	1	2		
Kao Qiao	3			1	2	
Yuan Zi	3		2	1		
Geng Kou	6		4	1	1	
Total	36	1	14	7	11	3

Guangdong Province

The pattern of collective income distribution in a province in South China will now be considered. The same method will be followed in proceeding from the provincial level to the team level.

Table 7.5 shows the distribution of per capita collective income in Guangdong Province for 1978.

The data show the income intervals within which the 297 100 production teams in the province are located. The average per capita collective income in the province is 73.4 yuan, well below the national average of 87.1 yuan for that year. Most of the teams in the province fall within the 51–100 yuan size class. A comparison with the data for Hebei reveals a similar pattern for both provinces. However, the level of

TABLE 7.5 *The Distribution of Collective Income in Guangdong Province, 1978*

Per capita income (yuan)	*Number of production teams*	*Percentage of teams*
0–40	55 400	18.7
41–50	43 300	14.6
51–100	150 600	50.7
101–150	33 000	11.1
More than 150	14 800	4.9

inequality in Guangdong is somewhat higher than in Hebei. In Guangdong, for example, 18.7 per cent of the teams fall in the lowest income interval of 0–40 yuan, whereas in Hebei, only 13.9 per cent fall in the same interval. Similarly, a slightly larger percentage of teams in Guangdong have a per capita income greater than 150 yuan.

Income distribution data for all the counties in Guangdong is not available. I do have data for the distribution of collective income in Fo Gang County. This is a county in the north of the Province. The region is hilling and difficult to farm. Only part of the land is irrigated and, moreover, the industrial sectors of the communes in the county are not well developed. The data on collective income per capita for the twelve communes in Fo Gang County in 1978 are given in Table 7.6. The mean collective income per head in the county for 1978 was 80.9 yuan, just slightly above the provincial average. The ratio of highest income to lowest income is only 1.48 and indicates a low level of inequality between the communes in the county.

The distribution of per capita collective income for Tang Tang Commune in Fo Gang County is shown in Table 7.7.

TABLE 7.6 *The Distribution of Collective Income per head in Fo Gang County, Guangdong Province, 1978*
(yuan)

Commune number	
1	92.00
2	91.70
3	86.00
4	85.00
5	85.00
6	84.00
7	82.00
8	80.00
9	76.80
10	74.00
11	72.60
12	62.00
Mean	80.93
Range	30.00
High/Low	1.48
Standard deviation	8.54
Coefficient of variation	0.11

TABLE 7.7 *The Distribution of Collective Income per head in Tang Tang Commune, Guangdong Province, 1978 (yuan)*

Brigade number	
1	111.00
2	106.00
3	104.00
4	101.00
5	98.00
6	97.00
7	97.00
8	95.00
9	85.00
10	82.00
11	80.00
12	77.00
13	72.00
14	72.00
15	70.00
16	69.00
17	69.00
Average brigade* income per head	84.00
Ratio of highest to lowest income	1.61
Total population	32 771

* The average given here is a weighted average in order to take into account population differences between brigades.

These data are arranged by brigade. The average brigade collective income per head was 84 yuan in 1978. The commune can therefore be considered an 'average' commune in the county. The ratio of highest income to lowest income was 1.61 and this ratio conforms closely to the county average (1.48). The distribution of collective income, therefore, is relatively equal both within the county and within Tang Tang Commune.

It should be interesting to see the extent to which the pattern of income distribution in Tang Tang Commune as a whole is reflected in the distribution among the teams of the *poorest* brigade in the commune. These data are presented in Table 7.8, and show the collective income per head among the 19 teams of Xin Tang Brigade in 1978. The average collective income per head for all teams was 69 yuan in 1978. Perhaps surprisingly, the ratio of highest income to lowest income was 4.95. This ratio is considerably higher than for the commune as a whole. Yet nearly

TABLE 7.8 *The Distribution of Collective Income per head Among the ninteen teams of Xin Tang Brigade, Tang Tang Commune, 1978*

Team	*Per capita income*
1	109
2	93
3	83
4	80
5	79
6	73
7	73
8	71
9	70
10	59
11	59
12	59
13	55
14	54
15	51
16	39
17	36
18	27
19	22
Brigade average[a]	69
Ratio of highest to lowest income	4.95
Standard deviation	22.2

[a] This is a weighted average to account for population differences between teams.

70 per cent of all the teams in the brigade had, in 1978, a collective income per head within one standard deviation of the unweighted mean (62.7 yuan). Moreover, in interviews with accountants from the brigade and from the poorest team, I learned that severe flooding had in recent years destroyed much of the housing and land of the poorest teams. Yet the data in Table 7.8 do indicate a larger degree of inequality in the poorest brigade in the commune than for the commune as a whole. But it must be remembered that these data refer only to collective income and do not include private income. In Section 3 it will be argued that income earned in the private sector is particularly important in supplementing the collective income of poor households. Hence, the data in Table 7.8 may overstate the level of inequality within this brigade.

To summarize the analysis so far, the cross-sectional data presented above indicate a low level of inequality in the distribution of collective income at the production team, brigade and commune levels. Indeed, there are good reasons to expect that economic growth in rural China has been accompanied by a narrowing over time in the distribution of collective income.

2. COMMUNE ORGANIZATION AND THE DYNAMIC PATTERN OF COLLECTIVE INCOME DISTRIBUTION

In order to analyse the dynamic aspects of collective income distribution the approach must be broadened to include time-series data. Not surprisingly, the availability of such data is limited, but I do have evidence from three communes from which to develop the argument.

Time-series data shall first be considered from two communes in Hebei Province, namely, Wu Gong Commune and Qie Ma Commune. Data on the pattern of income distribution over time for Wu Gong Commune are shown in Table 7.9.

Although the range of income increased during 1966–78 this increase was proportionately less than the rise in the mean income. This suggests a decline in inequality. Moreover, the ratio of highest income to lowest income declined steadily over the period and the coefficient of variation also declined.

In Table 7.10 data for the per capita collective income in Qie Ma Commune are given for 1970 and for 1978.

During this period the mean income per head increased by nearly 25 per cent. Yet the range of incomes decreased from 46.7 yuan to 42.0 yuan. Moreover, the ratio of highest income to lowest income declined

TABLE 7.9 *Changes Over Time in the Distribution of Per Capita Collective Income Among Brigades in Wu Gong Commune, 1966 and 1978*

	1966	*1978*
Mean income (yuan)	39.2	99.5[a]
Income range (yuan)	65.0	121.5
Ratio of highest to lowest income	4.25	2.83
Standard deviation	18.4	36.7
Coefficient of variation	0.47	0.37

[a] This figure stands for a simple mean of brigade incomes and therefore differs from the weighted mean figure presented in Table 7.3.

TABLE 7.10 *The Distribution of Collective Income per Head in Qie Mai Commune, 1970 and 1978*

	1970	*1978*
Mean income (yuan)	77.9	97.3
Income range (yuan)	46.7	42.0
Ratio of highest to lowest income	1.84	1.52
Standard deviation	15.4	12.5
Coefficient of variation	0.20	0.13

considerably from 1.84 to 1.52. The standard deviation and the coefficient of variation also declined substantially. These data indicate a tendency for a decline in inequality during the 1970s at Qie Ma.

The third commune for which time-series data are available is Evergreen Commune in the Beijing Municipality. Like the communes in the Shanghai Municipality, Evergreen is very prosperous; in 1978 the collective income per capita in the commune was 196 yuan. The commune has a well-developed industrial sector and in 1978 this sector accounted for 60 per cent of the commune's income.

In Table 7.11 a complete set of time-series data is presented for the distribution of collective income per capita at Evergreen for 1961–77. The mean per capita collective income in the commune increased by 20 per cent from 1961 to 1977. During this period the degree of inequality in the commune diminished. The ratio of highest brigade income to lowest brigade income, for example, declined from 2.02 in 1961 to 1.33 in 1977. This was not a steady decline, however: some fluctuations were evident during the early 1970s. The standard deviation and the coefficient of variation also displayed a marked tendency to decline during the period. The coefficient of variation, for example, decreased from 0.18 in 1961 to 0.09 in 1977.

The evidence from the sample of three communes indicate that the dispersion of incomes around the mean was lower in the 1970s than in the 1960s. Moreover, in two communes (Wu Gong and Qie Ma) the growth of per capita income was inversely correlated with the initial level of income. The analysis of these data suggests a relationship between the structure and the operation of the commune organization and a diminishing over time in the level of inequality.

Policy Mechanisms for Redistribution

Since 1962 the government has issued several key policy documents concerning the structure and the function of the commune. The first

TABLE 7.11 *Per Capita Distribution of Collective Income at Evergreen Commune, 1961–77*

Brigade	*1961*	*1962*	*1963*	*1964*	*1965*	*1966*	*1967*	*1968*	*1969*	*1970*	*1971*	*1972*	*1973*	*1974*	*1975*	*1976*	*1977*
1	181	187	146	134	147	164	152	114	102	125	123	129	117	164	164	183	164
2	197	186	160	167	185	167	173	147	125	146	157	162	166	194	193	204	199
3	218	201	187	158	158	168	182	132	140	177	174	192	197	204	204	225	197
4	108	131	97	115	122	121	122	111	122	136	162	165	176	165	163	184	184
5	150	168	144	145	150	161	139	138	139	143	154	180	174	173	173	200	202
6	170	177	172	152	168	168	162	153	144	164	173	186	203	209	207	209	222
7	122	140	137	135	130	129	131	112	110	147	135	124	141	127	145	149	167
8	163	162	145	133	148	144	144	109	88	126	117	88	158	185	185	196	205
9	153	185	165	140	143	126	167	123	103	141	161	170	197	197	198	210	216
10	160	190	159	143	165	170	204	136	148	182	174	125	153	159	157	181	201
11	173	212	220	183	210	222	211	112	160	173	173	160	181	181	181	195	198
12	152	179	162	137	154	157	172	155	138	151	163	160	152	146	165	184	n.a.
Mean	162.3	176.5	158.0	145.1	156.7	157.3	163.3	134.3	126.6	150.1	155.4	153.4	167.9	175.3	177.9	193.3	195.9
Standard deviation	29.8	23.4	29.2	17.9	23.7	27.0	27.5	22.3	21.9	18.7	19.9	30.7	25.4	24.5	19.9	19.3	18.0
Coefficient of variation	0.18	0.13	0.18	0.12	0.15	0.17	0.17	0.17	0.17	0.12	0.13	0.20	0.15	0.14	0.11	0.10	0.09
Ratio of highest to lowest	2.02	1.62	2.22	1.59	1.72	1.83	1.73	1.67	1.82	1.46	1.49	2.18	1.74	1.65	1.43	1.51	1.33

document was circulated in September 1962, and a revised version was issued by the Third Plenary Session of the Eleventh Central Committee in December 1978. Both documents suggest explicit guidelines for redistributing income to poor teams from the accumulation funds of the industrial enterprises in the commune. The 1962 document states, for example, that 'in addition to being used for enlarging reproduction in enterprises and developing the production undertakings of the commune, part of the profits of commune enterprises should be set aside to aid those production teams experiencing difficulties in prodution'.[3] The 1978 'regulations' reiterated this policy as follows:

> A good portion of the state's investment in the people's communes as financial aid should be used to support poor communes or brigades in developing their enterprises . . . The representative conferences [within the commune] have the right to decide how to use the profits in the enterprises. In addition to investment to enlarge the enterprises' reproduction, the profits will mainly be used to purchase additional farm machinery, to develop farmland capital construction, and to aid the poorer brigades to develop production; furthermore, a portion of the profits may also be distributed to commune members.[4]

The policy of redistributing commune industrial profits to poor teams often took the form of explicit grants or low-interest loans to poor teams from the commune level or the brigade level. At Cheng Dong Commune, for example, over 80 000 yuan from industrial accumulation was allocated in 1978 as 'aid to poor teams'. A further 451 000 yuan from industrial accumulation was allocated as 'contribution to the circulating fund for lower units'. This refers to the working capital funds of the production teams. When this contribution was combined with the direct 'aid to poor teams' an important policy mechanism operated actively within the commune for redistributing a substantial proportion of the surplus from the industrial sector. The operation of this policy can be seen more clearly by considering a poorer commune, i.e. Tang Tang Commune in Guangdong Province. In 1977, for example, over 40 per cent of the total industrial accumulation in the commune was allocated to the weaker production brigades and teams in the form of grants.

Such redistributive policies also operated directly between the state (usually the county-level government) and the poor brigades and teams within the commune. Indeed, the revised 'regulations' explicitly stipulate that 'a good portion of the state's investment in the people's commune as financial aid should be used to support poor communes or brigades in developing their enterprises'.[5] In 1978, for example, the three richest brigades in Wu Gong Commune received grants and loans equivalent to 8 per cent of their net income. The three poorest brigades, by contrast, received grants and loans equivalent to 40 per cent of their net income.

The county-level government used several other policy mechanisms to help poor brigades and teams. If a brigade or team encountered production or management difficulties, it was not uncommon for specialists from the county to be seconded there. More importantly, the county government arranged for poor teams to have priority in the procurement of scarce modern inputs. In 1978, for example, the poorest commune in Fo Gang County in Guangdong Province was allocated substantially more chemical fertiliser than the other communes in the county. The county government has often given grants or low interest loans to poor brigades specifically earmarked for purchasing tractors, irrigation pumps or harvesters.

Redistributive policy mechanisms also operated actively within a brigade. In Tang Tang Commune, for example, some brigades organised water conservancy projects to help their poor teams who suffered from flooding. They also organised work groups to help poor teams or households who were short-handed in busy seasons, or who wished to expand their area of cultivated land. Members of such work groups came from other teams in the brigade. Each production team assigned workpoints to the members of these work groups and these workpoints were claimed not from the funds of the recipient poor team, but rather from the funds of the donor team. This was in effect an explicit redistributive policy mechanism from rich teams to poor teams within a brigade.

Two other redistributive mechanisms should be mentioned. First, most communes established credit co-operatives which often made low-interest loans to poor teams or households. These loans were used to procure technical inputs for agriculture, or, for example, to finance the establishment of an industrial enterprise at the team level. Second, it was often the policy in the communes that I visited for the commune-level and brigade-level factories to employ a disproportionate share of their workers from poor teams. Since a large proportion of the wages of such workers were paid directly to the teams from which these workers come, such outside employment was not only lucrative for the team, but also redistributive in its effects. This can be illustrated by the following example from Xin Tang Brigade in Tang Tang Commune. In 1978 the average value of a workday in a brigade enterprise was 0.8 yuan. This value was 23 per cent higher than the average team–workday value of

0.43 yuan for an average team in the brigade, and four times higher than that for the poorest team. Moreover, for all the teams in the brigade in 1978, the average percentage of a team's labour force employed outside the team was 24.3. For the four poorest teams, however, this average was 36 per cent or 48.2 per cent higher than the brigade average. This policy was clearly a redistributive one.

3. PRIVATE ECONOMIC ACTIVITY AND THE DISTRIBUTION OF INCOME

I have so far considered only collective income generated in the three collective levels of the commune. I have omitted the income generated at the fourth level of the commune, namely, private economic activity at the household level. This is a serious omission. For the available evidence indicates that income earned in the private sector is an important supplement to income earned in the collective sector. What effect can private income have on the distribution of *total* income in rural China? I shall tackle this question by analysing the effects of private activity on income distribution among households within the commune. Although the available data are limited there are good reasons to believe that private activity can improve the distribution of income.

Household Level within the Commune

An important determinant of collective income for a household is the number of able-bodied workers who can engage actively in collective production. That is, the more that can be earned in collective production the larger is the household's collective income. Yet the greater the number of dependants in the household (e.g. infants, small children, grandparents, etc.) the lower will be collective income per head in the family. Thus households with a high ratio of dependants to able-bodied workers would be relatively disadvantaged in generating collective income compared to households with strong labour power and few dependants. This suggests, therefore, an important potential source of income inequality between households in a commune.

The Chinese government is well aware of the inverse relationship between the dependency ratio and collective income per head in the household. As such the government has explicitly encouraged households with unfavourable dependency ratios to compensate for their disadvantaged position concerning the collective sector by engaging actively in private econmic activity. The 'Regulations on the Work of the People's Communes', for example, state that:

> Households with too many members but too little manpower should be assigned appropriate field work and helped to develop domestic side occupations so that they are able to increase their income. . . .[6]
>
> Help should be given those commune members who experience difficulty of living. The production team should help them solve their difficulties and increase their income through family sideline production such as hog-raising, knitting and making mats etc.[7]

An April 1980 article in *People's Daily* argued further that:

> Those households with a strong labour force and good techniques have greatly increased their income; most of the households with difficulties and manpower shortages have also increased their income because of their efforts to raise work efficiency, give full scope to the role of their supplementary labour force and promote household sideline occupations with relatively better success.[8]

Indeed, most private activities such as tending animals, vegetable plots and weaving are done in and around the house. Families which have high dependency ratios would have relatively more labour available to engage in these activities for more hours of the day. Without a private sector option this labour would otherwise remain idle.

Yet to suggest that private economic activity can be an equalizing factor between households in a commune it is necessary empirically to show that the relative importance of private income declines as the level of per capita collective income increases. Unfortunately there are few available data to support this argument. The results of a recent study by Alison Ansell, Roger Hay and Keith Griffin do, however, lend tentative support. In 1979 a random sample was conducted of eleven teams in the Zhang Qing Commune in Suzhou Municipality. From these teams ninety-two households were interviewed. Their test consisted of a regression equation in which private income as a percentage of collective income (PY/CY) was regressed on collective income per head (CY/N). The regression equation is given below:

$$(2)\ PY/CY = 31.85 - 0.07\ (CY/N); \quad r^2 = 0.14.$$ [9]

The regression coefficient is negative as expected, and significant at the

1 per cent level. Their results indicate that the lower is the level of collective income per head the greater is the relative importance of the private sector. In this commune, at least, private economic activity has reduced inequality in the distribution of income between households.

Because of a lack of data one must be careful not to generalize on the basis of one study. It should be useful, however, to explore further the relationship between demographic factors and the distribution of income among households.

One reason why some households have a low level of collective income is simply that they have an above-average number of elderly people or of infants. Collective income, then, should be inversely associated with the number of dependants each collective worker must support. This can be seen from the data presented in Table 7.12 below. These data indicate that collective income per head is higher the lower is the dependency ratio, i.e. the size of household divided by the number of workpoint earners. Households in which three-quarters or more of the members earn income from collective activities (a dependency ratio of 1.33 or less) have a higher than average per capita collective income. Households where only half the members generate collective income (a dependency ratio of 2.00) have a lower than average collective income.

The fact that demographic phenomena are a source of inequality of collective income among households in China naturally leads one to inquire about the significance of inequality among households. Unfortunately, this is difficult to determine since most available data refer to aggregated collective units and not to households. The data in Table 7.12, however, permit one to gain an impression of differentials at the level of the household. The richest household listed in the Table is 2.7 times richer than the poorest – a moderate level of inequality within one team. Shujing Commune, however, is in one of the wealthiest regions of rural China and it is marked by a low level of inequality. If one can expect a range of household collective income, say, of 1:3 in a wealthy region, then what range might we expect in a region below the national average per capita income?

Data have recently become available which shed some light on this topic.[10] In July 1982 fifty-four households were sampled in a production team in a commune in Yunnan Province. The per capita distributed collective income was 128 yuan, indicating that this was indeed a poor team in a relatively poor province. The ratio of richest to poorest household in the team was approximately 1:11 and the coefficient of variation was 0.36. Although the distributed collective income for most of the households was clustered close to the mean for the team, the data

TABLE 7.12 *Twenty-three Households from a Production Team of Shujing Commune, Shanghai Municipality, 1980*

Household number	*Collective income per head (yuan)*	*Dependency ratio*	*Private income as percentage of collective income*
20	745.7	1.00	17.0
22	662.5	1.00	0.0
23	468	1.33	19.2
3	465	1.20	22.9
6	460	1.50	0.0
7	452.2	1.25	19.7
11	421	1.33	24.0
16	412.6	1.50	20.2
13	403	1.50	19.3
10	378.8	1.25	22.1
2	376.7	1.00	12.1
8	372	1.33	30.2
17	351	2.00	35.8
1	341	1.33	20.5
14	323	1.67	38.3
18	322	2.00	15.5
4	319	2.00	11.6
19	313	1.67	22.1
12	311	1.50	8.2
5	310	2.00	8.1
21	300	1.50	13.9
15	275	2.00	33.9
9	272	2.00	17.5

SOURCE Elizabeth J. Croll, *The Chinese Household and its Economy: Urban and Rural Survey Data* (Queen Elizabeth House, Contemporary China Centre, Resource Paper, Oxford, 1982) tables 20 and 49.

nevertheless suggests that a substantial level of inequality in the distribution of collective income still prevails within villages in specific regions of rural China. This inequality is most evident at the household level, where labour-poor households are at a disadvantage.

These results are surprising yet perhaps not alarming. This is because there are several important ways in which the data presented above do not give a full picture of household-level income distribution. First, poor households have often benefited more than proportionately by supplementing their collective income with income earned off-commune (e.g. in county-level enterprises). Second, a significant proportion of grain distributed within a production team (e.g. 50 per cent) has been distributed on a per capita basis (i.e. according to 'need'). This has helped to offset income differentials generated by unfavourable dependency ratios. Third, the 'guaranteed' provision of food, clothing, shelter, education, health-care and other 'basic needs' has been implicitly redistributive in its effects. Such 'in-kind' payments provided an income flow to the poor, labour-short households, thereby narrowing real income differentials still further.

A fourth and perhaps most important means for labour-short households to increase their income is through private economic activity. In Chapter 6 the private sector in rural China was described and the evidence suggested that private income provided an important supplement to collective income. The data in Table 7.12 provide further evidence in support of this argument. These data indicate that households with a high dependency ratio tended to obtain a higher proportion of their income from the private sector.

The fragmentary evidence available indicates, then, that households which are relatively disadvantaged toward the collective sector can generate relatively more income from the private sector. Without this option the distribution of income between households in rural China might perhaps be less equal.

4. RECENT REFORMS AND THE DISTRIBUTION OF RURAL INCOME

So far I have only referred briefly to the post-1978 reforms in rural China. While a detailed analysis of these reforms will be given in the next chapter it should be useful here to see whether the reforms have effected the distribution of income.

The reforms have a clear legacy from the 1956–7 period. At that time the opposition group in the government took issue with the orthodox Marxist–Leninist view of socialist agriculture. The opposition argued that China's agriculture had characteristics which resembled horticulture. It was seasonal and dependent upon the vagaries of the weather. Because of these and other factors involving incentives, crop production, it was argued, should be best handled at the level of the household or of small groups of households. Yet the opposition group were not able to convert these views into concrete policies for implementation.

By 1978, however, the opposition consolidated their power following the death of Mao Zedong and the fall of the 'Gang of Four'. The new leadership immediately formulated and began to implement a decentralization of decision-making in crop production from the team or brigade level to the household (or small groups of households) level.

Under this new system the teams conclude contracts with households. The contract includes the amount of land the households must till, the output to be produced and what the brigade or the team must provide. The contracted household organizes its own work and makes its own decisions. The household sells its quota of output to the team and, depending on the crop, sells any remaining amounts in the free market.

There are very important incentive effects under these new arrangements. These effects derive from the fact that decisions are decentralized to the level of households and a maximum level of participation is generated in production decisions. Under the old arrangements brigade and team leaders were mainly responsible for organizing the daily allocation of labour and of materials; peasants were paid by the working day according to set norms. Under the new arrangements peasants keep what is left of their output after meeting their collective quota, after paying agricultural taxes and after contributing to the team's welfare funds. Households receive clear and direct benefits and they know they can earn more income from an increased quality as well as quantity of labour.

There are two important potential sources of increased inequality under the new so-called 'responsibility system' described above. The first concerns land. Under the new system the land is still owned by the co-operative organization (usually the team). Households make contracts for land use with the organization. These contracts have recently been extended to fifteen years' duration.[11] The organization usually allocates land to each household on a per capita basis, or, less frequently, on a per worker basis. In the latter case differences in household demography could be a potential source of increased inequality. Under the former case (land allocated on a per capita basis) there are *a priori* reasons why income inequalities might be less than under the previous workpoint system. It is reasonable to assume under this system that output per mou would be similar from one household to another. Thus collective income per head would depend on the number of mou per head. Under the old system, by contrast, collective income per head depended more upon the dependency ratio within the household. If the variation in mou per head, therefore, is less than the range of dependency ratios, then the new 'responsibility' arrangements should produce less inequality over time.

A second important potential source of increased inequality could come from the ability of richer households to accumulate capital equipment for use on their contracted land. Under the old arrangements households were allowed to own small tools and implements for use in private production. This policy has recently changed. Households can now buy larger pieces of equipment (e.g. land tractors and trucks) for use on contracted land. By the end of 1983 Chinese peasants privately owned 2.12 million tractors, a 110 per cent increase from 1982.[12] There were 89 000 individually owned trucks for agricultural use in 1983, compared to 10 000 in 1982.[13] The recent reforms encourage state banks to make loans to households to finance the purchases of such equipment. In some provinces, moreover, households are encouraged to buy draft animals and other assets from the team.

The private accumulation of capital could therefore become a source of increased inequality because of differences in household savings rates and in the rate of return on household projects. The dispersion in profit rates among projects could be converted into greater inequality among households.

Yet if the recent reforms contain features which may increase inequality they also contain policies designed explicitly to counteract these tendencies. These policies are normally formulated at the provincial level. In Yunnan Province, for example, special funds are earmarked for the development of backward areas and 'special subsidies are given to poor production brigades and teams'.[14] Farm loans are offered free of interest to poorer households and teams. In an important interview, Du Runsheng, head of the Rural Policy Research Institute in the Secretariat of the Central Committee, stressed that 'the government has earmarked certain funds' and that 'banks grant special loans to help poor households'.[15] The government is also considering setting up a taxation system to counteract any significant widening in the distribution of income. This was first indicated by Deng Xiaoping in an interview in which I took part in 1979. More recently, Du Runsheng indicated that the plan had been under active consideration by the Central Committee in May 1984.[16]

It is important, nevertheless, to try to determine the empirical effects of the recent reforms on the distribution of income in rural China. The data in Table 7.13 allow one to form a preliminary impression of these effects. The analysis should perhaps be divided into two periods 1978–81 and 1981–2. From 1978 to 1981 the data are striking. First, the reforms have substantially reduced the percentage of households with per capita incomes under 100 yuan, from 33.3 per cent in 1978 to 4.6 per cent in 1981. The reforms clearly have gone a long way toward alleviating the problem of poverty in the Chinese countryside. Second, whereas 64.3 per cent of households in 1978 fell in the 100–300 yuan range, by 1981 this proportion had increased to 71.8 per cent. Thus, the

TABLE 7.13 *The Distribution of Income in Rural China, 1978–82*

	1978	*1981*	*1982*
Average per capita income in rural China (yuan)	133.6	223.4	270.1
Range of per capita income (yuan)	*Percent of households*		
0–100	33.3	4.6	2.4
100–200	49.3	37.3	24.4
200–300	15	34.5	37
300>	2.4	23.6	36.2
500>	n.a.	n.a.	6.7

SOURCE Interview with Du Runsheng, in *Beijing Review*, no. 18, 1984.

percentage of households in rural China clustered within a 3 : 1 range of per capita income increased significantly from 1978 to 1981. During the same period the proportion of households with per capita incomes of more than 300 yuan increased from 2.4 per cent to 23.6 per cent. It is likely that most of this group fell in the 300–500 range. If this is true, then by 1981 the reforms would seem to have had little effect on the level of inequality in rural China. Indeed by 1981 nine out of ten households probably fell in the 100–500 yuan range of per capita income.

For 1981–2, however, the data reveal a slight tendency for the range of per capita incomes in rural China to widen. This widening occurred at the high end of incomes. By 1982 nearly 7 per cent of households had incomes greater than 500 yuan; only 2.4 per cent, however, had incomes below 100 yuan. Thus by the end of 1982 a 100–500 yuan range for more than 90 per cent of rural households was maintained. Indeed, most of these households remained within 100 yuan of the mean per capita income for that year.

On balance, then, the data in Table 7.13 indicate that rural China has retained a relatively low level of inequality in the distribution of income from 1978 to 1982. There has indeed been a small widening of range for 90 per cent of households – from 4 : 1 in 1978 to 5 : 1 in 1982. But this should be counterbalanced by the fact that a quite remarkable reduction in rural poverty occurred during the period of the recent reforms.

The macroeconomic analysis above has received some support from several recent empirical studies of the effects of the reforms on income distribution at the microeconomic level. Keith Griffin and Kimberly Griffin concluded their analysis as follows:

there is no evidence that the reforms have been associated with an increase in the degree of inequality at the local level. As long as collectively owned land is allocated at least partly on a per capita rather than a per worker basis, and as long as land is periodically reallocated to take into account changes in the size of households, a high degree of equality is likely to persist indefinitely.[17]

Yet the new opportunities for entrepreneurial households to take risks, to borrow money, to buy capital equipment (such as trucks and tractors) and to reap benefits from these activities are perhaps reflected in the fact that by 1982 nearly 7 per cent of households were earning more than 500 yuan per capita. This tendency can be seen more clearly in Table 7.14. Of China's 2350 counties, those with a per capita income greater than 500 yuan increased from nine in 1982 to sixty-six in 1983. While only one county in China in 1982 had a per capita income greater than 600 yuan, by 1983 the number of such 'rich' counties had increased to twenty-two.

In rural China today there are clearly some very prosperous areas and some relatively 'wealthy' households. This suggest that at the extremes a considerable level of inequality remains. Indeed, even given the data presented in the last two chapters, household number 8 in Table 6.16 had a per capita collective income of 58.5 yuan while household number 20 in Table 7.12 had a per capita collective income of 746 yuan. The ratio, thus, is approximately 1 : 13. There are, no doubt, households with a distributed collective income considerably below 58.5 yuan and considerably above 746 yuan. Thus a reasonable guess about the range of collective income differentials for the whole country might be closer to 1 : 25 (e.g. 40 yuan and 1000 yuan). While employment outside the

TABLE 7.14 *County-level Distribution of Above-average Income in Rural China, 1982–3*

Range of income (yuan)	*Number of counties* 1982	1983
300–400	280	453
400–500	71	163
500–600	8	44
600–700	1	18
700	0	4

SOURCE *Zhongguo Nongmin Bao*, 10 Apr 1984, p. 1 in *FBIS, JPRS*, 27 June 1984, p. 9.

commune combined with private sector income might narrow this differential somewhat, this estimate does suggest that on a national scale a substantial level of inequality remains both within and between regions.

Yet it must be remembered that when one considers the ranges of income differences, one is dealing with the extreme observations. Most available studies indicate that the coefficients of variation are quite low (<0.35). Thus, the per capita income of most collective units and indeed for most households are more likely to lie within one standard deviation of the mean. It is this observation that allows one to conclude that in the main rural China is characterized by a low level of inequality in the distribution of income.

8 Rural Economic Performance, 1952–84

1. INTRODUCTION

Since 1956 China's rural economy has consisted largely of collective organizations. In the preceding chapters I have discussed some important reasons why such organizations can promote economic growth and development. These reasons have been largely microeconomic ones (e.g. the relationship between participation in decision-making and the rate of accumulation within the organization). Yet the government, not unreasonably, is inclined to judge these organizations by the criteria of their macroeconomic performance. When this performance was judged to have shortcomings the government demonstrated a willingness to experiment with some of the organizational arrangements in the countryside.

In 1957–8 substantial reforms were introduced in the rural organizations. On this occasion the reforms proved to be ill-considered. Performance from 1958 to 1961 was disastrous and by 1961–2 the government had to introduce a new set of policies. These policies solved some important problems. A powerful accumulative institution – rural small-scale industry – was successfully introduced into the countryside.

Yet other problems remained unsolved. The organization of crop production based on large groups, for example, proved to be ill-suited to the characteristics of Chinese agriculture. In 1978–9 the government decided to grasp this elusive nettle and it boldly decentralized decision-making in crop production to the level of the household. This decision (discussed in detail in Section 3 of this chapter) has so far been remarkably successful.

Such radical change, however, is not without its attendant risks. For the pre-1979 arrangements did prove to be successful on two important counts: great progress was made toward rural capital construction (particularly water control) and toward the establishment of rural small-scale industry. This can be seen from the data in Tables 8.1 and 8.2. The

TABLE 8.1 *Growth of Selected Inputs and Outputs in Chinese Agriculture, 1952–79*

	1952	*1952/57*	*1977*	*1976/80*	*1979*	*Percentage change*
Grain output (million metric tonnes)	–	169	–	304	–	+80
Arable area (million hectares)	–	109.9	–	–	99.3	−9.6
Sown area (million hectares)	–	150	150	–	–	–
Multiple cropping Index	–	136.6	151	–	–	+10.5
Irrigated area (million hectares)	21.3	–	–	–	45	+111.2
Grain yields (tonnes per hectare)	–	1.35	–	2.57	–	+90.4
Agricultural employment (million)	173	–	–	–	299.3	+73.0
Tractors (number)	1300	–	467 000	–	666 800	–
Power-driven drainage and irrigation machines (million h.p.)	0.1	–	60.0	–	71.2	–
Chemical fertilizer (million tonnes of domestic production of nutrient)	0.04	–	7.24	–	10.65	16.5

SOURCES Data on grain output, arable area, sown area and grain yields are from K. Walker (1981) pp. 216, 221, 222. Data for agricultural employment, irrigated area, tractors, machinery and chemical fertilizer are fromWorld Bank (1981) pp. 62, 65, 66. The figures for 1952/7 and 1976/80 are averages for the period.

TABLE 8.2 *Comparison of Average Annual Growth Rates of Grain Production and Brigade Enterprise Production, Selected Periods, 1952–79*

	Grain production	*Brigade enterprises*
1952–7	3.3	4.0
1957–65	0	6.6
1965–7	3.1	10.5
1957–77	1.8	8.9
1977–9	9.3	12.5
1952–79	2.6	8.3

SOURCE: World Bank (1981) p. 51.

data presented in Table 8.1 suggest that the increase in grain production over the period can be attributed almost entirely to increases in the productivity of land. Indeed, the amount of arable land decreased by 9.6 per cent over the period. Thus the increase in grain output can be explained by the substantial increase in grain yields. The data show that grain yields nearly doubled, from an average of 1.35 tonnes per hectare during 1952–7 to an average of 2.57 tonnes per hectare during 1976–80.

The data in Table 8.1 indicate that the doubling of grain yields can be explained by two developments. First, a substantial investment in water control occurred over the period (the amount of irrigated land more than doubled). By 1979 approximately 45 million hectares of land were irrigated, representing approximately 45 per cent of the arable land. This is a very high proportion, especially when it is contrasted with an estimated average of 17 per cent for other developing countries.[1] China's success in water-control construction was largely the result of extensive mobilization of labour in the countryside. James Nickum, for example, estimates that between 30 and 100 million persons participated annually during 1964–77 in rural water-control construction projects.[2] Most of these projects were organized at different levels of the commune organization and took place mainly during the Winter and Spring.

In Chapter 4 it was argued that effective water control is a major precondition for agricultural growth in the Chinese countryside. The complementarities between water and other modern inputs require that basic investment in irrigation should take place before substantial quantities of modern inputs are introduced. The commune organization was an effective institution for mobilizing off-peak labour for such construction. The commune could take advantage of important financial and planning economies of scale in the organization of these projects. The analysis of agricultural growth at Wu Gong Brigade provided empirical support for this argument. The data in Table 8.1 suggest that this pattern of agricultural growth also occurred at a national level. That is, labour was mobilized by the communes for investment projects and, simultaneously or subsequently, modern inputs were introduced. This interactive process perhaps provides the best explanation for the substantial growth in grain yields in rural China during 1952–79.

A second important achievement of the pre-1979 organizational arrangements was the growth of commune industry. Rural small-scale industry can have substantial indirect employment effects. This would occur if it can produce a steadily increasing flow of tools, pumps, cement and other construction materials which would help to raise the return to labour-intensive farmland capital construction projects. This in turn would raise the rate of absorption of rural under-employed labour.

The major benefit of commune industry, however, was its ability to promote a rapid accumulation of capital. Indeed the empirical findings in Chapter 5 suggested that commune industry was the 'engine of growth' in the countryside. This can also be seen at the national level from the data in Table 8.2. These data compare the average annual growth rates of grain production with corresponding rates for brigade-level industry. The rapid growth of rural small-scale industry is revealed clearly from these data. During 1957–77, for example, brigade industry grew at an average annual rate of 8.9 per cent. In the same period grain production grew at an annual rate of 1.8 per cent. Rural industrial growth thus played an important role within the commune in helping to compensate for slow agricultural growth during the difficult periods of the Great Leap Forward (1958–61) and the Cultural Revolution (1966–9). By 1979 the gross value of commune-level and brigade-level industrial output was 49.1 billion yuan, or more than a quarter of the gross value of light industrial production in the country.[3]

In contemplating substantial reforms after 1978, then, the government was well aware that the reforms could jeopardize the successful track record of rural capital construction and of small-scale industry. The organizational arrangements from 1962 to 1978 promoted investment and growth in these two vital sectors. Nevertheless from late 1978 to the present day the government has pressed on with a significant reform programme. This suggests that the government perceives 1957–77 as a period marked by unresolved problems and harmful fluctuations. Indeed, the current government considers the causes of these problems to be deep-rooted and therefore threatening to the long-term development of China. Before discussing the latest reforms it should be useful in the next section to see whether the government has good grounds for this perception.

2. ANALYSIS OF FLUCTUATIONS IN AGRICULTURAL GROWTH, 1957–77

The macroeconomic performance of the Chinese economy during 1949–79 has, on balance, been impressive. From 1953 to 1979, for example, the average annual growth rates for national income, agricultural production and industrial production were 6.0 per cent, 3.4 per cent, and 11.1 per cent respectively. In a recent article Liu Guoguang and Wang Xiangming compared these rates of growth with corresponding rates for West Germany, the United States, the Soviet Union and Japan. These comparisons are shown in Table 8.3. The data show that Chinese growth rates for agriculture and industry exceeded corresponding rates for these countries, with the exception of the industrial growth rate of Japan.

China's aggregate performance is also impressive when compared with other developing countries. Data comparing China's performance with the performance of selected developing countries are shown in Table 8.4. The average annual growth of gross domestic product (GDP) in China was more than 5 per cent for the 1960–79 period, surpassing corresponding rates of growth in India, Indonesia, Bangladesh and in the average low-income country. Whereas Chinese agricultural growth during the 1960–70 period was slow in comparison with other developing countries, in 1970–9 China's agricultural growth was very impressive. During this period China's agricultural output grew by 3.2 per cent per year, a rate surpassing by a wide margin the average low-income country, and by a narrow margin the average middle-income country. China's rate of industrial growth during both periods was very impressive when compared to industrial growth rates in the other developing countries. Indeed, only Indonesia achieved a faster rate of industrial and agricultural growth during the 1970–9 period.

Yet if one aspect of China's economic performance has been the achievement of high rates of growth during 1949–79 (particularly when compared to other developing countries), another aspect was the sharp fluctuations in these rates of growth both annually and over different plan periods. Between 1949 and 1978, for example, gross industrial and agricultural output value declined in four years; national income

TABLE 8.3 *Comparison of Chinese Industrial and Agricultural Growth Rates (1953–79) with Corresponding Growth Rates from Developed Countries (1950–79)*

Country	*Average annual rate of agricultural growth*	*Average annual rate of industrial growth*
China	3.4	11.1
West Germany	1.8	4.5
United States	1.9	4.5
Soviet Union	3.3	9.7
Japan	2.7	12.4

SOURCE Liu Guoguang and Wang Xiangming (1980) p.16.

TABLE 8.4 *Comparison of Chinese Industrial and Agricultural Growth Rates with Corresponding Rates in Selected Developing Countries, 1960–79 (Average annual rates of growth)*

Country	*GNP per capita (US$, 1979)*	*Gross domestic product 1960–70*	*1970–9*	*Agricultural growth 1960–70*	*1970–9*	*Industrial growth 1960–70*	*1970–9*
China	260	5.2	5.8	1.6	3.2	11.2	8.7
India	190	3.4	3.4	1.9	2.1	5.5	4.4
Pakistan	260	6.7	4.5	4.9	2.1	10.0	4.9
Bangladesh	90	3.6	3.3	2.7	1.9	7.9	7.0
Indonesia	370	3.9	7.6	2.7	3.6	5.2	11.3
Low-income countries	240	4.3	3.8	2.7	1.9	6.6	3.6
Middle-income countries	1420	6.1	5.5	3.6	3.0	7.4	6.5

SOURCE World Bank, *World Development Report* (Washington, 1981) pp.134 and 136. The data for low-income countries are averages for thirty-six countries with a GNP per capita between US$ 80 and US$ 370. The data for the middle-income countries are averages for fifty-nine countries with a GNP per capita between US$ 380 and US$ 4380. The data for the low-income countries exclude India and China, and their combined population in 1979 was, thus, 2260 million. The population (1979) of China, India, Indonesia, Pakistan and Bangladesh was 964.5, 659.2, 142.9, 79.7, 88.9 million respectively. The combined population of the middle-income countries in 1979 was 985.0 million.

declined in six years; and agricultural, heavy industrial and light industrial output each declined in five years.[4]

What was the record of agricultural performance during 1957–77? The data in Table 8.5 give an indication of the rates of growth during this period. Gross agricultural output increased at an average annual rate of 2.1 per cent. Because of rapidly increasing production costs, however,

TABLE 8.5 *Rates of Growth of Agricultural Output, 1957–77 (average annual rates)*

	1957–77
Gross agricultural output	2.1
Grain output	1.8
Cotton and oils	0.5
Other crops	2.2
Animal husbandry and fisheries	3.3
Net output of agriculture	1.6
Agricultural labour force	2.1
Population	1.9
Gross agricultural output per capita	0.2
Net agricultural output per capita	–0.5

SOURCE World Bank (1981) pp.51, 54, 73.

the annual rate of growth of net agricultural output was only 1.6 per cent. Moreover, the size of the agricultural labour force increased very rapidly over the period, at an average annual rate of 2.1 per cent. As a result, net agricultural output per worker declined, on average, by 0.5 per cent each year. This is a disturbing empirical finding, for it suggests that labour productivity in the countryside displayed little or no growth over the period.

The data in Table 8.6 show the per capita availability of selected food items during 1957–77. The per capita availability of unmilled grain declined from 248 kilogrammes in 1957 to 239 kilogrammes in 1977. The per capita availability of oils also daclined over the period. By 1977, however, the per capita availability of meat and vegetables had increased substantially.

An important reason for the slow rate of agricultural growth per capita during 1957–77 was the correspondingly rapid rate of growth of the population over the same period. Population increased by over 300 million in this period. As a result the man–land ratio increased sharply. By 1979 this ratio had risen to eight persons per hectare.[5] The corresponding ratio for India is less than half as high as in China, and in the United States the ratio is 300 times less.[6]

But if the rate of growth of grain output had been higher during 1957–77, or if the rate of growth of agricultural production costs had been lower, or both, then the per capita availability of grain and the net productivity per worker would not have declined.

Discussions of this record of growth in the recent Chinese literature often include remarks such as 'we should have achieved much greater successes', and 'agriculture, the foundation of industry and of the

TABLE 8.6 *Per Capita Availability of Selected Food Items, 1957–77 (Kilogrammes per capita)*

Item	*1957*	*1965*	*1970*	*1977*
Grain (unmilled)	248	215	232	239
Meat	6.2	–	–	8.3
Oils	2.7	2.1	1.9	1.7
Vegetables	79	–	78	94
Fish	4.7	–	–	5.0
Fruit	5.6	–	4.1	6.0
Sugar	1.3	–	–	1.8
Tea	0.2	0.1	0.2	0.3

SOURCE World Bank (1981) p. 56.

economy as a whole, is still extremely backward', and 'labour productivity in China's agriculture is too low'.[7] I shall argue below that the uneven performance of agriculture during 1957–77 should perhaps be attributed not to structural faults in the rural collective organizations, but rather to the ideological dogmatism reflected in the policies of that period. In part this can be explained by the differences between the 'opposition' in the leadership and the group led by Mao Zedong.

Policy within the Communes

In Chapter 2 I argued that there were two important reasons for the fall in grain production from 1958 to 1960 (output fell from 200 million tonnes in 1958 to 143 million tonnes in 1960). First, there was a tendency among certain members of the central government to favour a large scale in crop production. It was argued that this tendency reflected an 'orthodox' interpretation of Marxism–Leninism. Second, it was argued that the remuneration arrangements which operated within the early commune organization were damaging to incentives. A large share of income was distributed 'according to need'. Moreover agricultural workers often were organized in large groups, assigned specific tasks and paid according to pre-established norms. I suggested that the costs of monitoring effectively such large groups were high, and 'free-rider' problems could easily arise. As a result effort-discretion would be reduced, incentives would be damaged and, consequently, labour productivity would suffer. By 1961 the government had corrected some of these problems. The '60 Articles' were published in 1962 and embodied the more pragmatic policies of the 'opposition' group in the government. These policies restored a vigorous private sector at the level of the household and permitted rural village markets to exist. The amount of income distributed 'according to need' was reduced and a policy of distribution 'according to work' was promoted. The '60 Articles' also stipulated that a 'job-contract and responsibility' system of remuneration should operate within the commune organization. In this system small groups comprising several households within a production team could sign contracts for the delivery of a specific quantity of output at a certain date. Decisions concerning labour allocation and crop management were thus considerably decentralized. Such a decentralization of decision-making within the commune organization should have improved productivity. Indeed, grain production increased by 27 per cent from 1961 to 1964.

Yet during 1964 Mao Zedong and his supporters launched an ideological offensive against the 'opposition' and the policies of the '60 Articles'. The offensive started as a 'Socialist Education Movement' in the countryside and by 1966 it became part of the 'Cultural Revolution'. The rural embodiment of these political movements was the selection, by Mao personally, of the Dazhai production brigade in Shanxi Province to serve as a national 'model'. From 1964 to 1977 Mao and his supporters alleged that Dazhai's success in production and in capital accumulation was due to 'hard work', to 'self-reliance', and to placing 'politics in command'. A 'Learn from Dazhai' campaign was launched throughout the country. China's peasants were told that participation in the private sector was tantamount to 'taking the capitalist road'. According to the Dazhai model, remuneration should not be based on material incentives ('according to work'), but should be based on 'ideological' criteria. As such, a 'Dazhai workpoint system' was promoted throughout the countryside in which a workers's remuneration often depended as much upon political attitudes as upon the amount of work accomplished. Moreover a tendency toward 'large scale' in crop production reappeared. It was suggested that labour allocation by small 'work groups' would lead to a 'restoration' of capitalism. Indeed, communes were urged to follow Dazhai's example and to press for the amalgamation of production teams so that the brigade level would become the sole unit of account.

I have provided elsewhere an extensive analysis of the Dazhai model and the 'Learn from Dazhai' campaign.[8] I argued that although Mao recognized that the modernization of Chinese agriculture depended mainly upon the application of modern inputs, he nevertheless believed that an emphasis on such 'production forces' would undermine the importance of 'class struggle'. He was, in short, worried about the emergence of 'bourgeois relations of production' in the countryside. Yet evidence was provided to suggest that scarce technical aid and inputs were channelled clandestinely into Dazhai in order to ensure the success of the model.[9] The hope was that China's rural workforce would attribute agricultural growth as much to 'ideology' as to 'technique'.

The essence of the Dazhai model, then, was that agricultural growth derives from 'placing politics in command' rather than 'technique in command'. This 'law' was generalized by Mao's supporters in the 1960s and early 1970s to mean that continuous changes in the relations of production toward 'communism' would promote corresponding growth in the forces of production. Thus communes were encourgaged to change the level of ownership and accounting from production team to production brigade. According to this argument the smaller the scale of organization and management of crop production, the more 'capitalist' were the prevailing relations of production. Because Marx advocated distribution 'according to need' under conditions of full communism (i.e. when scarcity and consequently class struggle are eliminated, and goods are available in abundance) it was thought during 1964–76 that incentive arrangements and remuneration procedures should reflect a steady movement toward communism.

These views are now termed 'ultra-leftist' and occasionally 'sham-Marxism' by the present government. Indeed, I argued in Chapter 1 that Marx assigned primacy to the forces of production. In his model sustained growth of the forces of production can be 'fettered' by the prevailing relations of production. The relations of production were divided into two components, namely, ownership relations and work relations. It was argued that the redistribution of land in rural China and the subsequent establishment of collective production organizations resolved the most important structural impediments to the development of the forces of production. Sustained economic growth should thus depend upon the rate and efficiency of investment. Yet the insistence by the dominant group in the government of the need to continue to change production relations after 1962 in the direction of 'communism' would, according to Marx's own model, impede the growth of the forces of production, given their low 'initial' level. It is likely that the 'lessons' of the Dazhai model (e.g. elimination of the private sector, remuneration according to 'need' and to 'political attitude', centralization of scale) contributed to a dampening of incentives within the commune organizations and to a decline in labour productivity in agriculture.

There is evidence, moreover, that the implementation of these policies was accomplished through a return to 'commandist' practices which marked the 1956 and 1958–9 periods. Since 1978 a number of articles have been published which indicate that in many communes during 1964–76 'the sovereignty of the production teams has not been respected' and that 'the burden of the peasants must be lightened and the illegal acts of the cadres must be corrected'.[10] The phrase 'burden of the peasants' most likely refers to the tendency during this period of some cadres to requisition labour for brigade-level projects without proper compensation for production teams. There is also evidence that some cadres used 'commandist' tactics to increase the proportion of accumulation in the commune accounts rather than the proportion of distribution. According to Yao Wenyuan (one of the 'Gang of Four'), for example, the slogan 'Eat more, distribute more!' was supposed to lead to a 'restoration of capitalism'.[11] One of the earliest critics of Cultural Revolution policies, Xu Xiyu (Chairman of the Jiangsu Provincial Government) remarked in a 1971 speech:

> While making revolution it is not necessary to equalise the rich and the poor. . . . There are people who condemn the private property and the sideline occupations as 'tails of capitalism' although they are explicitly permitted by Party policy. This way of thinking is Left in form but Right in substance. Such people think that the more left they are, the better. They don't notice that they alienate themselves from reality. . . . On no account should there be in the future a desire to accumulate the means of the collective too quickly to the detriment of standards of living.[12]

In a recent book, Xue Muqiao, one of China's leading economists, emphasized this view in the following way:

> The Gang of Four argued that at no time can production forces grow without a change in the relations of production and advocated an unconditional, continual change in the social relations of production. This was an anti-Marxist view.[13]
>
> After the publication of the '60 Articles' in 1962, the relations of production in rural areas were stabilised. . . . Practice shows that objective economic laws are not to be violated, or else people will suffer. Problems arose in 1958 mainly because we expected to do too much through a change in the relations of production, including ownership, overlooking the law that the relations of production must conform to the growth of productive forces. Production resumed its growth [in 1978] as soon as we corrected our mistakes by readjusting the relations of production to the level of the production forces.[14]
>
> . . . farm output has not increased fast enough and has remained far below the targets set in the Five Year Plans. The basic cause lies in the errors we committed in the countryside. For a time a 'communist wind' was stirred up, under which egalitarianism won the day and human and material resources were transferred in disregard of the collectives to which they belonged. Arbitrary decisions were issued to collectives and peasants for doing one thing or another. All this infringed upon the rights of the commune, production brigades and production teams to make their own decisions, affecting the peasants' livelihood and their enthusiasm in socialist collective production.[15]

Policies 'exogenous' to the Commune Organisation

Recent Chinese criticism of the economic policies of 1964–77 have emphasized their implicit 'negation' of certain 'objective economic laws'. The two most important of these laws are the 'law of value' and the 'law of planned and proportionate development'.

An important concern of the 'law of planned and proportionate development' is the determination of the correct ratios of state investment between sectors in order to achieve balanced growth. In Chapter 2 it was argued that the government decided to allocate most of its investment funds to heavy industry during the First Five-Year Plan Period. It was thought that an industrial base had to be established before modern inputs for agriculture could be produced and distributed. Mao was nevertheless convinced that short-term productivity gains could be achieved in the countryside by establishing collective organizations to mobilize under-employed resources. He succeeded in convincing cadres at grass-roots levels of the logic of this argument, despite the opposition of many of his colleagues in the central government. I suggested, however, that although the logic of the 'collectivisation before mechanisation' argument was valid from a short-term perspective, the long-term prospects for Chinese agriculture would depend upon the ability of the industrial sector to produce and to allocate efficiently modern inputs for agriculture. Yet during the Great Leap Forward the policy of mobilizing underemployed resources reached the point of diminishing returns: without the application of chemical fertilizers, farm machines, improved seeds, etc. it became very difficult to employ productively larger amounts of labour. The statistical results in Chapter 4 support this view. In the 'traditional' period at Wu Gong Brigade (1953–68), the coefficient for the labour input in the brigade's production function was not statistically significantly different from zero. In the 'modern period' (1968–79), however, the coefficient for the labour input was large and highly significant. It was argued that the shift to double-cropping at Wu Gong, which was made possible by the establishment of the irrigation system and by the application of technical inputs, raised substantially the average and marginal productivity of labour above that which prevailed when traditional technology was used.

During 1961 and 1962 the government recognized the importance of redirecting the industrial sector to provide modern inputs for agriculture. The slogan 'agriculture as the foundation and industry as the leading factor' was advanced. This priority was to be reflected in a larger allocation of state investment to agriculture. Moreover the composition of industrial output was to be changed to reflect the needs of agricultural modernization.

Statistics indicating the pattern of government investment now reveal that the decisions reached during 1962–5 were not properly implemented in subsequent years. Although the share of state capital construction investment that was allocated to agriculture increased from 9.4 per cent in 1957 to 14.6 per cent in 1965, this proportion declined to 8.8 per cent in 1970.[16] Agriculture's share increased only moderately from 1970 to 1978. A similar pattern is evident for the allocation of state investment to light industry. The data show that the heavy industrial sector received the largest share of state investment, and that this proportion increased from 57.2 per cent in 1957 to 64.8 per cent in 1970.[17]

Yet if the composition of heavy industrial output reflected the needs of agricultural modernization, then this pattern of investment allocation would not be so alarming. The data in Table 8.7 suggest, however, that the composition of heavy industrial output did not change substantially over the period to support the modernization of agriculture. The share of investment in farm machinery, chemical fertilizer and pesticides in total heavy industrial investment increased only marginally between 1965 and 1975.

In presenting these data Yang Jianbai and Li Xuezheng argued that:

> Up to now, the pattern of China's heavy industry has not been adapted to the need to accelerate the growth of agriculture and light

TABLE 8.7 *Share of Farm-related Investments in Total Investment in Heavy Industry, 1953–78*

Period	*Investment in heavy industry (million yuan)*	*Investment in farm machinery chemical fertilizer and pesticides*	*Share of farm-related investment in total heavy industry investment*
1st FYP (1953–7)	22 599	758	2.9
2nd FYP (1958–62)	66 627	3 827	5.4
Readjustment (1963–5)	20 126	1 968	9.7
3rd FYP (1966–70)	52 477	4 773	8.0
4th FYP (1971–5)	92 058	9 338	10.1
1976–8	65 783	7 316	11.1
1952–78	324 163	27 993	8.6

SOURCE Yang Jianbai and Li Xuezheng (1980) p. 200

> industry. This is a major cause of the disproportions between the three sectors and an important lesson we should learn. . . . The trouble is that giving undue prominence to heavy industry has become a habit, a habit far stronger than the Party's guidelines and policies.[18]

The Chinese now argue that this "habit" resulted in a 'negation' of the 'basic economic law of socialism', namely, that the purpose of production is not 'for the sake of production' but rather to meet the material needs of the people. The persistance of this 'habit', however, begs the following question: why did the government continue to 'develop heavy industry only for the sake of heavy industry'?[19] The implications of this question have been examined recently by Cyril Lin.[20] He argues that the basic concept of growth underlying Chinese development planning derives from two sources. The first was Marx's model of simple and expanded reproduction in volume II of *Capital.* The second was the Soviet interpretation of Marx's model and the resulting policy implications for investment strategy and sectoral priorities. The Soviet interpretation was formalized in the growth model of Fel'dman. In his model the growth rate of national income and ultimately of consumption depends on the proportion of the producer goods sector's output that is reinvested within that sector. In this way the rate of growth of heavy industrial output is accelerated, thereby enhancing that sector's ability to provide at a future date an increasing stock of producer goods.

Lin also argues that in the late 1950s and early 1960s leading Chinese economists 're-examined previously held notions on the priority growth of the producer goods sector as inherited from Stalinist dogma and formulated their own growth models which emphasized the limiting conditions posed by the consumer goods sector on the producer goods sector, and hence on the rate of growth of national income'.[21] These economists were attacked in 1964 and many were subsequently purged during the 'Cultural Revolution'. As a result the dogmatic policy of 'developing heavy industry only for the sake of heavy industry' resulted in a neglect of the technical requirements of agricultural modernization.

A final 'exogenous' influence on agricultural productivity involved the 'negation' of 'the Law of Value'. This law presupposes the existence of commodities as a legitimate socialist economic category and implies commodity production and commodity exchange (based on equal value). Debates concerning the 'Law of Value' were conducted by Chinese economists in the 1950s and the early 1960s. These debates were concerned with the problem of transforming values into prices. One of China's leading economists, Sun Yefang, argued that 'plans and proportions of material quantities based on gross output value express only statistical and technological relationships rather than economic ones'.[22] Sun argued that the value of a commodity should express the (average) amount of 'socially-necessary' labour embodied in it. If this is so the 'Law of Value' can operate as a principle of efficient resource allocation in the economy. The 'Law of Value' has important implications for planning reform and, consequently, for investment efficiency. Sun Yefang and many of his colleagues envisaged an economy

> steered through various value parameters such as prices, profits, taxes, interest rates etc. . . . enterprises would enjoy considerable autonomy in production and marketing decisions, and would be profit-maximizing, on the basis of centrally-regulated prices conveying preference-scarcity information. 'Socialist competition' would prevail, which, acting in conjunction with other related reforms, becomes a 'magic whip', propelling a rapid and dynamic development of production forces.[23]

Cyril Lin has argued recently that the reform proposals of Sun and his colleagues

> were too unorthodox to be acceptable to the majority of Chinese ideologists weaned on standard Stalinist formulations postulating an irreconcilable and mutually exclusive relationship between the Law of Value and parametric value planning on one hand and the Law of Planned and Proportionate Development and physical – command planning on the other. The reformers' challenge to traditional orthodoxy went beyond purely economic questions . . . and contained serious ideological – political implications. . . . In addition, reform proposals advocating greater enterprise autonomy challenged the received doctrine of the definition of socialism and democratic centralism. Socialism had long been equated with centralization, and the more centralized the economic system the more socialist it was supposed to be. Democracy was a concept more applicable, where it was applicable, to relations between units within the Party and state apparatus rather than between the individual and the apparatus.[24]

Not surprisingly, during 1966–76 planning decisions were often arbitrary, physical controls predominated and the collection of aggregate statistical information was neglected. How did such an 'exogenous' economic environment affect the communes? There were three principal ways. First, the irrationality of the price system was reflected in the rapidly rising material costs of agricultural production. Yang Jianbai and Li Xuezheng, for example, argued recently that:

> The high prices set for agricultural producers' goods or means of production account for the rising costs in farming. Yet the state purchasing prices have either remained unchanged for years or increased too little to compensate for the rising costs. A survey conducted in 1,296 production teams in 22 provinces shows that during 1962–76, although the average per mou yield of six grain crops rose by 91 kg and the output value by 16.61 yuan, the production costs, including manpower, rose by 20.3 yuan, tax rose by 0.39 yuan, and net returns dropped by 4.11 yuan. Thus there appeared not only 'poor production teams with high yields' but also 'poor counties with rich harvests'. Isn't this a result of unreasonable pricing?[25]

An important reason for the 'unequal exchange' between industry and agriculture during this period was the need to make the agricultural sector 'pay' for the substantial decline in the efficiency of industry. The 'output effect of industrial investment' $\Delta Y/I$, where Y is output, and I is investment) declined from 0.319 in the Third Five Year Plan Period to 0.170 in the Fourth Plan Period.[26] Whereas 100 yuan of industrial investment yielded 35 yuan of national income in the First Plan Period, this yield dropped to 26 yuan and to 16 yuan in the Third and Fourth Plan Periods respectively.[27]

The steady decline in the efficiency of industrial investment (a consequence of the problems in the planning and price system) not only resulted in 'unequal exchange' between agriculture and industry, but also in the production of farm machinery of poor quality or inadequate design. Liu Guoguang and Wang Xiangming, for example, recently stated that 'a considerable part of farm machinery produced by heavy industry as aid to agriculture proved practically useless because of poor quality, unsuitable specifications, or lack of accessories'.[28]

A second consequence for the rural economy of the irrationality of the price and planning system during 1966–76 was its effect in promoting a 'backward and irrational pattern' of cropping. The policy of 'taking grain as the key link' was reinforced through a system of arbitrary physical controls and prices. As a result grain was produced 'at the expense of animal husbandry' and other crops (e.g. cotton); forests were destroyed, beaches and lakes were filled in and many other distortions in the efficient allocation of resources occurred within the communes.[29]

These policies 'damaged natural resources, disrupted ecological balance, and led to disastrous consequences' for agricultural performance.[30]

A final consequence for the rural economy of 'ultra-left' policies during 1966–76 was their effect on agricultural research and extension. As a result of the policy of placing 'politics in command' most agricultural research institutes and technical training schools were closed. Researchers were not allowed to conduct experiments and to test new techniques in conditions appropriate to specific areas. Indeed many scientists and technicians were 'encouraged' to participate in farm work rather than to pursue their research and training. The negative effects of these policies on agricultural productivity are difficult to assess, but it is reasonable to assume that they would have been substantial.

3. RECENT ECONOMIC REFORMS, 1978–84

Following the death of Mao Zedong and the arrest of the 'Gang of Four' in 1976, a different group in the government gained control of economic policy formulation. This is the group which throughout this book have been labelled 'the opposition' (e.g. Deng Xiaoping, Chen Yun, Bo Yibo). By 1978 their political position was consolidated and they proceeded rapidly to restore most of the rural policies that prevailed during 1962–4. Moreover, many of the economists who had been attacked in previous years have been rehabilitated.

The restoration of the views of economists such as Sun Yefang has had important implications for recent economic policy. At a conference on economic theory convened in Sichuan Province in 1978, for example, Zhao Ziyang (then First Secretary of the Provincial Party Committee) stated that planning and the market 'are not absolutely opposed to each other; they can be combined'.[31] He declared that 'it is absolutely impossible to devise plans which cover all contingencies'.[32] Hence it was 'very necessary to organise a market economy covering a certain sphere as a supplement'.[33] Zhao stressed the importance of solving the problems of combining the market with planning. The proceedings of the conference suggested that the government intended to use a regulated market with an efficient system of prices and other value parameters, in order to improve the efficiency of the economy.

The conference was soon followed by the Third Plenary Session of the Eleventh Central Committee. During this session two documents were approved which set out explicitly the rural economic policies of the current government. To some extent these policies are simply a restatement and clarification of the policies embodied in the '60 Articles' of 1962. The 'new 60 Articles' published after the Third Plenum restate most of these policies. The most important are as follows: (i) the existence of the private sector of the commune and the rural village markets are guaranteed; (ii) distribution should mainly be 'according to work', rather than 'according to need'; and (iii) the 'job contract and responsibility system' should operate widely.

A second document, entitled 'Party Decisions on the Acceleration of Agricultural Development' was also ratified at the Plenary Session. This document urged the adoption of 'a specific series of policies and measures in the next two or three years in order to accelerate agricultural development, lighten the peasants' burden, increase their income, and gradually realise agricultural modernization'.[34] These policies encourage crop specialization and the creation of agricultural zones and marketable grain base areas in accordance with principles of comparative advantage. The goal is to create a diversified agricultural sector, accomplished through a judicious mixture of quantity controls and the price mechanism.

The government also announced a quite extraordinary shift in the terms of trade in favour of agriculture. The most important element in this new policy was a large increase in grain procurement prices. In a recent government document it was stipulated that both the agricultural tax and the state purchase quota will remain fixed at the 1971–5 level[35] (although some reductions were made in 1980 and 1981[36]). The grain procurement price was raised by 20 per cent starting in 1979 while the price for the amount purchased above the quota was raised an additional 30 per cent.[37] The government also announced a rise in the purchase price for cotton, oil-bearing crops, sugar, animal by-products and aquatic and forestry products. The factory price and market price of farm machinery, chemical fertilizer, insecticides, plastics and other manufactured goods for farm use was cut by 10 to 15 per cent in 1979–80 and 'these benefits will in general be passed on to the peasants'.[38] Further price adjustments were made in 1980 and 1981. These changes increased the overall level of base prices by 3.5 per cent and by 2.4 per cent respectively.[39] In 1981 about 40 per cent of grain sold to the state was purchased at the base price. The remaining 60 per cent was sold at above-quota or negotiated prices, compared to less than 1 per cent in 1977.[40]

With the terms of trade between agriculture and industry significantly improved for the peasant, the government shifted their programme of reform after 1980 from prices to organizational arrangements. In the previous chapter I suggested briefly that the 'responsibility' system was an important part of this reform programme. Under this system the production team forms a contract with specialized groups, households or individuals. The contract usually includes the amount of land to be farmed and the output to be produced and sold to the collective. Bonuses are paid for overfulfilment of quotas and, in many cases, 'above quota' output can be sold by the household in the free village markets.

Perhaps the most important aspect of the responsibility system is its substantial decentralization of decision-making in crop management. The contracted household organizes its own work and makes its own decisions every day. This contrasts sharply with the previous organization of production by cadres where payments were awarded on a piece-work or workpoint basis. Under the piece-work system a specific task was given workpoint values commensurable with their difficulty, with the time required for completion and with their overall importance in the process of production. The member then received that number of points upon completion of the task. In another variant of the workpoint system members themselves were given ratings: an older, more skilled male might have received ten workpoints per day while a younger, less-experienced member may have received only six. Either variant of this system resulted in more workpoints for more work. At the end of the year the value of a single workpoint was determined by dividing total distributable income by the number of workpoints accumulated by all the members of the 'work group'. Payments equal to that value times the number of workpoints accumulated by each household were then made.

Whenever the size of the 'work group' was enlarged (or the level of account changed from the team to the brigade), the size of the unit in which the workpoint value was calculated increased, say, tenfold. This substantially weakened the relationship between individual effort and material reward. This relationship was dealt a severe blow during the late 1960s and early 1970s with the implementation of the Dazhai workpoint system. Under this system the determination of workpoints for a given task depended not just upon an individual's intensity of work or on his productivity, but also on his 'political attitude', as determined by cadres and by 'peer assessment'.

The responsibility system, on the other hand, has the advantage of avoiding many of the problems of imperfect information, monitoring, 'free-rider' abuse and so forth, that were discussed in Chapter 1. It is perhaps useful here to repeat Joseph Stiglitz's perceptive point about the relationship between incentives, screening and the productivity of the work group within an organization:

> incentives are a problem mainly because of difficulties in monitoring individuals' inputs and outputs. . . . Thus the magnitude of this problem depends on how we organise the production process. . . . If we hired workers to pick weeds, and paid them by the weight of weeds picked, they would pick the largest weeds, not necessarily the ones which would most likely interfere with the growth of the vegetables; if we hire workers to grow vegetables, and pay them in proportion to their output of vegetables, they will pick the correct weeds.[41]

In China today a household or a group of households are no longer dependent upon the judgement of cadres who have the power arbitrarily to decide the quality and quantity of their work effort. Indeed the potential for accumulation and growth in the co-operative organizations has always depended upon the strength of the links between individual benefit and collective interests. The current government is hoping that the 'production responsibility' system will strengthen these links and thereby improve the prospects for growth in the rural economy.

By 1984 more than 90 per cent of China's rural households had embraced the responsibility system.[42] In a series of central directives (Party Document Number 1 in January 1983 and in January 1984) the government has elaborated on this new system. The 1984 document stipulates that the period of individual land contracts can be extended to fifteen years in order to 'ensure the long-term implementation of the contract system'.[43] The transfer of land contracts can now be negotiated between households, as long as the transfer is 'registered' with the production team. The government stresses, however, that the land is still owned by the members of the co-operative organization and therefore that 'free trading in land is prohibited'.[44] One purpose of the new regulations is to encourage the cultivation and management of land by a smaller pool of 'talented' farmers. In a recent interview Du Runsheng, head of the Rural Policy Research Institute of the Central Committee, suggested that the new responsibility system has unmasked a surplus of labour in crop cultivation. He argued that such peasants should:

> leave their land and engage in other undertakings. . . . If cultivated land is gradually concentrated and tilled by 30 to 40 per cent of the peasant households, who can thus specialise in crop growing, the size of land tilled by each household could be two, three, or four times the present size. . . . Under such a situation we encourage the peasants to readjust land distribution and transfer the land contracts they have signed.[45]

But what should happen to the 'non-specialised' households who no longer engage principally in crop cultivation? The government is now promoting in Zhao Ziyang's recent words, 'economic associations of various descriptions organised by the peasantry on a voluntary basis'.[46] By 'associations' Zhao means co-operative enterprises engaged in various activities ranging from livestock, poultry, forestry and fish-breeding to trades and crafts requiring specialized skills. This policy was recently spelled out by Du Runsheng:

> [Peasants] are allowed to leave their land and run small-scale industries with their partners, or run cooperative commercial or transportation enterprises and large-scale animal husbandry. Different factors of production are allowed to circulate freely, which means a free flow of workers, capital and technology. The policy of free circulation was reaffirmed in the 1984 No. 1 document.[47]

Households or groups of households who form such associations can under certain circumstances hire a small number of labourers. Craftsmen with specialized skills 'are allowed to have no more than six or seven apprentices and helpers. Within this limit they are still small individual proprietors, not capitalists.'[48] While one can debate whether differences between these two categories are semantic or real it seems clear that the boundaries between the collective and private sectors in rural China are becoming blurred. What is perhaps most interesting is that the present government is encouraging this blurring in the name of efficiency.

One must remember, however, that rural China is still composed of participative co-operative organizations. Indeed, the recent reforms have emphasized this pattern of organization by simplifying and clarifying the organizational structure in the countryside. I shall argue below that the democratic nature of this organizational pattern has been significantly strengthened and extended.

The previous commune arrangements encompassed both political and economic features. Commune-level and brigade-level management committees not only co-ordinated the work of their own co-operative industrial enterprises, but they also managed education, health and other social-welfare duties. The government now argues that the administrative personnel, methods and controls needed to manage such civic functions are quite inappropriate when applied to the management of industrial enterprises. Since each production enterprise is itself a co-operative organization it is now argued (not unreasonably) that they should be managed only by an elected committee drawn from the enterprise's own members. An enterprise's management should be primarily concerned, after all, with the economic interests of its own organization. At the level of the village, agricultural activities and farmland capital projects are still co-ordinated by the village co-operative, i.e. the production team. This has not been changed and the government has indicated that it has no intention of changing this important pattern of organization.

The new reforms, therefore, have separated the management of co-operative economic organizations in the countryside from the civic and political functions required of a local government. These civic duties are now the responsibility of the township government (as they were in 1955–6). By the end of 1983 more than 22 000 township governments had been established in about half of the counties of China.[49] This process will have been completed by the end of 1984.

A township may be composed of dozens of villages. The recent reforms also include the decentralization of the township government to the village level, through the establishment of village committees. The new constitution of China stipulates that 'the village committee is a mass organization of self-management'.[50] It manages the public affairs and social services of the village, in liaison with the township government. The village committees and their leaders are elected by the villagers. The committees include a mediation group, a public security group and a public health group. By the end of 1983 170 000 village committees had been established in rural China; 600 000 more village committees will have been set up in 1984.[51]

China is breaking new ground in exploring combinations of market and planning, of agriculture and industry, of political and economic organization. By introducing separate political organizations at village and township levels in the countryside, China's 800 million peasants can gain important experience in some of the principles of political democracy. This could have profound long-term effects for China, the implications of which may perhaps be drawn from John Stuart Mill:

> We do not learn to read or write, to ride or swim, by merely being told how to do it, but by doing it. So it is only by practising popular government on a limited scale, that the people will ever learn how to exercise it on a larger.[52]

4. RURAL ECONOMIC PERFORMANCE, 1978–83

How has China's rural economy performed in the first five years of the new policies? Table 8.8 shows the main indicators of growth in the countryside from 1978 to 1983. The gross value of agricultural production nearly doubled over the period, increasing at an average annual rate of 16.2 per cent. Grain production was also impressive, increasing rapidly at an annual rate of 4.5 per cent. The emphasis on comparative advantage and specialization in the new policies was in part reflected in the significant growth in cotton production: output increased at a remarkable average annual rate of 18.9 per cent from 1978

TABLE 8.8 *Economic Growth in Rural China, 1978–83*

	1978	*1979*	*1983*	*Average annual growth rate over the period*
Gross value of[a] agricultural production (billion yuan)	158.4	–	312.1	16.2
Grain production[b] (million metric tonnes)	304.7	–	387.3	4.5
Cotton production[c] (million metric tonnes)	2.167	–	4.637	18.9
Employment in commune[d] and brigade enterprises (million)	28	–	32	2.4
Gross output value[d] of commune and brigade enterprise (billion yuan)	–	68.2 (1980)	92.87	9.0
Chemical fertilizer[e] (million tonnes)	–	10.65	16.59	11.1
Irrigation[f] (million hectares)	–	45	50	2.2

SOURCES [a] 1978 figure from Ma Hong, *New Strategy for China's Economy* (Beijing: New World Press, 1983) p. 153; 1983 figure from *Beijing Review*, 14 May 1984, 'Communique on Fulfillment of China's 1983 Plan'.

[b] Grain production: 1978: State Statistical Bureau, *China's Statistical Yearbook 1983* (Beijing, 1984), p. 158; 1983; *Beijing Review*, 28 May 1984, p. 18.

[c] Cotton production: 1978: Ma Hong, op. cit. p. 154; 1983; *Beijing Review*, ibid. p. 18.

[d] 1983 figures from *Beijing Review*, 9 July 1984, p. 9. 1978 and 1980 figures from Ministry of Agriculture, Department of Commune and Brhgade Enterprises, cited in K. Griffin (ed.) (1984) appendix table 3.

[e] 1979 figure from Table 8.1; 1983 from *Beijing Review*, 14 May 1984.

[f] 1979 figure from Table i.1; 1983 figure from *Beijing Review*, 30 Apr 1984, p. 19.

to 1983. This might also have reflected the effects of the decentralization of decision-making in crop production: contracted households have been quick to perceive the benefits to growing cotton in regions well-suited for it.

The data in Table 8.8 also show a steady growth in rural collective industry. The commune and brigade enterprises have increased their employment from 28 million to 32 million people from 1979 to 1983. The value of industrial output in the communes increased by 9 per cent per year. From 1979 to 1982, moreover, these industrial enterprises contributed more than 8 billion yuan to investment in crop production.[53] This is an amount equivalent to 73 per cent of the state's investment in agriculture over the same period.[54] In 1983 these enterprises produced 75 per cent of the country's total output of bricks, tiles, sand, limestone and basic farming tools. But the industrial co-operatives in the countryside not only contributed significant shares of their surplus to investment in the local agricultural sector. In 1983 nearly 8 billion yuan were allocated from industrial surpluses to village welfare facilities in the countryside.[55]

Steady progress was also made in agricultural investment. The application of chemical fertilizer increased by 11.1 per cent per year. The amount of land brought under irrigation increased by five million hectares, or 2.2 per cent annually. This is an adequate, if slower, rate of growth and it perhaps suggests a shortcoming in the new policies. Under the new arrangements agricultural production co-operatives operate at the village level (the production team). Rural capital construction is no longer co-ordinated at higher levels. While this ought not to present problems for the organizing of small projects it may become increasingly difficult to co-ordinate large-scale projects – which require the combined efforts of several villages. Under the new policies the township governments would not be expected to plan and to manage such large projects; and the industrial enterprises are now concerned only with their own production programmes. Thus the government may soon find it necessary to encourage new organizational arrangements for co-ordinating large agricultural construction projects (particularly for water control).

Yet agricultural production clearly has fared well under the new policies; and peasant standards of living have perhaps fared even better. This can be seen from the data in Table 8.9. Net income per head in the countryside has increased by 132 per cent from 1978 to 1983, a staggering increase of 22 per cent per year. Much of this gain, however, can be attributed not to income derived from increased production, but

TABLE 8.9 *Net Income and Consumption in Rural China, 1978–83*

	1978	*1979*	*1980*	*1981*	*1982*	*1983*	*Average annual rate over period*
Net income per head[a] (yuan)	133.57	160.2	191.3	223.4	270.11	309.8	22
Adjusted net income[b] per head (yuan)	137.5	156.8	171.5	189.9	214.2	241.6	12.6
Housing per head[c] (square metres)	8.1	–	–	–	–	11.6	7.2
Consumption per head of:							
wheat and rice (jin)[d]	245	–	–	–	384	–	11.3
meat, poultry, fish (jin)[d]	13.69	–	–	–	22.29	–	12.5
cloth (metre)[d]	0.413	–	–	–	1.53	–	54.1

SOURCES [a] Net income per head: 1983 figure from *Beijing Review*, 14 May 1984; 1982 figure derived from *Beijing Review*, 28 May 1984, p. 18; 1981 and 1980 are from Lee Travers (1984) p. 244; 1978–9 are from Table 6.4.

[b] Adjusted net income per head: 1978–81 are from Travers (1984) p. 245; 1982–3 are derived from *Red Flag*, 16 May 1984 in *SWB*, FE/W1294/A/p. 1, 4 July 1984.

[c] Housing per head: from *SWB*, ibid. p. 1.

[d] State Statistical Bureau, *Selected Statistics of China, 1983*, cited in K. Griffin (1984) p. 306.

to income derived from the 'one-off' nature of the substantial corrections in the terms of trade between agriculture and industry. If one adjusts the figures to allow for these price effects then net income per head rose by a lower rate of 12.6 per cent per year. Nevertheless this is a remarkable average increase in the standard of living of 800 million peasants.

Other indicators of better living standards can also be seen in Table 8.9. Housing per head increased by 7.2 per cent per year from 1978 to 1983; many families used some of their increased income to build additions to their homes. The annual per capita consumption of grain and animal protein also rose significantly – by 11.3 per cent and 12.5 per cent respectively. The diet of the Chinese peasant has clearly improved both quantitatively and qualitatively in the past five years.

One indication that the post-1978 reforms have improved resource allocation is the growth in the consumption of cloth from 1978 to 1983. By adjusting prices more accurately to reflect scarcities the reforms have yielded both a substantial gain in cotton production (19 per cent per year) and a quite remarkable increase in cloth consumption per head (54.1 per cent per year).

The main indicators of performance, then, provide strong evidence that the reform policies were well-conceived and, so far, very effective. Growth in the countryside has accelerated and living standards have significantly improved. The scale of the achievements from 1978 to 1983 can be seen more clearly by comparing some of the rates of growth during this period with corresponding growth rates during 1957–77. These data are shown in Table 8.10. Perhaps the most important contrast between the two periods is in the consumption of grain. Grain consumption per capita displayed no tendency to increase over the twenty-year period (indeed it even declined slightly by 0.17 per cent per year). Since 1978, however, grain consumption has increased by more than 11 per cent per year. Adjusted net income has increased by more than four times and agricultural output by nearly eight times as much per year since 1978 as compared to 1957–77. Grain output from 1978 to 1983 has more than doubled its average annual rate of growth during 1957–77.

It should not be surprising, in view of this record of performance, if the reform policies of the current government receive the enthusiastic support of most of China's peasants. Their own decision-making power and participation have been significantly extended within the village co-operative organizations. The rural industrial enterprises are continuing to grow and are slowly absorbing surplus labour. Moreover an active

TABLE 8.10 *Comparison of Average Annual Growth Rates in the Rural Economy, 1957–77 and 1978–83*

	1957–77	*1978–83*
Net income per head (adjusted)	2.9[a]	12.6
Agricultural output:	2.1	16.2
grain	2.04[b]	4.5
cotton	1.46[b]	18.9
Consumption per head:		
grain	−0.17[c]	11.3[d]
meat	1.6[c]	11.46[d]

SOURCE [a] *Red Flag*, 16 May 1984, in *SWB*, FE/W12941/A/p. 1. This datum refers to 1958–78

[b] Ma Hong, op. cit., appendix table 2. These data are for 1957–78. Note that the corresponding data in Table 8.5 are likely to be slightly under-estimated.

[c] These data are from Table 8.6.

[d] State Statistical Bureau, op. cit., cited in K. Griffin (ed.) (1984) p. 306. All other data are from Tables 8.5, 8.8 and 8.9.

and productive private sector has been explicitly encouraged by the government. Much of the evidence suggests that the peasants for their part have responded by working harder and by producing considerably more output per person. Their increased efforts in turn have so far been well-rewarded by a substantial increase in living standards in the past five years.

It is worth emphasizing, finally, that the policies of 1958–60 and 1966–76 were based on a dogmatic interpretation of Marxism–Leninism. Indeed the argument that continuous change in the relations of production in the direction of full communism can promote steady growth in the forces of production represents a fundamental misconception of Marx's development model. Marx was mainly concerned with determining whether or not an appropriate *correspondence* existed between relations and forces of production.

Between 1956 and 1962 the Chinese searched for an appropriate structure of work relations within the rural organizations. Because of the importance of introducing an 'industrial sector' into the countryside, confusion arose within the government over the appropriate economies of scale for crop management on the one hand and the optimal financial and planning economies of scale for rural capital construction and industry on the other. By 1962 the government had, it seemed, reached a consensus regarding the optimal structure of work relations within the rural organizations. Unfortunately dogma rather than common sense prevailed and these work relations were again altered in a substantial way. These dogmatic views were also evident in macroeconomic policy (e.g. the planning and price system and state investment priorities) which in combination with the problems in the communes had adverse effects on rural economic growth.

Xue Muqiao, perhaps China's leading economist, in the introduction to his 1981 book, recognized the danger of ideological dogmatism in the determination of economic policy. He argued:

> Socialism is a new system. In studying the laws of motion of the Socialist economy, we must always base our work on actual conditions . . . Marx and Lenin showed us the laws governing the transition from capitalism to communism through socialism . . . However, the classics they authored are insufficient for a study of the socialist economy because socialism never actually existed in their lifetime . . . We must never take what is said by Marx, Engels, and Lenin in their works as dogma or as a panacea.[56]

This view was also reflected in a 1981 article by two prominent economists, Tian Jianghai and Zhang Shuguang. They argued as follows:

> The problems regarding balance and regulation, economic structure and setup, however, happened not only in China, but in other socialist countries as well. What then is the reason? We hold that, from an epistemological point of view, it is because people had a dogmatic understanding of Marxist views on socialism for a long period of time, which has resulted in negating the existence of a commodity economy within the socialist economy; writing off the relative independence and right of socialist enterprises to manage their own affairs, taking the model of a highly centralized planning economy practised in the Soviet Union under Stalin as the sole socialist economic model, taking plans as the only means of organizing and regulating the development of socialist economy, trying to depend on one planning center to organize the production of hundreds of thousands of different products and direct the economic activities of the entire society, and negating the regulating role of the market mechanism in the socialist economy.[57]

The views of these economists received official approval in an authoritative article in the Communist Party's theoretical journal, *Red*

Flag on 1st October 1984 and in editorials in the *Peoples' Daily* on 7 and 8 December 1984. The front-page commentary in *Peoples' Daily* stated:

> There are many things that Marx, Engels and Lenin never experienced or had any contact with, and we cannot depend on the works of Marx Lenin to solve all our modern day questions.[58]

The impressive performance of the Chinese economy since 1978 is attributable in part to the refutation of the ideological dogmatism of 1958–60 and 1966–76. If the 'cycle' of dogmatism does not reappear, then the recent record of growth provides good grounds for optimism about the future performance of the rural economy.

9 Conclusion

The organizational structure in rural China, based on co-operatives, is generating steady growth and consequently proportional improvements in their members' welfare. Indeed the achievement of maximum 'social welfare' has always been assigned an important role by the theorists of orthodox economics. This body of theory has elegantly demonstrated how maximum social welfare can be attained by employing a specific *procedure*, namely the use of the market mechanism under competitive conditions. It has been shown, for example, that for some 'initial' endowment, the use of the market mechanism will, under certain assumptions, lead to a general equilibrium in an economy.[1] In this theoretical model, after all trades have been completed, the value of each agent's final bundle of goods will depend on the value of his initial bundle of goods. Moreover under certain general assumptions the market mechanism will ensure that the final allocation of resources will be a Pareto-efficient one. Yet the theory has never attempted to address the following question: how is the initial endowment of resources to be determined? In my view the issue of institutions and organizations has arisen in economics in part because the conventional theory has not tackled this question. In the context of low-income countries this neglect is particularly disturbing. For if the initial endowments of hundreds of millions of peasants are not sufficient for them to acquire a 'final bundle' which is adequate to meet their basic needs (e.g. nutrition, health, shelter, etc.) then in what sense is the Pareto-efficiency of the final outcome a *just* outcome?

Amartya Sen has recently criticized conventional economic analyses of poverty, starvation and famine from this perspective. That is, he argues that we 'need to view the food problem as a relation between people and food in terms of a network of entitlement relations'.[2] In *Poverty and Famines* Sen concentrates on the ability of different groups of the population to 'establish command' over food through the entitlement relations operating in a country. These relations, he argues, depend on the prevailing legal, economic, political and social characteristics of a society. In criticizing the 'market' approach of orthodox economists Sen argues as follows:

> Adam Smith's proposition is, in fact, concerned with efficiency in meeting a market demand, but it says nothing on meeting a need that has not been translated into effective demand because of a lack of market-based entitlement and shortage of purchasing power . . . . Viewed from the entitlement angle there is nothing extraordinary in the market mechanism taking food away from famine-stricken areas to elsewhere. Market demands are not reflections of biological needs or psychological desires, but choices based on exchange entitlement relations. If one doesn't have much to exchange, one can't demand very much, and may thus lose out in competition with others whose needs may be a good deal less acute, but whose entitlements are stronger.[3]

The theory of entitlements has been examined by Robert Nozick.[4] He argues that a determination of the justice of an initial endowment depends on historical considerations. Nozick follows Locke in arguing that any initial appropriation of property by an individual is just, provided that it 'does not worsen the situation of others'.[5] Yet in many developing countries the pattern of appropriation of the most important physical asset – land – has been a *fait accompli* for many decades. Thus the people born in recent years neither have any 'unowned objects' (in Locke's sense) to appropriate nor have they any *legal* claims on the unearned wealth (e.g. land) owned by the descendants of the original appropriators. It is not surprising then that Sen concludes *Poverty and Famines* as follows:

> The focus on entitlement has the effect of emphasizing legal rights. Other relevant factors, for example market forces, can be seen as operating *through* a system of legal relations (ownership rights, contractual obligations, legal exchanges, etc.). The law stands between food availability and food entitlement. Starvation deaths can reflect legality with a vengeance.[6]

The dilemma posed by the obstacle of existing legal 'rules' in the promotion of justice has recently been addressed by Ronald Dworkin.[7] The classical economists, however, also recognized the nature of the problem. John Stuart Mill, for example, argued that 'society is fully entitled to abrogate or alter any particular right of property which on sufficient consideration it judges to stand in the way of the public good'.[8] Karl Marx was less concerned with justifying the transformation of institutions (the relations of production) in terms of ethical criteria. He argued that the requirements of sustained economic growth would eventually result in a rearrangement of the institutions in a country. Thus the implication of Mill's and Marx's arguments for a poor country are similar: the prevailing legal arrangements governing property rights may have to be altered if a just pattern of growth is to be promoted and sustained.

In China the Communist Party, with the support of the poor peasants (70 per cent of the rural population), confiscated the land of the landlords and much of the land of the rich peasants and redistributed it to the poor peasants. Clearly, formal legal rules were 'abrogated' in the process. Yet within a few years the pattern of land ownership which had prevailed for centuries was altered and the 'initial endowments' of the majority of peasants were substantially improved. Although the land redistribution in rural China changed fundamentally the social fabric of the countryside the existing 'initial conditions' (e.g. the high man–land ratio, the fragmentation of landholdings, the low level of agricultural productivity and of per capita income, the income elastic demand for food grains, etc.) left unresolved some important problems concerning economic growth. The new government had still to determine an appropriate organization of rural production.

How should such organizations be structured? In Chapter 1 I discussed this question in general terms by drawing from diverse strands in the economics literature. The object was to construct a framework with which to analyse the Chinese experience. I argued that the problem of organizational structure involves the determination of appropriate work relations of production. This is an important issue. For just as inappropriate ownership relations can impede development, so too can inappropriate work relations impede growth.

In this book I have argued that economic growth depends upon investment. A useful interpretation of investment is to see it as the cost of change, or as 'a present sacrifice of consumption in the hope of subsequent gain'. It has been argued that co-operative organizations can under certain conditions facilitate a sacrifice of present consumption by its members. I suggested that a member's attitude toward investment and growth would therefore depend upon his cost–benefit valuation of the structure, the incentive system and the investment programme of the organization.

The empirical findings in this book support the view that investment and growth depend in an important sense upon an individual's perception of these aspects of the organization. In the microeconomic case-studies in Chapters 4 and 5 I found that economic growth at Wu Gong and Cheng Dong Communes was accompained by steady increase in the accumulation–distribution ratios over time. A similar result was obtained from the data for all the communes in Hebei Province and in Jia Ding County. The industrial 'sector' of the commune organization was an increasingly important source of accumulation. That is, the industrial 'sector' accounted for a large share of the available surplus within the commune. Moreover, a large share of the industrial surplus was allocated to accumulation.

An important reason for the decision by the government in 1957–8 to establish commune organizations in the countryside was the need to promote rural industry. There was much logic behind this policy. Indeed, the rate of accumulation in China's rural communes has in recent years been very rapid. Between 1965 and 1979, for example, the average annual rate of growth in China's rural communes was 13.3 per cent.[8] This is a very impressive rate of growth and, to a large extent, it can be attributed to the growth of commune industry.

In the empirical study in Chapter 4 one could see that a large share of commune agricultural investment (e.g. funds for the purchasing of technical inputs) was derived from commune industrial accumulation. I suggested that such patterns of investment allocation should have an important effect on the attitudes of the commune members (most of whom are engaged in agricultural production at the level of the production team) and, hence, on their willingness to sacrifice present consumption in the hope of future gain.

Another important share of accumulation funds in the 'case-study' communes was allocated to investments in health and education services for commune members. Such services provide 'basic needs' for members. The consumption of such services over time, therefore, constitutes an important part of the 'future benefits' obtained from the decisions to sacrifice present consumption. Thus, the expectation of 'capturing' such benefits could have a substantial effect on an individual member's valuation of the commune's investment programme. I did not have data from the case-study communes to examine the flows of such 'basic needs' services over time. However, macroeconomic data indicating levels of health and education attainment in China are now available. Moreover these data allow one to compare indicators of Chinese health and education levels with corresponding levels attained in other developing countries. In Table 9.1, for example, data comparing recent

TABLE 9.1 *Comparison of Indicators of Educational Levels in China with Selected Developing Countries, 1960–81*

Country	*Number enrolled in primary school as percentage of age group (6–11)*		*Number enrolled in secondary school as percentage of age group (12–17)*		*Literacy rate (1981)*[a]
	1960	*1981*	*1960*	*1981*	
China	109	118	21	44	69
India	61	79	20	30	36
Indonesia	71	100	6	30	62
Pakistan	30	56	11	17	24
Bangladesh	17	35	8	15	26
Low-income countries	80	94	18	34	40
Middle-income countries	75	102	14	41	65

SOURCE World Bank, *World Development Report* (1984) p. 266; (1981) p. 178.
[a] The literacy rate is the percentage of persons aged 15 and over who can read and write.

indicators of education in China with indicators in India, Indonesia, Pakistan, Bangladesh and the low-income and middle-income countries as groups are shown. In China all of the children aged 6 to 11 are enrolled in primary schools and 44 per cent of children aged 12 to 17 are enrolled in secondary schools. These levels of education are substantially higher than the average of the low-income countries (94 per cent and 34 per cent respectively). Indeed, a higher percentage of children are enrolled in secondary schools in China than in the average for the middle-income countries. Moreover the literacy rate in China in 1981 was 69 per cent compared to 36 per cent in India, 24 per cent in Pakistan, 26 per cent in Bangladesh, 40 per cent in the 'average' low-income country and 65 per cent in the 'average' middle-income country.

The data in Table 9.2 show a comparison of health-related indicators in China with corresponding indicators for the same group of countries. These data are particularly interesting because they show the rapid progress over time in the provision of health care in China. Between 1960 and 1980 the ratio of population to physician and to nursing person declined rapidly in China. In absolute terms this ratio in 1980 was substantially lower than in all the other countries, including the averages for the middle-income countries. The data also show that from 1950 to 1982 life expectancy at birth in China increased from 36 years to 67 years.

TABLE 9.2 *Comparison of Health-related Indicators in China and Corresponding Indicators in Selected Developing Countries, 1950–80*

Country	*Population per:* Physician 1960	Physician 1980	Nursing person 1960	Nursing person 1980	*Life expectancy at birth* 1950	1982	*Infant mortality rate*[b] *(aged 0–1)* 1960	1982	*Daily per capita calorie supply* Total 1981	As percentage of requirement[c] 1981
China	8 390	1 810	4 050	1 790	36	67	165	67	2 526	107
India	4 850	3 690	9 630	5 460	38	54	165	94	1 906	86
Indonesia	46 780	11 530	4 510	2 300	35	53	150	102	2 342	110
Pakistan	5 400	3 480	16 960	5 820	43[d]	50	162	121	2 313	106
Bangladesh	–	10 940	–	24 450	43[d]	49	159	133	1 952	84
Low-income countries	37 092	15 931	9 759	9 716	37[a]	51	163	114	2 082	91
Middle-income countries	10 430	5 414	3 838	1 886	48	60	126	76	2 607	111

SOURCE World Bank, *World Development Report* (1984) pp. 262 and 264

[a] This datum includes China and India.

[b] These data refer to the number of infants who die before reaching 1 year of age per 1000 live births in a given year.

[c] The daily calorie requirement per capita refers to the calories needed to sustain a person at normal levels of activity and health, taking into account age and sex distributions, average body weights and environmental temperatures.

[d] These data refer to 1960.

The average low-income country, by contrast, started at about the same level in 1950, but, by 1982, had improved life expectancy to only 51 years. Indeed, the average middle-income country started higher than China (48), but ended lower (60). The infant mortality rate in China in 1982 was also substantially lower (67 per thousand) than the corresponding rate in India (94 per thousand), in Bangladesh (133 per thousand) and in Indonesia (102 per thousand).

These data suggest that China's rural organizations have been remarkably successful in providing health and educational services to their members. China's success is all the more impressive when compared to corresponding indicators for other developing countries. The World Bank commented on these (and other) comparative data as follows:

> China's most remarkable achievement during the past three decades has been to make the low-income groups far better off in terms of basic needs than their counterparts in most other poor countries. They all have work; their food supply is guaranteed through a mixture of state rationing and collective self-insurance; most of their chldren are not only at school but are also being comparatively well taught; and the great majority have access to basic health care and family planning services. Life expectancy – whose dependence on many other economic and social variables makes it probably the best single indicator of the extent of real poverty in a country – is (at 67 years) outstandingly high for a country at China's per capita income level.[9]

Throughout this book I have argued that the members of China's rural organizations have perhaps been inclined to sacrifice present consumption in order to receive for themselves and their families a 'stream' of future benefits. The data presented above enable one to determine the composition of an important part of this 'stream' of benefits. The provision of health and educational services, shelter and a basic level of food are, after all, very important components of the well-being of a poor peasant family. The attainment of a high level of these basic needs in rural China is thus an important reflection of the *pattern* of economic growth. By participating in the decisions involving the determination of the investment programme the members of the organizations have, in effect, contributed to the determination of that pattern of growth.

Another important characteristic of the pattern of economic growth is the distribution of the flow of income from that growth. The empirical findings in Chapters 6 and 7 indicated that the commune organization promoted a low level of inequality among its collective units in the distribution of income within specific regions. The evidence also indicated that the structure of the collective organizations and the policies which operate within them have led to a narrowing over time in the distribution of rural income at local levels. At the same time I presented evidence which suggested that considerable inequality remains, particularly among households in different regions. Differentials of 1:13 were observed among households in two different regions and it is therefore likely that on a national scale a substantial level of inequality still persists. Whether the effects of the recent policies will lead to a widening in distribution of income remains to be seen. So far the effects appear to be neutral. As the more entrepreneurial peasants prosper, however, the distribution could begin to widen. Yet the government has indicated that it might use macroeconomic policies (such as a personal income tax) in order to control such tendencies, should they emerge.

The distribution of income and wealth in capitalist countries is determined in part through the price system. Payments are made through the price system to the owners of factors of production. To an important extent this distributive function of the price system has been subsumed in rural China by the democratic procedures of the production organizations. Yet a price system also has an allocative function – to convey scarcity and preference information. I argued in Chapter 8 that the allocative role of prices has to an important extent been 'negated' in contemporary China. It was perhaps thought that the allocative function of the market mechanism could be undertaken by central planning and resources could be allocated mainly by administrative methods.

The allocative efficiency of a socialist economy has long been the subject of debate among economists. Challenges were first raised by Mises, Hayek and Robbins.[10] Mises argued that private ownership of the means of production is indispensable for a rational allocation of resources: without such a pattern of ownership efficient choices between competing alternatives cannot be made. Taylor, Lerner, Lange and others followed Barone in demonstrating how shadow prices could be determined for the valuation of capital goods and, consequently, how efficient choices could be made in a socialist economy.[11] Hayek and Robbins subsequently conceded the theoretical possibility of obtaining an efficient allocation of resources in a socialist economy; they doubted, however, that a satisfactory organizational solution to the problem could be found. Yet the 'concession' by Hayek and Robbins was important because it implied that the fundamental feature of the market mechanism is the allocative efficiency of the price system and not the specific pattern of ownership of property.

Nevertheless the debate over the organizational efficacy of a socialist economy has continued to this day. In China the operation of an effective price system for allocating resources has been inhibited by dogma and by ideological disputation among the leadership. Recent Chinese proposals, however, envisage the use of a 'regulated' market mechanism in the economy. The central government would make only 'strategic' macroeconomic decisions involving the approximate rate of growth of national income, the distribution of central investment funds between sectors, the main investment trends for heavy industry and the determination of output targets of the most important commodities in the economy. The rest of the economy, comprising production organizations and households, would operate with considerable autonomy and should 'communicate' with each other and with the central government via the market. The market is 'regulated' in the sense that the central government can 'influence' the allocation of resources through parametric value planning.

Whether such an economic system will evolve in China remains to be seen. A prerequisite for the implementation of such a system is the decentralization of economic decision-making. This, in turn, involves a transfer of power from the state government to the collective organizations. Włodzimierz Brus has argued eloquently that such a real transfer of power, and the consequent efficiency of a socialist economy, will ultimately depend upon the extent to which genuine democracy operates within the system.[12] This view was emphasized in China in a recent article by Jiang Yiwei entitled 'The Theory of an Enterprise-Based Economy'. Jiang argued that:

> economic democracy is the basis of political democracy. A major defect in China's existing economic structure is the excessive concentration of power . . . . In fact, this is an inevitable result of managing the whole national economy as a single 'big enterprise'.[13]

Jiang suggests that a transfer of decision-making power from the central government to the production organizations would, under certain conditions, improve the efficiency of the economy:

> This is a question of who wields power in an enterprise . . . an enterprise should be a body controlled by all its workers and staff

> members. The key to applying this principle lies in establishing and perfecting a system of democratic management.[14]

Economic growth, if it is to be sustained, must ultimately depend upon an efficient allocation of resources throughout China's economy. Production organizations must 'communicate' with each other and with the government through the language of an accurate price system. It is difficult to imagine how resources can be allocated efficiently without a proper transmission of scarcity and preference information. This is perhaps a bitter pill for the Communist Party and the state bureaucracy to swallow – since a substantial transfer of decision-making power to the production organizations is required for an efficient price system to operate in the economy.

It is hard, then, to escape the conclusion that the achievement of sustained economic growth and development depends as much upon genuine democracy at national political levels as it does upon democracy operating at the level of the collective organizations. In Włodzimierz Brus's words the achievement of national political democracy in a socialist country requires that:

> A fundamental change is necessary – from totalitarian dictatorship, unrestricted monopoly and uncontrolled power in the hands of a narrow leading elite, to effective dependence of government on society, i.e. the creation of a mechanism which permits legal questioning, modification and ultimately rejection of government policy and its replacement by a different policy enjoying the support of the majority. Effective dependence of government on society or – to formulate the same point in a different way – effective social control over government assumes real freedom of speech, freedom of association, the rule of law and, above all, the necessity of periodically seeking a social mandate for power by way of elections in which there are both personal and political alternatives. This is equivalent to allowing, on the basis of socialism, centres of political initiative which are independent of the government, and thus, to call things by their proper names, legal forms of opposition.[15]

Yet John Stuart Mill believed that true national democracy and macro-economic efficiency will ultimately depend upon the proper practice of democracy in organizations. If this is so then China's rural organizations have perhaps established an important foundation for the achievement of sustained growth and development and for the promotion of national democracy.

Notes and References

INTRODUCTION

1. G. Meier (1976) pp.1 and 5.

1 AN ORGANIZATIONAL APPROACH TO GROWTH

1. See, for example, M. Scott (1980); C. Kennedy and A. Thirlwall (1972); A. Heertje (1977).
2. For a good summary and discussion of equilibrium growth theory see A. Dixit (1976).
3. See, for example, M. Scott (1980); C. Kennedy and A. Thirlwall (1972); W. A. Eltis (1973).
4. R. Solow (1957).
5. B. Massel (1961); M. Abromowitz (1956); S. Fabricant (1959).
6. D. Jorgenson and Z. Griliches (1967) p. 271.
7. Ibid. p. 274.
8. Ibid. p. 272. In Denison's reply he attacked methodological errors in Jorgenson's and Griliches's article. See E. F. Denison (1969).
9. P. Chinloy (1980); W. Waldorf (1973).
10. S. Star (1974).
11. Ibid. p. 134. Emphasis in original.
12. M. Scott (1980); M. Scott (1976); R. Nelson (1964); R. Nelson and S. Winter (1974); R. Nelson (1973); R. Nelson (1980); and R. Nelson (1981).
13. R. Nelson (1973) p. 465. Emphasis added.
14. C. Kennedy and A. Thirlwall (1972) p.19.
15. R. Nelson and S. Winter (1974).
16. Ibid. p. 886.
17. W. Nordhaus and J. Tobin (1972) p. 2.
18. R. Nelson (1980) p. 62. Emphasis in original.
19. A. Heertje (1977) pp. 205–6.
20. R. Nelson and S. Winter (1974) p. 903.
21. J. Schumpeter (1934).
22. Ibid. p. 68.
23. M. Scott (1976) p. 317.
24. Ibid. p. 318. Emphasis in original.
25. K. Arrow (1974) p. 16.

26. J. R. Commons (1970) p. 34.
27. J. Mirrlees (1976) p. 131. See also R. Radner (1972).
28. See, for example, O. E. Williamson (1973); and A. Alchian and H. Demsetz (1972).
29. See M. Spence (1973), and G. Akerlof (1970).
30. J. Stiglitz (1975) p. 576.
31. R. Radner (1972); J. Stiglitz, ibid.; A. Alchian and H. Demsetz (1972); O.Williamson (1975).
32. P. Steer and J. Cable (1978); and H. Armour and O. Teece (1978).
33. M. Olson (1965).
34. See, for example, the survey article by H. Leibenstein (1979).
35. *The Times*, 16 Oct 1981.
36. H. Arnold, M. Evans, R. House (1980).
37. Ibid. p. 135.
38. Ibid. p. 137.
39. Ibid. p. 139.
40. H. Simon (1978). See also H. Simon (1959).
41. A. Sen (1979b).
42. C. Pateman (1970) p. 43.
43. J.-J. Rousseau, *The Social Contract* (1963).
44. Ibid. p. 41.
45. C. Pateman (1970) p. 27.
46. J.-J. Rousseau (1963) p. 387.
47. J. S. Mill, in G. Himmelfarb (ed.) (1963) p. 186.
48. J. S. Mill (1909) pp. 760–1.
49. Ibid. pp. 772–3.
50. Ibid. p. 761.
51. Ibid. pp. 778–9.
52. Ibid. pp. 789–90.
53. Ibid. p. 792.
54. Ibid. pp. 792–3.
55. K. Marx (1969 and 1970) vol. I, p. 159.
56. See G. A. Cohen (1978).
57. See K. Marx (1904).
58. Organization of Economic Co-operation and Development (1976) p. 32.
59. Ibid. pp. 35–6.
60. Ibid. p. 32, Emphasis in original.
61. J. Gäbler (1977) p. 58.
62. See, for example, A. Ingham (1977). For an application of this approach to agriculture see, for example, S. Cheung (1969).
63. OECD (1976) p. 61.
64. J. Schumpeter (1970) p. 167.
65. W. Brus (1975) p. 186.
66. See, for example, Oscar Lange (1970).
67. W. Brus (1975) p. 27.
68. Ibid. p. 27.
69. Ibid. p. 30.
70. Ibid. p. 194.
71. O. Lange (1970) p. 135.

72. W. Brus (1975) pp. 72–3.
73. W. Brus (1973) pp. 77–8.
74. A. Sen (1979d) p. 192.
75. W. Brus (1972); W. Brus (1975).
76. M. Scott (1981) p. 213. For Kalecki's views see M. Kalecki (1972) Chap. 3 and 4. For Brus's view see W. Brus and K. Laski (1972).
77. S. Marglin (1963); A. Sen (1961).
78. A. Sen (1967) p. 114.
79. Ibid.
80. J.-J. Rousseau (1963); See also A. Sen and W. Runciman (1965).
81. W. Baumol (1952) p. 92.
82. J. S. Mill (1909) pp. 760–1.
83. B. Ward (1958); E. Domar (1966); J. Meade (1972).
84. J. Vanek (1969); J. Vanek (1970); B. Horvats (1975); J. Robinson (1967); D. Dubraucič (1970); W. Brus (1975) pp. 89–90; M. Schrenk (1981) pp. 55–9; R. McCain (1973); E. Furbotn (1973); and R. Carson (1977).
85. M. Schrenk, ibid.; C. Ardelan (1980). In Yugoslav enterprises today, extensive participation is promoted through the creation of basic organizations of associated labour (BOAL's) within the enterprise. A BOAL is often the smallest unit with a marketable output. Moreover, each enterprise in Yugoslavia has three overlaying aspects to its self-management: (i) professional 'operational' management; (ii) democratic self-management by BOAL members; and (iii) a social-political organization. All major enterprise decisions, especially personnel and distribution decisions, require consent by each BOAL.
86. M. Schrenk, op. cit. p. 57.
87. A. Steinherr (1978). For a survey of the literature on agricultural producer co-operatives see C. Obern and S. Jones (1981). For a survey of the literature on co-operatives in industrialized countries see D. Jones (1978).
88. J. Drèze (1976).
89. Ibid. p. 1127.
90. Ibid. p. 1138.
91. Ibid. p. 1137.
92. A. Steinherr (1977) p. 551.
93. A. Steinherr (1978) p. 551.
94. I shall not be concerned here with analysing the external environment (e.g. the operation of an economy-wide 'regulated' market mechanism, including an efficient price system; a limited, but important degree of central marcroeconomic co-ordination; and a substantial degree of political democracy at a national level). While these serious omissions will be addressed briefly in Chapters 8 and 9, they are not the central concerns of this book.

2 THE EMERGENCE OF THE RURAL ORGANIZATION

1. See *Selected Readings from the Works of Mao Zedong* (Peking: Foreign Languages Press, 1967) pp. 20–32.

2. See, for example, R. Ash (1976a); and D. Perkins, ed. (1975a).
3. R. Ash (1976a) p. 1.
4. State Statistical Bureau (1960) p. 34.
5. P. Schran (1969) p. 26.
6. Ibid. p. 26.
7. 'Report of Land Reform Work in South Kiangs', *Sunan Ribae*, 1 Jan 1952. Cited in R. Ash (1976b) p. 528.
8. R. Ash (1976b) p. 539.
9. F. Schurmann (1968) p. 437.
10. Mao Zedong, 'Request for Opinions on the Tactics for Dealing with Rich Peasants', Mar 1950, *Selected Works*, vol. 5, op. cit. p. 24.
11. For discussions about the quality of Chinese data published in the 1950s see: K. Chao (1965); A. Eckstein (1961); Li Choh-ming (1962); Ta-Chung Liu and K. C. Yeh (1965); N. Chen (1967); and Thomas Wiens (1975). Thomas Wiens argues that 'Chinese statistics for the 1949–1957 period are on the whole internally consistent to the extent that we can disaggregate and that they are also reconcilable with statistics from the Republican period.' See T. Wiens, ibid. Peter Schran, who compared official Chinese data for the period with western estimates concludes: 'The official 1952–1957 data probably understate the level of grain production as well as that of agricultural production in general to minor degrees. But . . . they state the trends in production reasonably accurately.' Peter Schran (1969) p. 122.
12. T. T. Hsueh and P. W. Liu (1980).
13. Ibid. pp. 388–9.
14. Ibid. pp. 388–9.
15. Ibid. pp. 388–9.
16. Ibid. p. 394.
17. *Model Regulations for an Agricultural Producers' Cooperative* (Peking: Foreign Languages Press, 1976) p. 4.
18. *Model Regulations for an Advanced Agricultural Producers' Cooperative* (Peking: Foreign Languages Press, 1976) p. 2.
19. Ibid. pp. 24–5.
20. Ibid. p. 25.
21. Ibid. p. 26.
22. C. Riskin (1971) p. 251.
23. R. Kojima (1967) pp. 55 and 59.
24. Liu Shaoqi (1956) p. 431.
25. Editorial, *People's Daily*, 14 Jan 1957.
26. Editorial, *People's Daily*, 3 Jan 1957.
27. Peking Home Radio Service, 2 Feb 1957, in British Broadcasting Company, *Summary of World Broadcasts* (*SWB*), Economic Supplement, 1–7, Feb 1957.
28. NCNA, 30 Sep 1958.
29. Central Committee, CCP, 'Resolution on Some Questions Concerning the People's Communes' (1958) p. 123.
30. *Gongren Ribao*, 8 Sep 1958, cited in G. Dutt (1967) p. 36.
31. K. Walker (1968) p. 445.
32. J. Dömes (1980) p. 37.
33. Ibid. p. 38.

34. Central Committee, CCP, 'Resolution on Some Questions Concerning the Communes' (1958) p. 136.
35. K. Walker (1968) p. 445.
36. A. Tang and B. Stone (1980) table 3, p. 26.
37. *Kung-tso Tung-hsun*, no. 6 (27 Jan 1961) pp. 6–7. Cited in B. Ahn (1975) p. 635.
38. We shall discuss the private sector of the rural economy in detail in Chapter 8.
39. Cited in G. Dutt (1967) pp. 108–9.
40. Central Committee, CCP (1962) pp. 695–725.
41. Ibid. pp. 704–15. Selected excerpts from Articles 20–38.
42. F. Crook (1975) p. 373.
43. G. William Skinner (1964) p. 394

3 ANALYSIS OF THE RURAL ORGANIZATION

1. A. Smith (1947) p. 115. Referring to farming, Smith further argued that 'After what are called the Fine Arts, and the liberal professions, there is perhaps no trade which requires so great a variety of knowledge and experience.' Ibid. p. 114.
2. See the discussion of this comparison by K. Wittfogel (1971) p. 12. See also N. Georgescu-Roegen (1969).
3. K. Marx, *Capital*, vol 1 (Harmondsworth: Penguin Books, 1976). See especially, section 10 on 'Large-scale Industry and Agriculture', pp. 636–9.
4. K. Wittfogel (1971) p. 15.
5. F. Engels, as cited in ibid. p. 12.
6. K. Kautsky (1899) p. 298.
7. L. Trotsky (1969) p. 63.
8. Ibid. p. 65.
9. Ibid. p. 102.
10. See, for example, V. I. Lenin (1963) pp. 428 and 326–7.
11. N. Jasny (1949).
12. Mao Zedong, *Selected Works* (1977) vol. 3, p. 156. Emphasis added.
13. Mao Zedong (1980) p. 134.
14. Mao Zedong, 'On the Cooperative Transformation of Agriculture', *Selected Works* (1977) vol. 5, p. 190.
15. See, for example, R. Myers (1975); and John Wong (1971).
16. See, for example, S. Goya (1966); and D. Pfanner (1969).
17. A. Tang and B. Stone (1980) p. 31.
18. F. Schurmann (1968) p. 454.
19. Central Committee, CCP (1956) pp. 411–12.
20. Ibid. p. 420.
21. Deng Zuwei, as quoted in F. Schurmann (1968) p. 204, note 30. Schurmann argues that Chen Yun supported Deng's position at the Third Plenary Session.
22. Central Committee, CCP (1957) pp. 500, 501.

23. Central Committee, CCP, 'Directive of the Central Committee of the CCP to Improve Agricultural Producer Cooperatives' Administration of Production', in ibid. pp. 505–6.
24. Ibid. pp. 508–9.
25. J. Stiglitz (1975).
26. Ibid. p. 576.
27. R. Radner (1972); J. Stiglitz, ibid.; A. Alchian and H. Demsetz (1972); O. Williamson (1973). See also J. Mirrlees (1976).
28. P. Steer and J. Cable (1978); H. Armour and D. Teece (1978).
29. J. Stiglitz (1975) p. 558, note 10.
30. The first models of decision-making and labour allocation in a producers' co-operative were developed by Benjamin Ward (1958); Evsey Domar (1966); Jaroslav Vanek (1969); and Amartya Sen (1966). A private sector was introduced into the framework by Walter Oi and Elizabeth Clayton (1968); and the model was elaborated more formally by Michael Bradley (1971) and by Norman Cameron (1973). The household's optimal allocation of labour between the collective sector, the private sector and leisure under conditions of uncertainty was developed by John Bonin (1977). Recent extensions in the Chinese context were developed by Dennis Chinn (1979) and (1980a); and in the Tanzanian context by Louis Putterman (1981).
31. L. Putterman, ibid. p. 384.
32. A. Sen (1966).
33. L. Putterman (1981) p. 388.
34. J. Schumpeter (1950) p. 68.
35. American Small-Scale Industry Delegation (1977) p. 71.
36. H. Chenery (1975).
37. See, for example, D. Wheeler (1980).
38. P. Streeten (1979); I. Adelman and C. Morris (1973); K. Griffin (1978).
39. D. Wheeler (1980) p. 436.
40. M. Lockeed, D. Jameson and L. Lau (1980). See also C. Colclough (1980).
41. M. Lockeed, D. Jameson and L. Lau, ibid.
42. Central Committee, CCP (1962) p. 713.
43. Ibid. p. 712.
44. Ibid. p. 696.
45. Ibid. p. 696.

4 A CASE-STUDY OF AGRICULTURAL GROWTH

1. The countries were Burma, Sri Lanka, Taiwan, Malaysia, India, Japan, South Korea, Pakistan, Philippines, Thailand and China.
2. S. Ishikawa (1967a) p. 108.
3. In June 1979 a delegation of six Oxford economists visited Wu Gong Commune in Hebei Province. During the visit we attended a series of meetings with leaders and accountants from the commune level, the brigade level and the team level. All of the data which follow in this chapter were obtained during this visit.

4. See, for example, S. Ishikawa (1967a); Y. Hayami, V. Ruttan and H. Southworth (1979); Y. Hayami and V. Ruttan (1971).
5. The data series and methodology for this regression analysis are from M. S. Marshall (D. Phil. thesis, Oxford, 1982) table 6.4.
6. These are unfortunately the only three years in which data on workpoint claims are available.

5 A CASE-STUDY OF RURAL INDUSTRIAL GROWTH

1. The Oxford delegation of economists visited Cheng Dong Commune in June 1979. The data which follow in this chapter were obtained in the meetings held there (and in Wu Gong Commune) with commune officials.
2. The time-series data for Cheng Dong cover only the period 1972–8. All data are totals for all enterprises at each level.
3. I shall assume that 'team activity' refers only to agriculture. While some teams do engage in very limited industrial production the data do not permit such disaggregation. Thus, the figures for team-level activity might overstate slightly the importance of agriculture.
4. In 1978 Cheng Dong established three brigades as 'accounting units'. In so doing the teams in the brigade are eliminated as accounting units. Thus all figures for these so-called 'transitional brigades' include some industrial activity and some agricultural activity. I shall assume that half of the income from these brigades derives from the activities of each sector.
5. See M. S. Marshall (1982) chaps 5, 9 and 10.

6 THE PRIVATE SECTOR IN THE RURAL ORGANIZATION

1. Central Committee of the CCP (1962) p. 715. The data in this chapter were collected during a field trip to China in June 1979. These data were supplied by officials and accountants at the provincial, county, brigade and team level. The data in this section and in the next section refer only to the distributed component of collective income.
2. Central Committee of the CCP (1978) p. 111.
3. S. J. Burki (1965) p. 38; F. Crook (1975) p. 403.
4. Central Committee of the CCP (1962) p. 715.
5. New China News Agency, in *SWB*, FE/6467/B11, p. 13, 26 July 1980.
6. Editorial, *People's Daily*, 11 May 1981, p. 1, in *SWB*, FE/6724/B11, p. 3, 15 May 1981.
7. New China News Agency, 22 July 1980, in *SWB*, FE/6481/B11, p. 13, 26 July 1980.
8. Interview with Wu Chun-Cheng, Deputy Head of People's Commune Section of the Hebei Provincial Office of Agriculture and Forestry, 19 June 1979; interview with Tang Tang Commune Management Committee

members, Guangdong Province, 26 June 1979; interview with Cheng Dong Commune Management Committee officials, Jia Ding County, Shanghai Municipality, 23 June 1979.
9. New China News Agency Chinese Service, 22 Apr 1980, in *SWB*, FE/6411/B11, p. 11, 3 May 1980.
10. Central Committee of the CCP (1962) p. 716.
11. New China News Agency, 27 Sep 1979.
12. Central Committee of the CCP (1978) pp. 110–11.
13. Central Committee of the CCP (1978) p. 105.
14. Interview with Tang Tang Commune officials, op. cit.
15. Interview with Li Siang Family in Qie Ma Commune, Hebei Province, June 1979. At this commune the sale of one pig to the state yields 90 yuan, 80 jin of maize and 40 jin of chemical fertilizer.
16. *People's Daily*, 11 Aug 1977, p. 2. In Hunan Province a Foodstuffs station has organized a laboratory to produce ampules, tablets and powder from medicinal herbs for the treatment of sick pigs, as well as earmarking 140 000 yuan to 'improve and purify the Liu shu-ho good-breed pigs'. Ibid. p. 2.
17. Shaanxi Provincial CCP Committee, Peking Home Service, in *SWB*, FE/6467/B11, p. 11.
18. NCNA Chinese Service, in *SWB*, FE/6467/B11, p. 3, 10 July 1980.
19. NCNA Daily Report, 9 Mar 1980, p. 7.
20. Inner Mongolia Regional Service, 9 July 1980, in *SWB*, FE/6474/B11, p. 2, 18 July 1980.
21. NCNA, 19 July 1980, in *SWB*, FE/6478/B11, p. 5, 23 July 1980.
22. Editorial, *Gongren Ribao*, 'The General Key to Solving Problems of Work', 27 June 1980, in *SWB*, FE/6471/C, p. 5, 15 July 1980.
23. Guangdong Provincial Radio Service, 9 June 1980, in *SWB*, FE/*1088/A, p. 1, 25 June 1980.
24. G. William Skinner (1964).
25. Central Committee of the CCP (1962) p. 716.
26. Ho Zhen and Wei Wen (1962) pp. 11–15.
27. Peking Home Radio Service, 'Lectures on the Commune: Village Fairs and Commune Management', in *SWB*, FE/6111/B11, pp. 1–2.
28. Central Committee of the CCP (1978) p. 112.
29. Peking Home Radio Service, 'Lectures on the Commune', op. cit. p. 1.
30. Ibid. p. 2.
31. NCNA, 8 May 1981, in *SWB*, FE/W1134/A/p. 9, 20 May 1981.
32. Ibid. p. 9.
33. Liu Jihan and Yi Fahai (1978).
34. These interviews were conducted in June 1979 with the assistance of Wang Gengjin, Vice-Director of the Institute of Agricultural Economics, Chinese Academy of Social Science.
35. S. J. Burki (1965), p. 40; J. Deleyne, (1978), p. 23; G. Etienne (ed.) (1974); T. Rawski (1979) p. 78; M. Whyte and W. Parrish (1978) p. 365.
36. F. Crook (1975) p. 404.
37. Editorial, *Sichuan Ribao*, 29 Jan 1980, in *SWB*, FE/6351/B11, p. 17, Feb 1980.
38. Guo Zhaoren and Wang Wenjun, *People's Daily*, 15 Dec 1979, in *SWB*, FE/6305/B11, pp. 7–8, 28 Dec 1979.

39. Jilin Provincial Radio Service, 5 May 1980, in *SWB*, FE/6421/B11, p. 8, 16 May 1980.
40. Ibid. p. 8.
41. Editorial, *People's Daily*, 11 May 1981, in *SWB*, FE/6724/B11, p. 2, 15 May 1981.
42. Central Committee, CCP (1979) p. 6.
43. See, for example, K. Griffin (ed.) (1984).

7 THE DISTRIBUTION OF RURAL INCOME

1. The data which follow in this and the next section were collected during a field trip to China in June 1979.
2. New China News Agency, 2 Jan 1981, p. 5.
3. Central Committee, CCP (1962) p. 720.
4. Central Committee, CCP (1978) pp. 110–11.
5. Ibid. pp. 110–11.
6. Central Committee, CCP (1978) p. 109.
7. Central Committee, CCP (1962) p. 717.
8. Article by Wu Ziang, *People's Daily*, 9 Apr 1980, in *SWB*, FE/6404/B11, p. 10.
9. This equation is reported in K. Griffin (1982). For details of the study see A. Ansell, R. Hay and K. Griffin (1982).
10. See K. Griffin (ed.) (1984) chap. 2.
11. *Beijing Review*, no. 18 (1984) p. 18.
12. *Beijing Review*, no. 27 (1984) p. 8.
13. Ibid. p. 8.
14. Kunming, Yunnan Provincial Service, 10 July 1984, in *SWB*, FE/W1297/A/p. 8, 25 July 1984.
15. *Beijing Review*, no. 18 (1984) p. 21.
16. Ibid.
17. K. Griffin (ed.) (1984) p. 102.

8 RURAL ECONOMIC PERFORMANCE, 1952–84

1. World Bank (1981) p. 62.
2. J. E. Nickum, *Hydraulic Engineering and Water Resources in the People's Republic of China* (Stanford, Calif., 1977). Cited in Thomas Rawski (1979) p. 111.
3. World Bank (1981) p. 4.
4. Yang Jianbai and Li Xuezheng (1980) p. 185.
5. World Bank (1981) p. 17.

6. Ibid.
7. Yang Jianbai and Li Xuezheng (1980) pp. 184 and 186.
8. M. S. Marshall (1979). An earlier draft of this paper was delivered at a seminar on Chinese politics at Stanford University in December 1975.
9. This argument was confirmed in an interview with Zheng Zhong, Vice-Minister of Agriculture, on 12 June 1979. A recent article in *Beijing Review* commented as follows: 'It was widely publicised that Dazhai never accepted any aid from the state. "It had built itself up." Not so. Between 1967 and 1977, the brigade got from the state 840 000 yuan, either in cash or in materials. The tiny village of Dazhai not only received enormous help in the form of material, funds and manpower from the state and various departments, but also at times sought assistance. . . . It is not unusual for the state and other departments to give help, but to falsely claim that no help at all was received and to create a "model" with funds and material and then expect others to emulate without the same access to funds and material is downright dishonest. Moreover, such a model cannot be very persuasive.' *Beijing Review*, no. 16, 20 Apr 1981, p. 25.
10. Xue Muqiao, *People's Daily*, 18 Oct 1978, as cited in J. Dömes (1980) p. 101.
11. Yao Wenhyuan, *Red Flag*, Mar 1975, p. 20, as cited in J. Dömes (1980) p. 83
12. Xu Xiyu, Jiangsu Provincial Service, 27 Feb 1971, as cited in J. Dömes (1980) p. 72.
13. Xue Muqiao (1981) p. x.
14. Ibid. p. 37.
15. Ibid. p. 181.
16. World Bank (1981) annex A, main report, p. 102.
17. Ibid.
18. Yang Jianbai and Li Xuezheng (1980) pp. 202–3.
19. Ibid. p. 205.
20. Cyril Lin (1985) chap. 2.
21. Ibid.
22. As cited in Cyril Lin (1981) p. 14.
23. Ibid. p. 15.
24. Ibid. pp. 18–19.
25. Yang Jianbai and Li Xuezheng (1980) pp. 207–8. See also an article by Sun Yefang where he makes the same point: Sun Yefang (1980).
26. Cyril Lin (1985), chap. 2, table 2.34.
27. Ibid.
28. Liu Guoguang and Wang Xiangming (1980) p. 27.
29. Ibid. p. 37.
30. Ibid.
31. Zhao Ziyang, Sichuan Provincial Radio Service, in BBC, *Summary of World Broadcasts (SWB)* FE/6038, 1979.
32. Ibid.
33. Ibid.
34. Central Committee, CCP, 'On some Questions Concerning the Acceleration of Agricultural Development', BBC, *SWB*, FE/6241/C1, pp. 4–5, 10 Oct 1979.
35. Ibid. p. 6.
36. See L. Travers (1984) p. 242.

37. Central Committee, CCP, 'Communique of the Third Plenary Session', *Peking Review*, no. 52, Dec 1978, p. 13.
38. Ibid. p. 13.
39. L. Travers, op. cit. p. 242.
40. Ibid.
41. J. Stiglitz (1975) p. 558, note 10.
42. *Beijing Review*, 27 Feb 1984, p. 16.
43. *Beijing Review*, 30 Apr 1984. p. 20.
44. Ibid. p. 20.
45. Ibid.
46. *Beijing Review*, 11 June 1984, p. 1.
47. *Beijing Review*, 30 Apr 1984, p. 18.
48. Ibid. pp. 19–20.
49. *Beijing Review*, 12 Mar 1984, p. 9.
50. Ibid.
51. Ibid.
52. J. S. Mill (1963) p. 186.
53. *Beijing Review*, 16 Apr 1984, p. 7.
54. BBC, *SWB*, July 1984, FE/W1298/A, p. 4.
55. *Beijing Review*, 16 Apr 1984, p. 7.
56. Xue Muqiao (1981) p. iv.
57. Tian Jianghai and Zhang Shuguang (1981) p. 49.
58. Editorial, *People's Daily*, 7 and 8 December 1984, p. 1. This quotation contains the correction published in *People's Daily* on 8 December 1984.

9 CONCLUSION

1. See, for example, K. Arrow and F. Hahn (1972) chap. 2.
2. A. Sen, *Poverty and Famines* (1981a) p. 159.
3. Ibid. p. 161.
4. R. Nozick (1980) chap. 7. See also R. Nozick (1973).
5. R. Nozick (1973) p. 75. Locke's theory is set out in section 27 of his *Two Treatises on Government*, ed. P. Laslett (1967).
6. A. Sen (1981a) pp. 165–6.
7. R. Dworkin (1977).
8. World Bank (1981) p. 58.
9. World Bank (1981a) p. 85.
10. See L. von Mises (1935), F. von Hayek (1935) and L. Robbins (1937).
11. See F. Taylor (1938), A. Lerner (1970), O. Lange (1938) and E. Barone (1935). See also G. Heal (1973).
12. W. Brus (1975) chap. 4.
13. Jiang Yiwei (1980) p. 64.
14. Ibid. pp. 69–70.
15. W. Brus (1975) p. 208.

Bibliography

Abramowitz, M. (1956) 'Resource and Output Trends in the United States since 1870', *American Economic Review*, May, pp. 5–23.

Adelman, I. and Morris, C. (1973) *Economic Growth and Social Equity in Developing Countries* (Stanford, Calif.: Stanford University Press).

Ahn, B. (1975) 'The People's Commune in China', *Journal of Asian Studies*, May, pp. 630–58.

Akerlof, G. (1970) 'The Market for Lemons', *Quarterly Journal of Economics*, Aug, pp. 488–500.

Alchian, A. and Demsetz, H. (1972) 'Production, Information Costs, and Economic Organization', *American Economic Review*, pp. 777–93.

American Small Scale Industry Delegation (1977) *Rural Small-scale Industry in the People's Republic of China* (Berkeley, Calif.: University of California Press).

Anderson, D. and Leiserson, M. (1980) 'Rural Nonfarm Employment in Developing Countries', *Economic Development and Cultural Change*, Jan, pp. 227–49.

Andors, S. (1977) *China's Industrial Revolution* (New York: Pantheon Books).

Ansell, A., Hay, R. and Griffin, K. (1982) 'Private Production and Income Distribution in a Chinese Commune', *Food Policy*, Feb, pp. 3–12.

Ardelan, C. (1980) 'Worker's Self-management and Planning: The Yugoslav Case', *World Development*, vol. 8, pp. 623–38.

Argyris, C. (1962) *Interpersonal Competence and Organizational Effectiveness* (Homewood, Ill.: Dorsey Press).

Armour, H. and Teece, D. (1978) 'Organizational Structure and Economic Performance: A Test of the "M" Hypothesis', *Bell Journal of Economics*, Spring, pp. 106–22.

Arnold, H., Evans, M. and House, R. (1980) 'Productivity: A Psychological Perspective', in S. Maital and N. Meltz (eds) *Lagging Productivity Growth* (New York: Harper & Row) pp. 131–81.

Arrow, K. (1951) *Social Choice and Individual Values* (New Haven, Conn.: Yale University Press).

Arrow, K. and Hahn, F. (1972) *General Competitive Analysis* (San Francisco: Holden Day).

Arrow, K. (1974) *The Limits of Organization* (New York: Norton).

Arrow, K. (1975) 'Vertical Integration and Communication', *Bell Journal of Economics*, Spring, pp. 173–83.

Arrow, K. (1979) 'Values and Collective Decision-making', in F. Hahn and M. Hollis (eds) *Philosophy and Economic Theory* (Oxford: Oxford University Press) pp. 110–26.

Ash, R. (1976a) *Land Tenure in Pre-Revolutionary China: Kiangsu Province in the 1920s and 1930s* (London: Contemporary China Institute).

Ash, R. (1976b) 'Economic Aspects of Land Reform in Kiangsu, 1949–52', *The China Quarterly*, June, pp. 261–92, and Sep, pp. 519–45.

Atkinson, A. B. (1973) 'Worker Management and the Modern Industrial Enterprise', *Quarterly Journal of Economics*, Aug, pp. 375–92.

Barone, E. (1935) 'The Ministry of Production in the Collectivist State', in F. Von Hayek (ed.) *Collectivist Economic Planning* (London: Routledge & Kegan Paul) pp. 247–90.

Baum, R. (1975) *Prelude to Revolution* (New York: Columbia University Press).

Baumol, W. (1952) *Welfare Economics and the Theory of the State* (Cambridge, Mass.: Harvard University Press).

Blau, P. (1981) 'Interdependence and Hierarchy in Organizations', in O. Grusky and G. Miller (eds) *The Sociology of Organizations* (New York: The Free Press) pp. 151–75.

Bonin, J. (1977) 'Work Incentives and Uncertainty on a Collective Farm', *Journal of Comparative Economics*, Mar, pp. 77–97.

Bradley, M. (1971) 'Incentives and Labour Supply on Soviet Collective Farms', *Canadian Journal of Economics*, vol. 4, pp. 342–52.

Bridgham, P. (1967) 'Mao's "Cultural Revolution" – Origin and Development', *China Quarterly*, no. 29, pp. 1–35.

British Broadcasting Corporation, *Summary of World Broadcasts*, Selected translations of Chinese newspaper and journal articles and Chinese radio programmes for various years. (Caversham: BBC).

Brus, W. and Laski, K. (1965) 'The Law of Value and the Problem of Allocation in Socialism', in *On Political Economy and Econometrics: Essays in Honour of Oscar Lange* (Warsaw: Polish Scientific Publishers) pp. 45–60.

Brus, W. and Laski, K. (1966) 'Growth with Full Employment of Productive Forces', in *Problems of Economic Dynamics and Planning: Essays in Honour of Michal Kalecki* (Warsaw: Polish Scientific Publishers) pp. 59–78.

Brus, W. and Laski, K. (1972) 'Problems in the Theory of Growth under Socialism', in A. Nove and M. Nuti (eds) *Socialist Economics* (Harmondsworth: Penguin Books) pp. 173–210.

Brus, W. (1972) *The Market in a Socialist Economy* (London: Routledge & Kegan Paul).

Brus, W. (1973) *The Economics and Politics of Socialism: Collected Essays* (London, Routledge & Kegan Paul).

Brus, W. (1975) *Socialist Ownership and Political Systems* (London: Routledge & Kegan Paul).

Buck, J. L. (1937) *Land Utilization in China* (Nanking: University of Nanking).

Buck, J. L., Dawson, O. and Wu, Y. (1966) *Food and Agriculture in Communist China* (London: Praeger).

Burki, S. (1965) *A Study of Chinese Communes* (Cambridge, Mass.: Harvard University Press).

Cameron, N. (1973) 'Incentives and Labour Supply in Cooperative Enterprises', *Canadian Journal of Economics*, vol. 6, pp. 16–23.

Carson, R. (1977) 'A Theory of Cooperatives', *Canadian Journal of Economics*, Feb, pp. 565–89.

Central Committee, Chinese Communist Party (1956) in Union Research

Institute, *Documents of the Chinese Communist Party Central Committee*, vol. 1 (Hong Kong: Union Research Institute).

Central Committee, Chinese Communist Party and State Council (1956) 'Joint Directive on Strengthening Production Leadership and Organizational Construction of Agricultural Producer Cooperatives', in R. Bowie and J. Fairbank (eds) *Communist China, 1955–59: Policy Documents* (Cambridge, Mass.: Harvard University Press, 1962) pp. 242–55.

Central Committee, Chinese Communist Party (1957), 'Directive of the CCP Central Committee to Overhaul Agricultural Producer Cooperatives', in Union Research Institute, *Documents of the Chinese Communist Party Central Committee* (Hong Kong: Union Research Institute, 1957) pp. 500–1.

Central Committee, Chinese Communist Party (1958) 'National Programme for Agricultural Development', in *Second Session of the Eighth National Congress of the Communist Party of China* (Peking: Foreign Languages Press) pp. 98–126.

Central Committee, Chinese Communist Party (1958) 'Resolution on Some Questions Concerning the People's Communes', in Union Research Institute, *Documents of Chinese Communist Party Central Committee* (Hong Kong: Union Research Institute, 1971) pp. 123–48.

Central Committee, Chinese Communist Party (1962) 'Regulations on the Work of the People's Commune', in Union Research Institute, *Documents of the Chinese Communist Party Central Committee* (Hong Kong: Union Research Institute, 1971) pp. 695–725.

Central Committee, Chinese Communist Party and State Council (1971) 'Decision to Launch a Campaign for Building Irrigation Projects', in Union Research Institute, *Documents of the Chinese Communist Party Central Committee* (Hong Kong: Union Research Institute) pp. 517–22.

Central Committee, Chinese Communist Party (1975) *Documents of the First Session of the Fourth National People's Congress of the People's Republic of China* (Peking: Foreign Languages Press).

Central Committee, Chinese Communist Party (1978a) 'Communique of the Third Plenum', *Beijing Review*, no. 52, 29 Dec.

Central Committee, Chinese Communist Party (1978) 'Regulations on the Work in the People's Communes', revised version, Dec 1978, in *Issues and Studies*, Aug 1979, pp. 100–12; and Sep 1979, pp. 104–12.

Central Committee, Chinese Communist Party (1979) 'On Some Questions Concerning the Acceleration of Agricultural Development', in British Broadcasting Corporation, *Summary of World Broadcasts* (FE/6241/C1), 10 Oct.

Central Committee, Chinese Communist Party (1980) *Main Documents of the Third Session of the Fifth National People's Congress of the People's Republic of China* (Peking: Foreign Languages Press).

Central Committee, Chinese Communist Party (1981) *Resoultion on CCP History* (Peking: Foreign Languages Press).

Chao, K. (1965) *The Rate and Pattern of Industrial Growth in Communist China* (Ann Arbor, Mich.: University of Michigan Press).

Chao, K. (1970) *Agricultural Production in Communist China, 1949–65* (Madison: University of Wisconsin Press).

Chao Kuo-Chun (1960) *Agrarian Policy of the Chinese Communist Party* (Bombay: Asia Publishing House).

Chen, E. (1976) 'The Empirical Relevance of the Endogenous Technical Progress Function', *Kyklos*, vol. 29, pp. 256–71.

Chen, E. (1977) 'Factor Inputs, Total Factor Productivity, and Economic Growth: the Asian Case', *The Developing Economies*, June, pp. 121–43.

Chen, N. (1967) *Chinese Economic Statistics* (Edinburgh: University of Edinburgh Press).

Chen Yun (1952) 'Agricultural Producers' Cooperatives of the Present Stage in China: High Level Forms of Mutual Aid', *Hsueh-hsi*, no. 4, pp. 28–32.

Chenery, H. (1975) *Redistribution with Growth* (London: Oxford University Press).

Cheung, S. (1969) *The Theory of Share Tenancy* (Chicago: University of Chicago Press).

Chinloy, P. (1980) 'Sources of Quality Change in Labour Input', *American Economic Review*, Mar, pp. 108–19.

Chinn, D. (1977) 'Land Utilization and Productivity in Pre-War Chinese Agriculture: Pre-Conditions for Collectivization', *American Journal of Agricultural Economics*, Aug, pp. 559–64.

Chinn, D. (1979) 'Team Cohesion and Collective Labour Supply in Chinese Agriculture', *Journal of Comparative Economics*, vol. 3, pp. 375–94.

Chinn, D. (1980) 'Cooperative Farming in North China', *Quarterly Journal of Economics*, Mar, pp. 279–97.

Chinn, D. (1980a) 'Diligence and Laziness in Chinese Production Teams', *Journal of Development Economics*, no. 7, pp. 331–44.

Cohen, G. A. (1978) *Karl Marx's Theory of History* (Oxford: Oxford University Press).

Colclough, C. (1980) *Primary Schooling and Economic Development* (World Bank: Staff Working Paper, no. 399), June.

Cole, G. D. H. (1919) *Self-Government in Industry* (London, Bell & Sons).

Commons, J. (1970) *The Economics of Collective Action* (Madison: University of Wisconsin Press).

Crook, F. (1975) 'The Commune System in the People's Republic of China, 1963–1974', in U.S. Congress, *China: A Reassessment of the Economy* (Washington, U.S. Government) pp. 366–411.

Croll, E. (1982) *The Chinese Household and Its Economy: Urban and Rural Survey Data* (Queen Elizabeth House, Contemporary China Centre, Oxford: Resource Paper).

Crouch, C. (1978) 'Inflation and the Political Organization of Economic Interests', in F. Hirsch and J. Goldthorpe (eds) *The Political Economy of Inflation* (London: Martin Robinson & Co.) pp. 217–39.

Cyert, R. and March, J. (1963) *A Behavioural Theory of the Firm* (Englewood Cliffs, N.J.: Prentice-Hall).

de Janvry, A. (1973) ' A Socioeconomic Model of Induced Innovations for Argentine Agricultural Development', *Quarterly Journal of Economics*, Aug, pp. 410–35.

Deleyne, J. (1978) *The Chinese Economy* (London: André Dutsch).

Denison, E. (1969) 'Some Major Issues in Productivity Analysis: An Examination of Estimates by Jorgenson and Griliches', *Survey of Current Business*, vol. 49, May (part II).

Dittmer, L. (1974) *Liu Shao-Ch'i and the Chinese Cultural Revolution* (Berkeley, Calif.: University of California Press).

Dixit, A. (1976) *The Theory of Equilibrium Growth* (London: Oxford University Press).

Dobb, M. (1933) 'Economic Theory and the Problems of a Socialist Economy', *Economic Journal*, pp. 588–98.

Dobrska, Z. (1963) 'The Choice of Techniques in Developing Countries', in M. Kalecki (ed.) *Essays on Planning and Economic Development*, vol. 1 (Warsaw: Polish Scientific Publishers) pp. 23–38.

Domar, E. (1966) 'The Soviet Collective Farm as a Producer Cooperative', *American Economic Review*, Sep, pp. 734–57.

Dömes, J. (1980) *Socialism in the Chinese Countryside* (London: Hurst & Co.).

Drèze, J. (1976) 'Some Theory of Labour-Management and Participation', *Econometrica*, vol. 44, pp. 1125–39.

Dubraucić, D. (1970), 'Labour as an Entrepreneurial Input: An Essay in the Theory of the Producer Cooperative Economy', *Economica*, Aug, pp. 297–310.

Dutt, G. (1967) *Rural Communes of China* (London: Asia Publishing House).

Dworkin, R. (1977) *Taking Rights Seriously* (London: Duckworth).

Eckstein, A. (1961) *The National Income of Communist China* (Glencoe, Ill.: The Free Press).

Ellman, M. (1979) *Socialist Planning* (Cambridge: Cambridge University Press).

Ellman, M. (1981) 'Agricultural Productivity Under Socialism', *World Development*, Sep, pp. 979–90.

Eltis, W. A. (1973) *Growth and Distribution* (London: Macmillan)

Elvin, M. (1969) *The Pattern of the Chinese Past* (Stanford, Calif.: Stanford University Press).

Etienne, G. (1974) *China's Agricultural Development* (Geneva: Asian Documentation and Research Centre).

Fabricant, S. (1959) *Basic Facts on Productivity Change* (New York: Columbia University Press).

Fel'dman, G. A. (1984) 'On the Theory of Growth Rates of National Income', in N. Spulber (ed.) *Foundations of Soviet Strategy for Economic Growth* (Bloomington, Ind.: University of Indiana Press) pp. 171–91, 304–31.

Fung, K. (1974) 'Output vs. 'Surplus' Maximization: the Conflicts between the Socialized and the Private Sector in Chinese Collectivized Agriculture', *The Developing Economies*, vol. 12, pp. 41–55.

Furubotn, E. (1973) 'The Long-Run Analysis of the Labour-Managed Firm: An Alternative Interpretaion', *American Economic Review*, Mar, pp. 104–123.

Gäbler, J. (1977) 'Participation and the Working of the Price Mechanism in a Market Economy', in D. Heathfield (ed.) *The Economics of Co-determination* (London: Macmillan) pp. 46–60.

Gao Zhihun (1980) 'What is the Best Economic Setup for China', *Social Sciences in China*, Mar, pp. 7–17.

Georgescu-Roegen, N. (1960) 'Economic Theory and Agrarian Economics', *Oxford Economic Papers*, Feb, pp. 1–40.

Georgescu-Roegen, N. (1969) 'Process in Farming versus Process in Manufacturing: A Problem of Balanced Development', in U. Papi and C. Nunn (eds) *Economic Problems of Agriculture in Industrial Societies* (London: Macmillan) pp. 497–528.

Griffin, K. (1978) *International Inequality and National Poverty* (London: Macmillan).

Griffin, K. and Saith, A. (1981) *Growth and Equality in Rural China* (Maruzen, for the International Labour Office).

Griffin, K. (1982) 'Economic Organization and Performance in Rural China', Magdalen College, Oxford, mimeo.

Griffin, K. (ed.) (1984) *Institutional Reform and Economic Development in the Chinese Countryside* (London: Macmillan).

Griffin, K. and Khan, A. (1978) 'Poverty in the Third World: Ugly Facts and Fancy Models', *World Development*, Mar, pp. 395–404.

Griliches, Z. (1964) 'Research Expenditures, Education, and the Aggregate Agricultural Production Function', *American Economic Review*, Dec, pp. 961–74.

Hawkins, C. (1977) 'Some Effects of Worker Participation and the Distribution of Income', in D. Heathfield (ed.) *The Economics of Co-Determination* (London: Macmillan) pp. 36–45.

Hayami, Y. and Ruttan, V. (1971) *Agricultural Development: An International Perspective* (Baltimore: Johns Hopkins Press).

Hayami, Y., Ruttan, V. and Southworth, H. (1979) *Agricultural Growth in Japan, Taiwan, Korea, and the Philippines* (Honolulu: University of Hawaii Press).

Hayek, F. Von (1935) 'The Nature and History of the Problem', Hayek, F. (ed.) *Collectivist Economic Planning* (London: Routledge & Kegan Paul) pp. 1–14.

Heal, G. (1973) *The Theory of Economic Planning* (Oxford: North-Holland Publishers).

Heertje, A. (1977) *Economics and Technical Change* (London: Weidenfeld & Nicolson).

Hirshleifer, J. and Riley, J. (1979) 'The Analytics of Uncertainty and Information – An Expository Survey', *Journal of Economics Literature*, Dec, pp. 1375–421.

Ho Zhen and Wei Wen (1962) 'On Village Trade Fairs', *Jingji Yenjiu*, no. 4, pp. 11–15.

Horvat, B. (1975) 'An Institutional Model of a Self-Managed Socialist Economy', in J. Vanek (ed.) *Self-Management, Economic Liberation of Man* (Harmondsworth: Penguin Books) pp. 127–44.

Horvat, B. (1980) 'Ethical Foundations of Self-Government', *Economic and Industrial Democracy*, Feb, pp. 1–21.

Horvat, B. (1981) 'Establishing Self-governing Socialism in a Less Developed Country', *World Development*, Sep, pp. 951–64.

Hseuh, T. and Liu, P. (1980) 'Collectivization of Chinese Agricultural Production, 1952–1957: A Land-Saving Organizational Change', *Journal of Comparative Economics*, no. 4, pp. 378–98.

Hu Qiaomu (1978) 'Observe Economic Laws, Speed Up the Four Modernizations', *Peking Review*, 10 Nov, pp. 7–12.

Hughes, T. and Luard, E. (1959) *The Economic Development of Communist China* (London: Oxford University Press).

Ingham, A. (1977) 'Participation and Risk', in D. Heathfield (ed.) *The Economics of Co-determination* (London: Macmillan) pp. 135–49.

Ishikawa, S. (1967a) *Economic Development in Asian Perspective* (Tokyo: Kinokuniya Bookstore Co.).

Ishikawa, S. (1967b) 'Resource Flow Between Agriculture and Industry', *The Developing Economies*, Mar, pp. 3–49.

Ishikawa, S. (1971) 'Changes in the Structure of Agricultural Production in Mainland China', in W. Jackson (ed.) *Agrarian Policies and Problems in Communist and Non-Communist Countries* (Seattle, Wash.: University of Washington Press) pp. 346–77.

Ishikawa, S. (1972) 'A Note on the Choice of Technology in China', *Journal of Development Studies*, Oct, pp. 161–86.

Jasny, N. (1949) *The Socialized Agriculture of the USSR* (Stanford, Calif.: Stanford University Press).

Jiang Yiwei (1980) 'The Theory of an Enterprise-Based Economy', *Social Sciences in China*, Mar, pp. 48–70.

Jin Dequn (1981) 'Criteria for Land Distribution During the Second Revolutionary Civil War', *Social Sciences in China*, Mar, pp. 55–67.

Johnston, B. and Kilby, P. (1975) *Agriculture and Structural Transformation* (London: Oxford University Press).

Jones, D. (1978) 'Producer Cooperatives in Industrialized Western Economies: An Overview', *Annals of Public and Cooperative Economy*, Apr, pp. 149–62.

Jones, H. (1975) *Modern Theories of Economic Growth* (London: Nelson).

Jorgenson, D. and Griliches, Z. (1967) 'The Explanation of Productivity Change', *Review of Economic Studies*, July, pp. 249–83.

Kalecki, M. (1967) 'The Difference Between Crucial Economic Problems of Developed and Underdeveloped Non-Socialist Economies', in M. Kalecki (ed.) *Essays on Planning and Economic Development*, vol. 3 (Warsaw: Polish Scientific Publishers) pp. 9–18.

Kalecki, M. (1972) *Selected Essays on the Economic Growth of the Socialist and the Mixed Economy* (Cambridge: Cambridge University Press).

Kalecki, M. (1976) *Essays on Developing Economies* (Chichester: Harvester Press).

Kautsky, K. (1899) *The Agrarian Question* (Stuttgart).

Kennedy, C. and Thirlwall, A. (1972) 'Surveys in Applied Economics: Technical Progress', *Economic Journal*, Mar, pp. 11–12.

Klatt, W. (1971) 'Comment' and 'Successes and Failures of Communist Farming', in W. Jackson (ed.) *Agrarian Policies and Problems in Communist and Non-Communist Countries* (Seattle, Wash.: University of Washington Press) pp. 65–8 and pp. 462–78.

Kojima, R. (1967) ' "Self-Sustained National Economy" in Mainland China', *The Developing Economies*, Mar, pp. 50–67.

Kosta, J. (1977) 'Workers' Councils in the "Prague Spring" of 1968', in D. Heathfield (ed.) *The Economics of Co-determination* (London: Macmillan) pp. 61–79.

Krishna, R. (1967) 'Agricultural Price Policy and Economic Development', in H. Southworth and B. Johnston (eds) *Agricultural Development and Economic Growth* (Ithaca, N.Y.: Cornell University Press) pp. 497–540.

Lange, O. (1938) *On the Economic Theory of Socialism*, B. Lippincott (ed.) (Minneapolis, Minn.: University of Minnesota Press) pp. 57–142.

Lange, O. (1970) *Papers in Economics and Sociology, 1930–1960* (Oxford: Pergamon Press).

Lardy, N. (1978) *Economic Growth and Distribution in China* (Cambridge: Cambridge University Press).

Lardy, N. (1983) *Agriculture in China's Modern Economic Development* (Cambridge: Cambridge University Press).

Leibenstein, H. (1960) *Economic Theory and Organizational Analysis* (New York: Harper & Bros).

Leibenstein, H. (1978) *General X-Efficiency Theory and Economic Development* (Oxford: Oxford University Press).

Leibenstein, H. (1979) 'A Branch of Economics is Missing: Micro-Micro Theory', *Journal of Economic Literature*, June, pp. 477–502.

Leibenstein, H. (1980) *Beyond Economic Man* (Cambridge, Mass.: Harvard University Press).

Lenin, V. I. (1963) *Collected Works*, vols I and III (Moscow: Progress Publishers).

Lerner, A. (1934) 'Economic Theory and Socialist Economy', *Review of Economic Studies*, Oct, pp. 51–61.

Lerner, A. (1970) *The Economics of Control* (New York: The Macmillan Co.).

Li Choh-Ming (1962) *The Statistical System of Communist China* (Berkeley, Calif.: University of California Press).

Li Yining (1981) 'The Role of Education in Economic Growth', *Social Sciences in China*, June, pp. 66–84.

Lin, C. (1981) 'The Reinstatement of Economics in China Today', *China Quarterly*, Mar, pp. 1–48.

Lin, C. (1985) 'Marxian Economic Categories and Problems of Centralization and Decentralization in Chinese Economic Planning', D.Phil. thesis, University of Oxford.

Liu Guoguang and Wang Xiangming (1980) 'A Study of the Speed and Balance of China's Economic Development', *Social Sciences in China*, Dec, pp. 15–43.

Liu Jinhan and Yi Fahai (1978) 'Encourage Commune Members to Develop Appropriate Family Sidelines', *Guangming Ribao*, 10 Apr.

Liu Shaoqi (1956) 'Report to the Eighth Party Congress', in R. Bowie and J. Fairbank (eds) *Communist China, 1955–1959: Policy Documents* (Cambridge, Mass.: Harvard University Press).

Liu T. C. and Yeh, K. C. (1965) *The Economy of the Chinese Mainland* (Princeton, N.Y.: Princeton University Press).

Locke, J. (1967) *Two Treatisès on Government*, P. Laslett (ed.) (Cambridge: Cambridge University Press).

Lockeed, M., Jameson, D. and Lau, L. (1980) 'Farmer Education and Farm Efficiency: A Survey', *Economic Development and Cultural Change*, Oct, pp. 37–76.

Ma Yinqu (1958) *My Economic Theory, Philosophy, and Political Standpoint* (Peking, Financial Publishers).

McCain, R. (1973) 'Critical Notes on Illyrian Economics', *Kyklos*, vol. 26, pp. 380–86.

Macpherson, C. B., (1980) 'Pluralism, Individualism and Participation', *Economic and Industrial Democracy*, Feb, pp. 21–30.

Macrae, J. (1970) 'Mobilization of the Agricultural Surplus in China for Rapid Economic Development, 1952–1957',, *The Developing Economies*, Mar, pp. 79–92.

Macrae, J. (1979) 'A Clarification of Chinese Development Strategy since 1949', *The Developing Economies*, vol. 17, pp. 266–94.

Mao Zedong (1974) *Mao Tse-tung Unrehearsed*, S. Schram (ed.) (Harmondsworth: Penguin Books).

Mao Zedong (1977) *A Critique of Soviet Economics* (London: Monthly Review Press).

Mao Zedong (1977) *Selected Works*, vol. 5 (Peking: Foreign Languages Press).

Mao Zedong (ed.) (1978) *Socialist Upsurge in China's Countryside* (Peking: Foreign Languages Press).

Mao Zedong (1980) 'Economic and Financial Problems', in A. Watson, *Mao Zedong and the Political Economy of the Border Region* (Cambridge: Cambridge University Press) pp. 57–251.

March, J. and Simon, H. (1981) 'Decision-Making Theory', in O. Grusky and G. Miller (eds) *The Sociology of Organizations* (New York: The Free Press) pp. 135–50.

Marglin, S. (1963) 'The Social Rate of Discount and the Optimal Rate of Investment', *Quarterly Journal of Economics*, Feb, pp. 95–111.

Marshall, M. S. (1979) 'Red and Expert at Tachai: A Sources of Growth Analysis', *World Development*, vol. 7, pp. 423–32.

Marshall, M. S. 'Institutional Transformation and Economic Growth in Rural China' (D.Phil. thesis, Oxford University, 1982).

Marx, K. (1904) *A Contribution to a Critique of Political Economy* (London: Kegan Paul).

Marx, K. (1957, 1961, 1962) *Capital*, vol. I, vol. II, vol. III (Moscow: Progress Publishers).

Marx, K. (1969, 1970) *Selected Works* (Moscow: Progress Publishers).

Marx, K. (1972) *Critique of the Gotha Programme* (Peking: Foreign Languages Press).

Maslow, A. (1954) *Motivation and Personality* (New York: Harper & Row).

Massel, B. (1961) 'A Disaggregated View of Technical Change', *Journal of Political Economy*, Dec, pp. 547–57.

Meade, J. (1972) 'The Theory of Labour-Managed Firms and of Profit Sharing', *Economic Journal*, Mar, pp. 402–28.

Meier, G. (1976) *Leading Issues in Economic Development*, 3rd ed. (New York: Oxford University Press).

Mill, J. S. (1909) *Principles of Political Economy* (London: Longmans Green & Co.).

Mill, J. S. (1962) *Utilitarianism*, M. Warnock (ed.) (Glasgow: Collins & Sons).

Mill, J. S. (1963) *Essays on Politics and Culture*, in G. Himmelfarb (ed.) (New York: Doubleday & Co.).

Mill, J. S. (1967) *Collected Works*, J. M. Robson (ed.) (Toronto: University of Toronto Press).

Mill, J. S. (1978) *On Liberty* (Harmondsworth: Penguin Books).

Mirrlees, J. (1976) 'The Optimal Structure of Incentives and Authority within an Organization', *Bell Journal of Economics*, Spring, pp. 105–31.

Mises, L. von (1935) 'Economic Calculation in the Socialist Commonwealth', in F. Hayek (ed.) *Collectivist Economic Planning* (London: Routledge & Kegan Paul).

Myers, R. (1975) 'Cooperation in Traditional Agriculture and its Implications for Team Farming in the People's Republic of China', in D. Perkins (ed.) *China's Modern Economy in Historical Perspective* (Stanford, Calif.: Stanford University Press) pp. 261–77.

Myrdal, G. (1969) *The Political Element in the Development of Economic Theory* (New York: Simon & Schuster).

Needham, J. (1963) 'The Past in China's Present', *Pacific Viewpoint*, Sep.
Nelson, R. (1964) 'Aggregate Production Functions and Medium Range Growth Projections', *American Economic Review*, Sep, pp. 575–606.
Nelson, R. (1973) 'Recent Exercises in Growth Accounting: New Understanding or Dead End?', *American Economic Review*, June, pp. 462–68.
Nelson, R. and Winter, S. (1974) 'Neoclassical vs. Evolutionary Theories of Economic Growth', *Economic Journal*, Dec, pp. 886–905.
Nelson, R. (1980) 'Production Sets, Technological Knowledge and R & D: Fragile and Overworked Constructs for Analysis of Productivity Growth?', *American Economic Review*, May, pp. 62–7.
Nelson, R. (1981) 'Research on Productivity Growth and Productivity Differences', *Journal of Economic Literature*, Sep, pp. 1029–64.
New China News Agency, Selected articles for selected years.
Niu Zhonghuang (1957) *Accumulation and Consumption in the National Income of China* (Peking, China Youth Publishers), translated in U.S. Government, *Current Background*, no. 511.
Ng, G. (1978) 'Operation and Control of Individual Economic Activities in Collective Agriculture: the Case of China' (Working Paper, International Labour Office, Geneva).
Nordhaus, W. and Tobin, J. (1972) 'Is Growth Obsolete?', in R. Gordon (ed.) *Economic Research: Retrospect and Prospect* (New York: National Bureau of Economic Research).
Nozick, R. (1973) 'Distributive Justice', *Philosophy and Public Affairs*, Autumn, pp. 45–126.
Nozick, R. (1980) *Anarchy, State and Utopia* (Oxford: Oxford University Press).
Nurske, R. (1953) *Problems of Capital Formation in Underdeveloped Countries* (Oxford: Blackwell).
Obern, C. and Jones, S. (1981) 'Critical Factors Affecting Agricultural Production Cooperatives', *Annals of Public and Cooperative Economy*, Sep, pp. 317–49.
Ohkawa, K. and Johnston, B. (1969) 'The Transferability of the Japanese Pattern of Modernizing Traditional Agriculture', in E. Thorbecke (ed.) *The Role of Agriculture in Economic Development* (New York, pp. 277–302).
Oi, W. and Clayton, E. (1968) 'A Peasant's View of a Soviet Collective Farm', *American Economic Review*, vol. 58, pp. 37–59.
Olson, M. (1965) *The Logic of Collective Action* (Cambridge, Mass.: Harvard University Press).
Organization of Economic Cooperation and Development (1976) *Workers Participation* (Paris: OECD).
Pateman, C. (1970) *Participation and Democratic Theory* (Cambridge, Cambridge University Press).
Pajestka, J. (1965) 'Investment in Infrastructure Versus Direct Production Facilities', in M. Kalecki (ed.) *Essays on Planning and Economic Development*, vol. 2 (Warsaw: Polish Scientific Publishers) pp. 51–61.
Perkins, D. (1964) 'Centralization and Decentralization in Mainland China's Agriculture, 1949–1962', *Quarterly Journal of Economics*, May, pp. 208–37.
Perkins, D. (1966) *Market Control and Planning in Communist China* (Cambridge, Mass.: Harvard University Press).
Perkins, D. (1975) 'Constraints Influencing China's Agricultural Performance',

in U.S. Congress, *China: A Reassessment of the Economy* (Washington, D.C.: U.S. Congress) pp. 350–66.

Perkins, D. (ed.) (1975a) *China's Modern Economy: A Historical Perspective* (Stanford, Calif.: Stanford University Press).

Perrow, C. (1979) *Complex Organizations: A Critical Essay* (Glenview, Ill.: Scott Foreman).

Pfanner, D. (1970) 'A Semi-subsistence Village Economy in Lower Burma', is C. W. Rowton (ed.), *Subsistence Agriculture and Economic Development* (Chicago: Aldire) pp. 47–60.

Putterman, L. (1981) 'Is a Democratic Collective Agriculture Possible?', *Journal of Development Economics*, vol. 9, pp. 375–403.

Radner, R. (1972) 'Normative Theories of Organization', in C. McGuire and R. Radner (eds.) *Decisions and Organizations* (London: North-Holland), pp. 177–88.

Rawls, J. (1972) *A Theory of Justice* (Oxford: Oxford University Press).

Rawls, J. (1974) 'Some Reasons for the Maximin Criterion', *American Economic Review*, May, pp. 141–6.

Rawski, T. (1979) *Economic Growth and Employment in China* (Washington, D.C.: Oxford University Press, World Bank).

Red Flag, Editorial Department (1968) *The Struggle Between the Two Roads in China's Countryside* (Peking: Foreign Languages Press).

Riskin, C. (1971) 'Small Industry and the Chinese Model of Development', *China Quarterly*, Apr, pp. 245–73.

Robbins, L. (1937) *Economic Planning and International Order* (London: Macmillan).

Robinson, J. (1967) 'Comment', *American Economic Review*, Mar, pp. 222–3.

Robinson, J. (1979) *Aspects of Development and Underdevelopment* (Cambridge: Cambridge University Press).

Rousseau, J.-J. (1963) *The Social Contract*, in E. Barker (ed.) *Social Contract, Essays by Locke, Hume and Rousseau* (London: Oxford University Press).

Schram, S. (1966) *Mao Tse-Tung* (Harmondsworth: Penguin Books).

Schram, S. (1969) *The Political Thought of Mao Tse-tung*, (London: Praeger).

Schram, S. (1971) 'Mao Tse-Tung and the Theory of the Permanent Revolution', *China Quarterly*, Apr, pp. 221–44.

Schram, S. (1981) 'To Utopia and Back: A Cycle in the History of the Chinese Communist Party', *China Quarterly*, Sep, pp. 407–39.

Schran, P. (1969) *The Development of Chinese Agriculture, 1950–1959* (Urbana, Ill.: University of Illinois Press).

Schrenk, M. (1981) 'Managerial Structures and Practices in Manufacturing Enterprises: A Yugoslav Case Study' (World Bank, Working Paper, no. 455), May.

Schultz, T. (1966) *Transforming Traditional Agriculture* (New Haven, Conn.: Yale University Press).

Schultz, T. (1968) 'Institutions and the Rising Economic Value of Man', *American Journal of Agricultural Economics*, Dec, pp. 1113–22.

Schumpeter, J. (1934) *The Theory of Economic Development* (Cambridge, Mass.: Harvard University Press).

Schumpeter, J. (1970) *Capitalism, Socialism and Democracy* (London: Unwin).

Schurmann, F. (1968) *Ideology and Organization in Communist China* (Berkeley, Calif.: University of California Press).
Scott, M. (1976) 'Investment and Growth', *Oxford Economic Papers*, Nov, pp. 317–64.
Scott, M. (1980) 'A Critique of Growth Theory' (Oxford: Nuffield College, mimeo).
Scott, M. (1981) 'The Contribution of Investment to Growth', *Scottish Journal of Political Economy*, Nov, pp. 211–26.
Sen, A. (1961) 'On Optimizing the Rate of Saving', *Economic Journal*, Sep, pp. 479–96.
Sen, A. and Runciman, W. (1965) 'Games, Justice and the General Will', *Mind*, Sep, pp. 554–62.
Sen, A. (1966), 'Labour Allocation in a Cooperative Enterprise', *Review of Economic Studies*, Oct, pp. 361–71.
Sen, A. (1967) 'Isolation, Assurance and the Social Rate of Discount', *Quarterly Journal of Economics*, Feb, pp. 112–24.
Sen, A. (1969) 'A Game-Theoretic Analysis of Theories of Collectivism and Allocation', in T. Majumdar (ed.) *Growth and Choice* (Calcutta: Oxford University Press) pp. 1–18.
Sen, A. (1973) 'Behavior and the Concept of Preference', *Economica*, May, pp. 241–59.
Sen, A. (1975) *Employment, Technology and Development* (Oxford: Oxford University Press).
Sen, A. (1979a) 'Utilitarianism and Welfarism', *The Journal of Philosophy*, Sep, pp. 463–88.
Sen, A. (1979b), 'Personal Utilities and Public Judgements: Or What's Wrong with Welfare Economics?', *Economic Journal*, Sep, pp. 537–58.
Sen, A. (1979c) 'Rational Fools: A Critique of the Behavioral Foundations of Economic Theory', in F. Hahn and M. Hollis (eds) *Philosophy and Economic Theory* (Oxford: Oxford University Press) pp. 87–109.
Sen, A. (1979d) *Collective Choice and Social Welfare* (Oxford: North-Holland).
Sen, A. (1981a) *Poverty and Famines* (Oxford: Oxford University Press).
Sen, A. (1981b) 'Public Action and the Quality of Life in Developing Countries', *Oxford Bulletin of Economics and Statistics*, Nov, pp. 287–319.
Shapiro, S. (1981) *Experiment in Sichuan* (Peking: New World Press).
Sigurdson, J. (1977) *Rural Industrialization in China* (Cambridge, Mass.: Harvard University Press).
Sik, O. (1980) 'Towards an Humane Economic Democracy', *Economic and Industrial Democracy*, Aug, pp. 313–42.
Simon, H. (1959) 'Theories of Decision-making in Economics and Behavioral Science', *American Economic Review*, June, pp. 253–83.
Simon, H. (1978) 'Rationality as Process and as Product of Thought', *American Economic Review*, May, pp. 1–16.
Skinner, G. W. (1964) 'Marketing and Social Structure in Rural China', Nov, *Journal of Asian Studies*, pp. 32–43.
Smith, A. (1947) *The Wealth of Nations* (London: Dent)
Solow, R. (1957) 'Technical Change and the Aggregate Production Function', *Review of Economics and Statistics*, Aug, pp. 312–320.
Solow, R. (1970) *Growth Theory* (Oxford: Oxford University Press).

Spence, M. (1973) 'Job Market Signalling', *Quarterly Journal of Economics*, Aug, pp. 355–74.

Star, S. (1974) 'Accounting for the Growth of Output', *American Economic Review*, Mar, pp. 123–35.

State Council of the People's Republic of China (1976) *Land Reform Law* (Peking: Foreign Languages Press).

State Council of the People's Republic of China (1976) *Model Regulations for an Agricultural Producer's Cooperative* (Peking: Foreign Languages Press).

State Council of the People's Republic of China (1976) *Model Regulations for an Advanced Agricultural Producer's Cooperative* (Peking: Foreign Languages Press).

State Statistical Bureau (1960) *Ten Great Years* (Peking: Foreign Languages Press).

Steer, P. and Cable, J. (1978) 'Internal Organization and Profit: An Empirical Analysis of Large U.K. Companies', *Journal of Industrial Economics*, Sep, pp. 13–30.

Steinherr, A. (1975) 'Profit-Maximizing vs. Labour-Managed Firms: A Comparison of Market Structure and Firm Behavior', *Journal of Industrial Economics*, Dec, pp. 97–104.

Steinherr, A. (1977) 'On the Efficiency of Profit-Sharing and Labour Participation in Management', *Bell Journal of Economics*, Autumn, pp. 545–55.

Steinherr, A. (1978) 'The Labour-Managed Economy: A Survey of the Economics Literature', *Annals of Public and Cooperative Economy*, Apr, pp. 128–47.

Steinherr, A. and Peer, H. (1975) 'Worker Management and the Modern Industrial Enterprise: A Note', *Quarterly Journal of Economics*, Nov, pp. 662–9.

Stewart, F. and Streeten, P. (1976) 'New Strategies for Development: Poverty, Income Distribution and Growth', *Oxford Economic Papers*, Nov, pp. 381–405.

Stiglitz, J. (1975) 'Incentives, Risk and Information: Notes Towards a Theory of Hierarchy', *Bell Journal of Economics*, Autumn, pp. 552–79.

Stiglitz, J. (1975a) 'The Theory of "Screening", Education and the Distribution of Income', *American Economic Review*, June, pp. 283–300.

Stiglitz, J. and Uzawa, H. (eds) (1969) *Readings in the Modern Theory of Economic Growth* (Cambridge, Mass.: MIT Press).

Streeten, P. (1972) *The Frontiers of Development Studies* (London: Macmillan).

Streeten, P. (1979) 'Basic Needs: Premises and Promises', *Journal of Policy Modeling*, vol. 1, pp. 136–46.

Sun Yefang (1980) 'What is the Origin of the Law of Value?', *Social Sciences in China*, Sep, pp. 155–71.

Tang, A. and Stone, B. (1980) *Food Production in the People's Republic of China* (Washington, D.C.: International Food Policy Research Institute).

Taylor, F. (1938) 'The Guidance of Production in a Socialist State', in B. Lippincott (ed.) *On the Economic Theory of Socialism* (Minneapolis, Minn.: University of Minnesota Press) pp. 41–54.

Tian Jianghai and Zhang Shuguang (1981) 'Organization, Planning and Efficiency – An Inquiry into the Superiority of the Socialist Economic System', *Social Sciences in China*, Dec, pp. 24–54.

Tinbergen, J. (1982) 'Ways to Socialism', *Co-existence*, Apr, pp. 1–13.

Travers, L. (1984) 'Post 1978 Rural Economic Policy and Peasant Income in China', *China Quarterly*, July, pp. 241–59.

Trotsky, L. (1969) *The Permanent Revolution and Results and Prospects* (New York: Pathfinder Press).

U.S. Congress (1978) *Chinese Economy Post-Mao: A Compendium of Papers* (Washington, D.C.: U.S. Congress, U.S. Government).

U.S. Government, *Joint Publications Research Service*, Selected Translations of Chinese journal and newspaper articles for selected years (Washington, D.C.: U.S.Government).

U.S. Government, *Survey of China Mainland Press*, Selected translations of Chinese journal and newspaper articles for selected years (Washington, D.C.: U.S. Government).

Usher, D. (1980) *The Measurement of Economic Growth* (Oxford: Blackwell).

Vanek, J. (1969) 'Decentralization Under Workers' Management', *American Economic Review*, Dec, pp. 1006–10.

Vanek, J. (1970) *The General Theory of Labour Managed Market Economies* (Ithaca, N.Y.: Cornell University Press).

Varian, H. (1979) 'Distributive Justice, Welfare Economics, and the Theory of Fairness', in F. Hahn and M. Hollis (eds.) *Philosophy and Economic Theory* (Oxford: Oxford University Press) pp. 134–54.

Vermeer, E. (1982) 'Income Differentials in Rural China', *China Quarterly*, Mar, pp. 1–33.

Wädekin, K. (1973) *The Private Sector in Soviet Agriculture* (Berkeley, Calif.: University of California Press).

Waldorf, W. (1973) 'Quality of Labour in Manufacturing', *Review of Economics and Statistics*, May, pp. 284–90.

Walker, K. (1966) 'Collectivization in Retrospect: the Socialist "High Tide" of Autumn 1955–Spring 1956', *China Quarterly*, Apr, pp. 1–43.

Walker, K. (1967) *Planning in Chinese Agriculture* (London: Cass Co).

Walker, K. (1968) 'Organization for Agricultural Production', in A. Eckstein, W. Galenson and T. Liu (eds) *Economic Trends in Communist China* (Edinburgh: University of Edinburgh Press) pp. 397–458.

Walker, K. (1981) 'China's Grain Production, 1975–80 and 1952–57: Some Basic Statistics', *China Quarterly*, June, pp. 215–47.

Wang Yongjiang (1981) 'What is the Aim of Socialist Production?', *Social Sciences in China*, Mar, pp. 5–13.

Ward, B. (1958) 'The Firm in Illyria: Market Syndicalism', *American Economic Review*, Sep, pp. 556–89.

Warriner, D. (1969) *Land Reform in Principle and Practice* (Oxford: Oxford University Press).

Weitz, R. (1965) 'Social and Political Structures Influencing Agricultural Development', in R. Weitz (ed.) *Rural Planning in Developing Countries* (London: Routledge & Kegan Paul).

Wheeler, D. (1980) 'Basic Needs Fulfillment and Economic Growth', *Journal of Development Economics*, vol. 7, pp. 435–51.

Whyte, M. and Parrish, W. (1978) *Village and Family in Contemporary China* (Chicago: University of Chicago Press).

Wiens, T. (1975) 'Agricultural Statistics in the People's Republic of China: Another Look' (Washington, D.C.: mimeo).

Wiles, P. (1964) *The Political Economy of Communism* (Oxford: Blackwell).
Wiles, P. (1977) *Economic Institutions Compared* (Oxford: Blackwell).
Williamson, O. (1973) 'Markets and Hierarchies: Some Elementary Considerations', *American Economic Review*, May, pp. 316–25.
Williamson, O. (1975) *Markets and Hierarchies, Analysis and Antitrust Implications: A Study in the Economics of Internal Organization* (New York: The Free Press).
Wilson, R. (1975) 'Informational Economies of Scale', *Bell Journal of Economics*, Spring, pp. 184–95.
Wilson, D. (ed.) (1977) *Mao Tse-tung in the Scales of History* (Cambridge: University of Cambridge Press).
Wittfogel, K. (1971) 'Communist and Non-Communist Agrarian Systems with Special Reference to the U.S.S.R. and Communist China: A Comparative Approach', in W. Jackson (ed.) *Agrarian Policies and Problems in Communist and Non-Communist Countries* (Seattle, Wash.: University of Washington Press) pp. 3–61.
Wong, J. (1971) 'Peasant Economic Behaviour: The Case of Traditional Agricultural Cooperation', *The Developing Economies*, Sep, pp. 332–49.
World Bank (1981) *China: Socialist Economic Development, Annex C, Agricultural Development*, and *Main Report* (Washington, D.C.: World Bank).
World Bank (1981a and 1984) *World Development Report* (Washington, D.C.: World Bank).
Xiao Liang (1980) 'Politics and Economics – How are They Related?', *Social Sciences in China*, Dec, pp. 5–12.
Xiao Zhuoji (1980) 'The Law of Price Movement in China', *Social Sciences in China*, Dec, pp. 44–60.
Xue Muqiao (1960) *The Socialist Transformation of the National Economy in China* (Peking: Foreign Languages Press).
Xue Muqiao (1981) *China's Socialist Economy* (Peking: Foreign Languages Press).
Yang Jianbai and Li Xuezheng (1980) 'The Relations Between Agriculture, Light Industry and Heavy Industry in China', *Social Sciences in China*, June, pp. 182–212.
Zhao Ziyang (1982) *China's Economy and Development Principles* (Peking: Foreign Languages Press).
Zheng Linzhuang (1981) 'Agricultural Modernization and Agricultural Production Efficiency', *Social Sciences in China*, Sep, pp. 104–20.
Zhou Enlai (1956) 'Report on Proposals for the Second Five Year Plan for the Development of the National Economy', in R. Bowie and J. Fairbank (eds) *Communist China, 1955–1959: Policy Documents* (Cambridge, Mass.: Harvard University Press, 1962) pp. 216–41.
Zimbalest, A. (1981) 'On the Role of Management in Socialist Development', *World Development*, Sep, pp. 971–8.

Index